AF574211

WANG YUYANG
CHAOSMOSIS

MOUSSE PUBLISHING

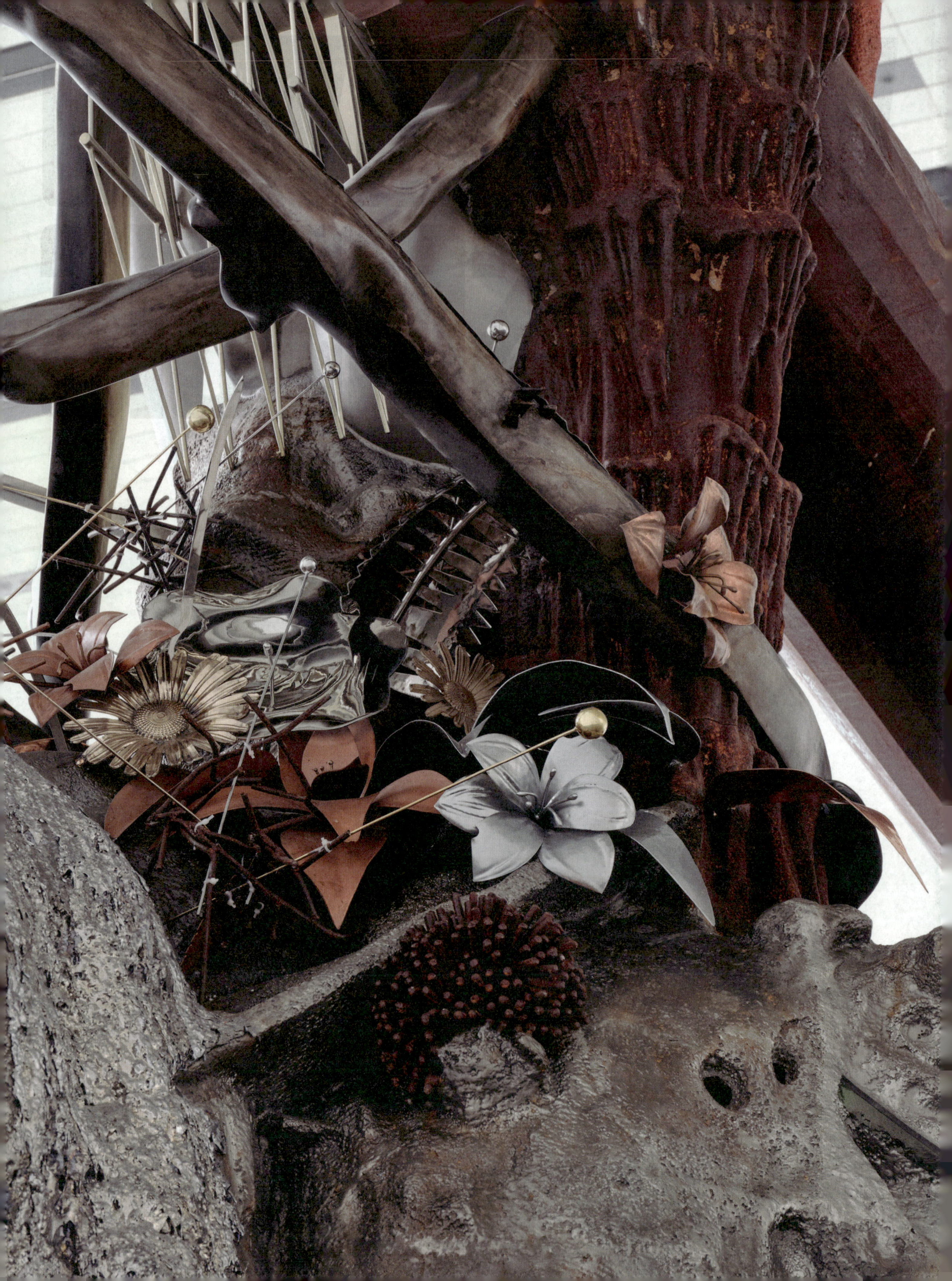

[01]

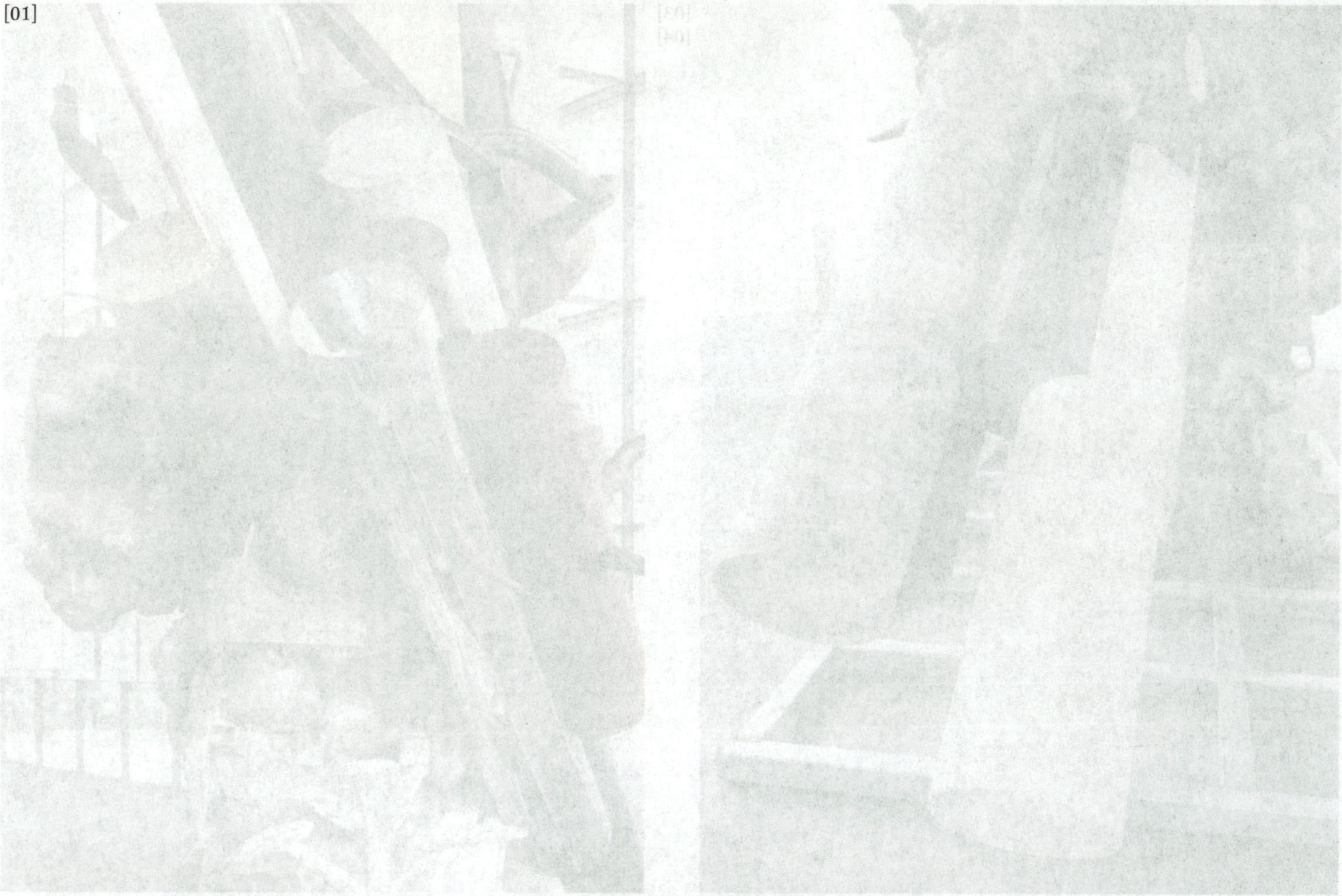

[01] [02]

Symbiosis – Out, 2024. Iron, stainless steel, brass, red copper, plaster, fiberglass, sand. 800 × 380 × 600 cm

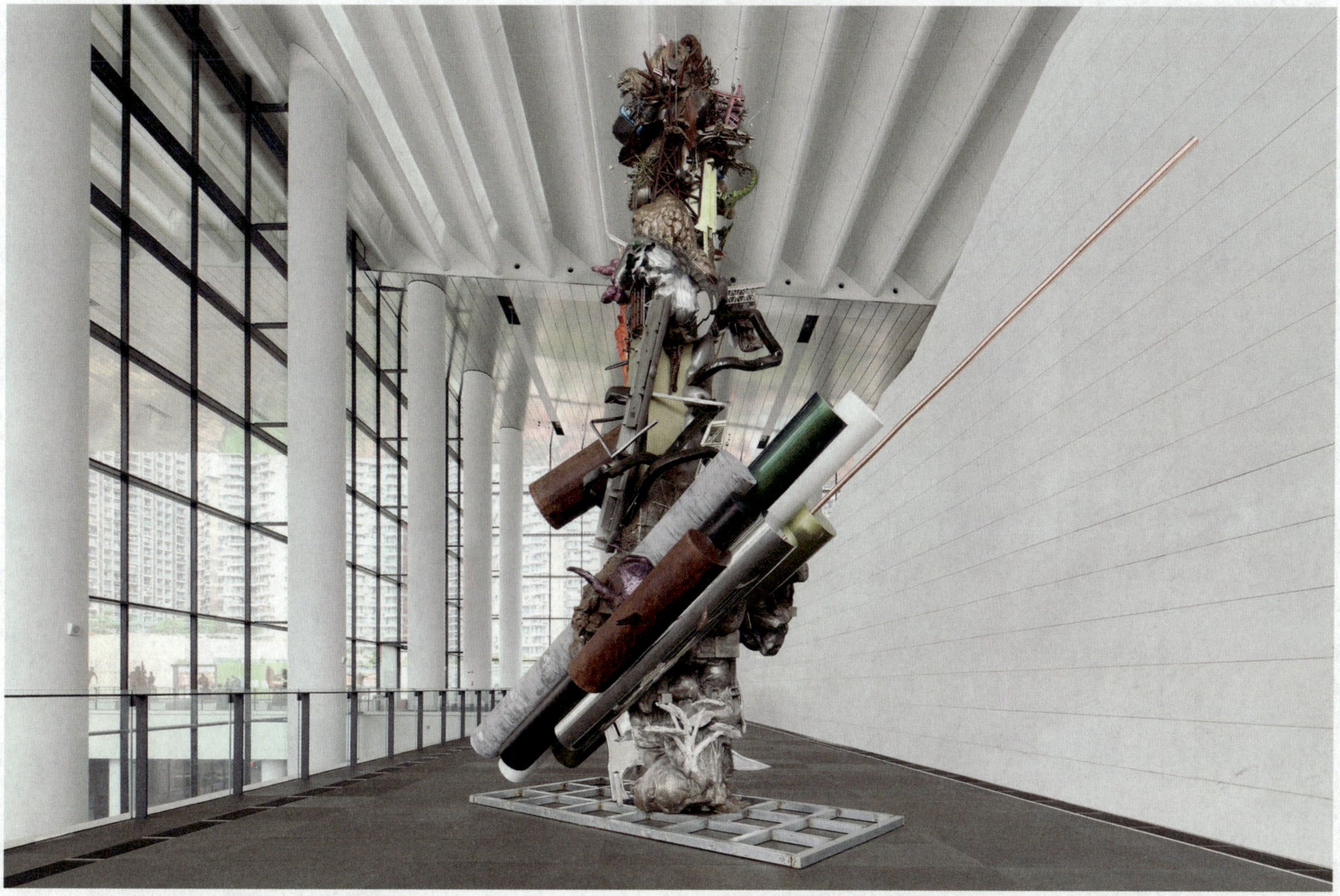

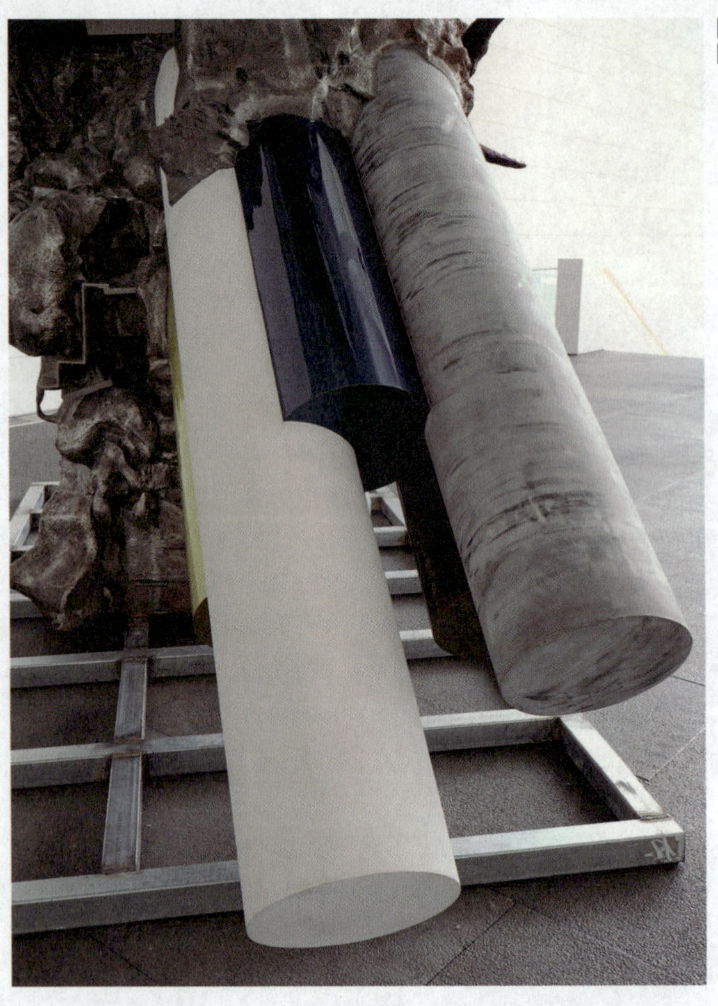

[03]
[04]

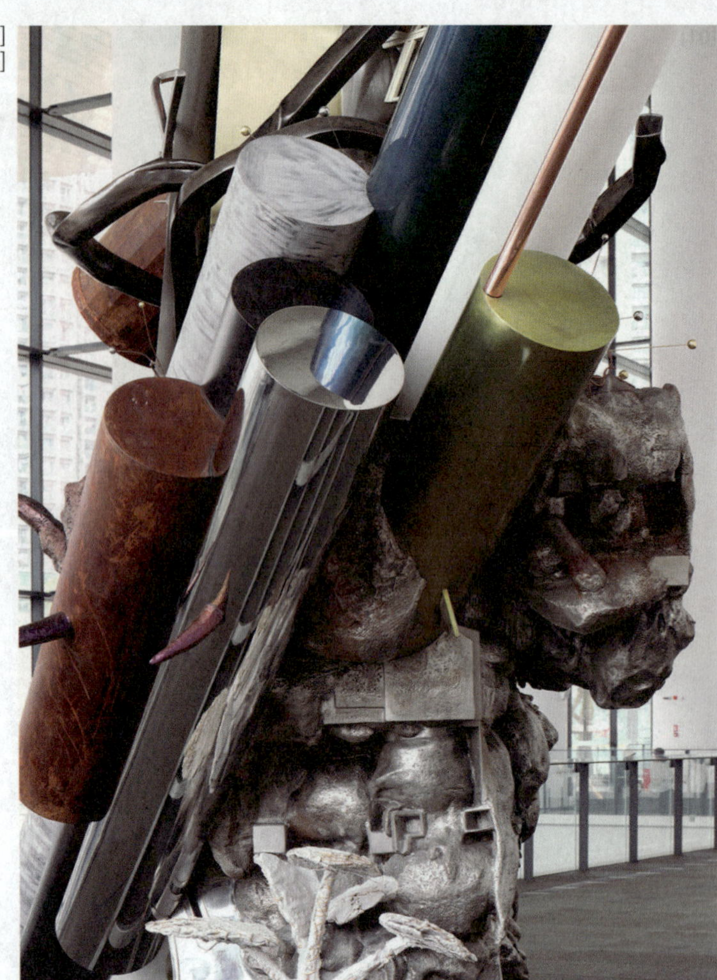

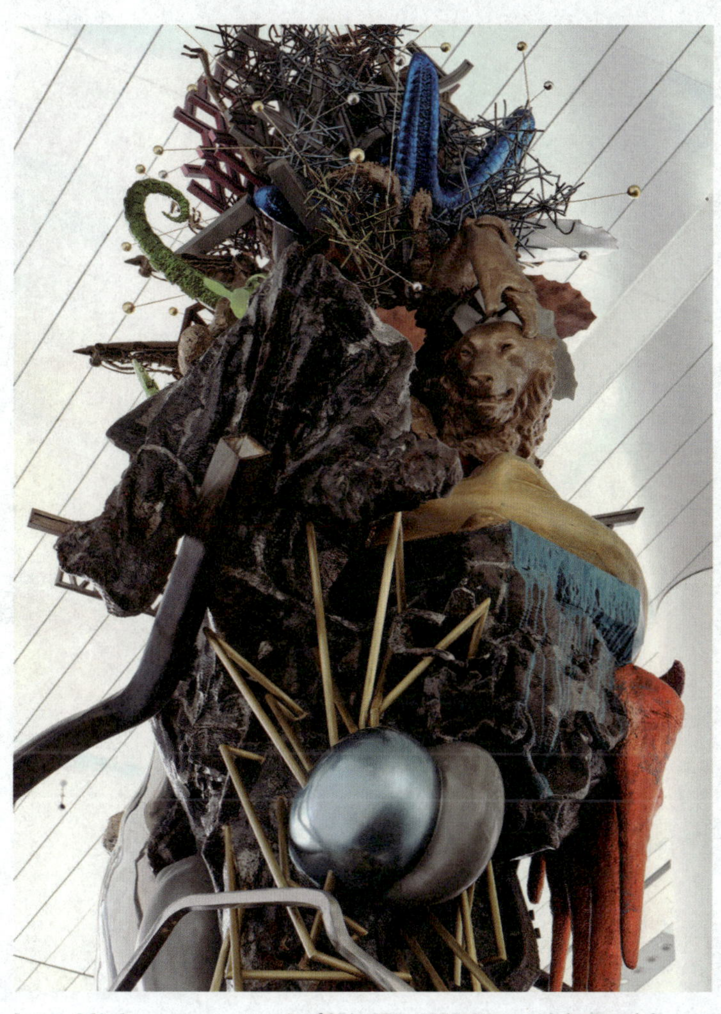

[05]

[03, 04] [05] *Symbiosis – Out*, 2024. Iron, stainless steel, brass, red copper, plaster, fiberglass, sand. 800 × 380 × 600 cm

[06] [07]

Symbiosis – Out, 2024. Iron, stainless steel, brass, red copper, plaster, fiberglass, sand. 800 × 380 × 600 cm

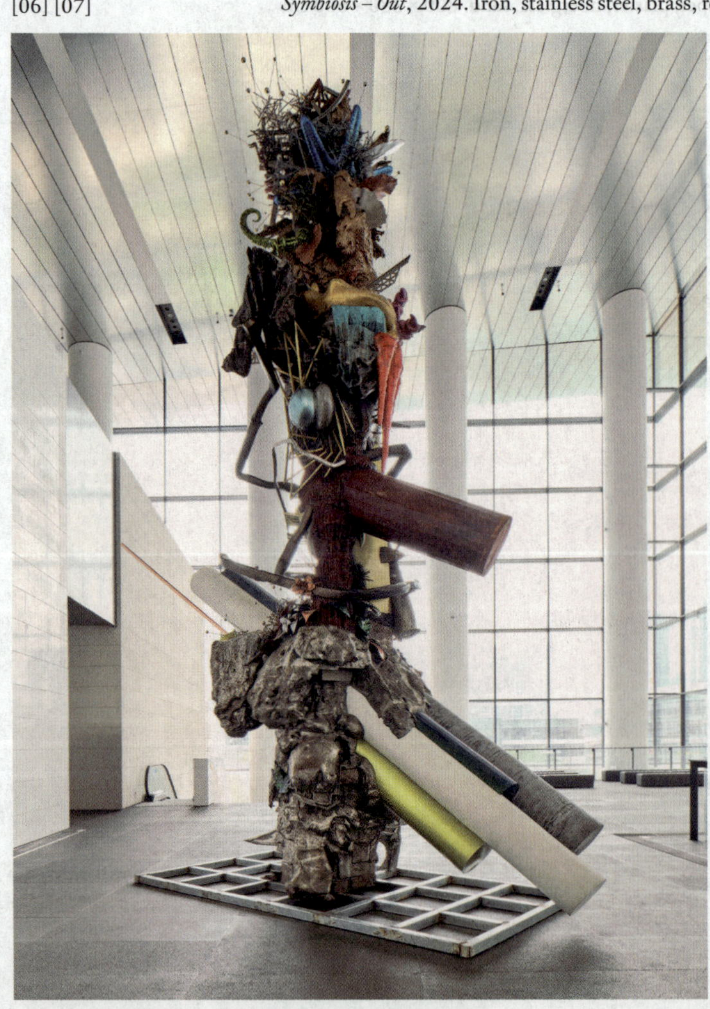

[06]

[07]

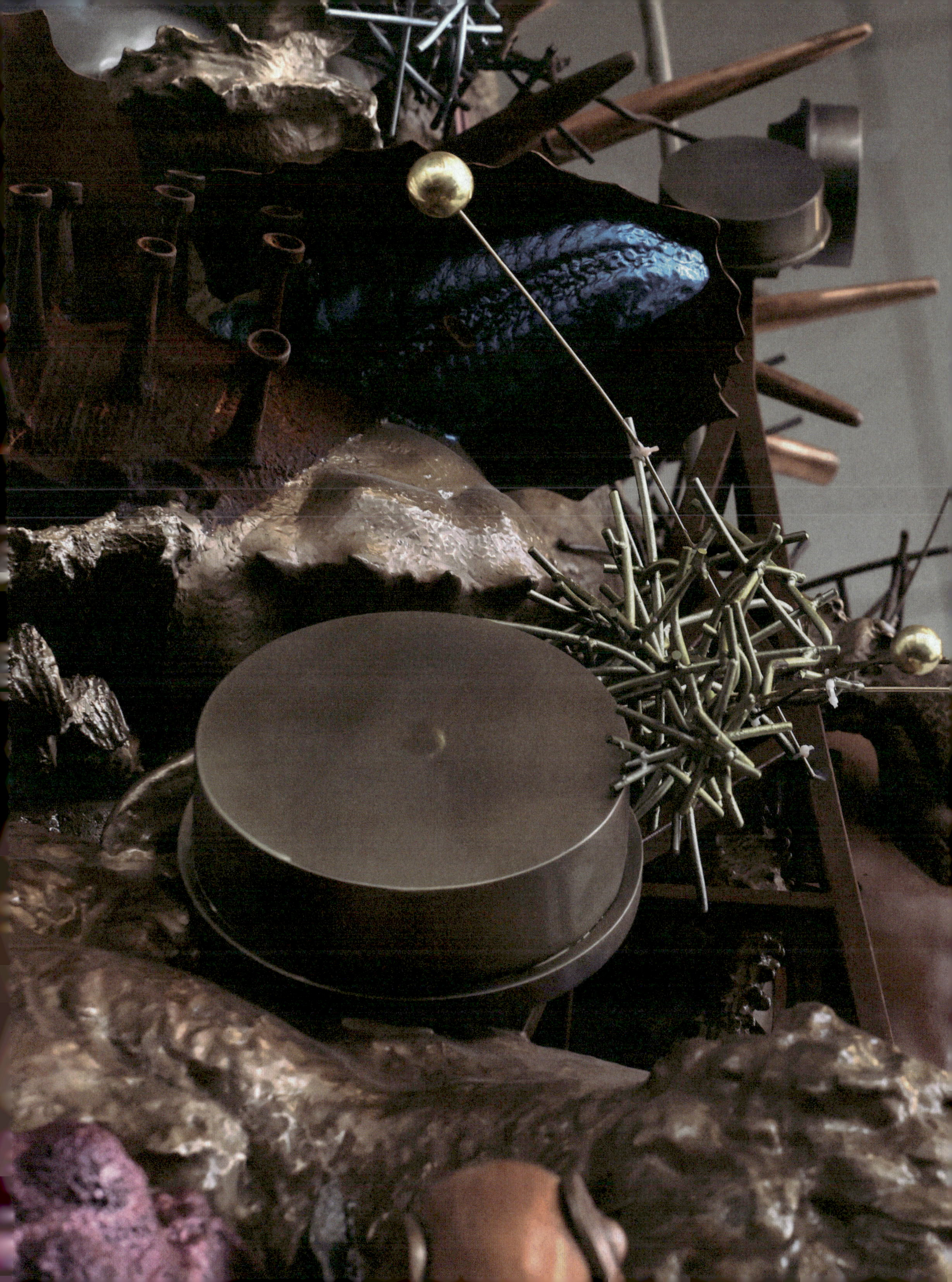

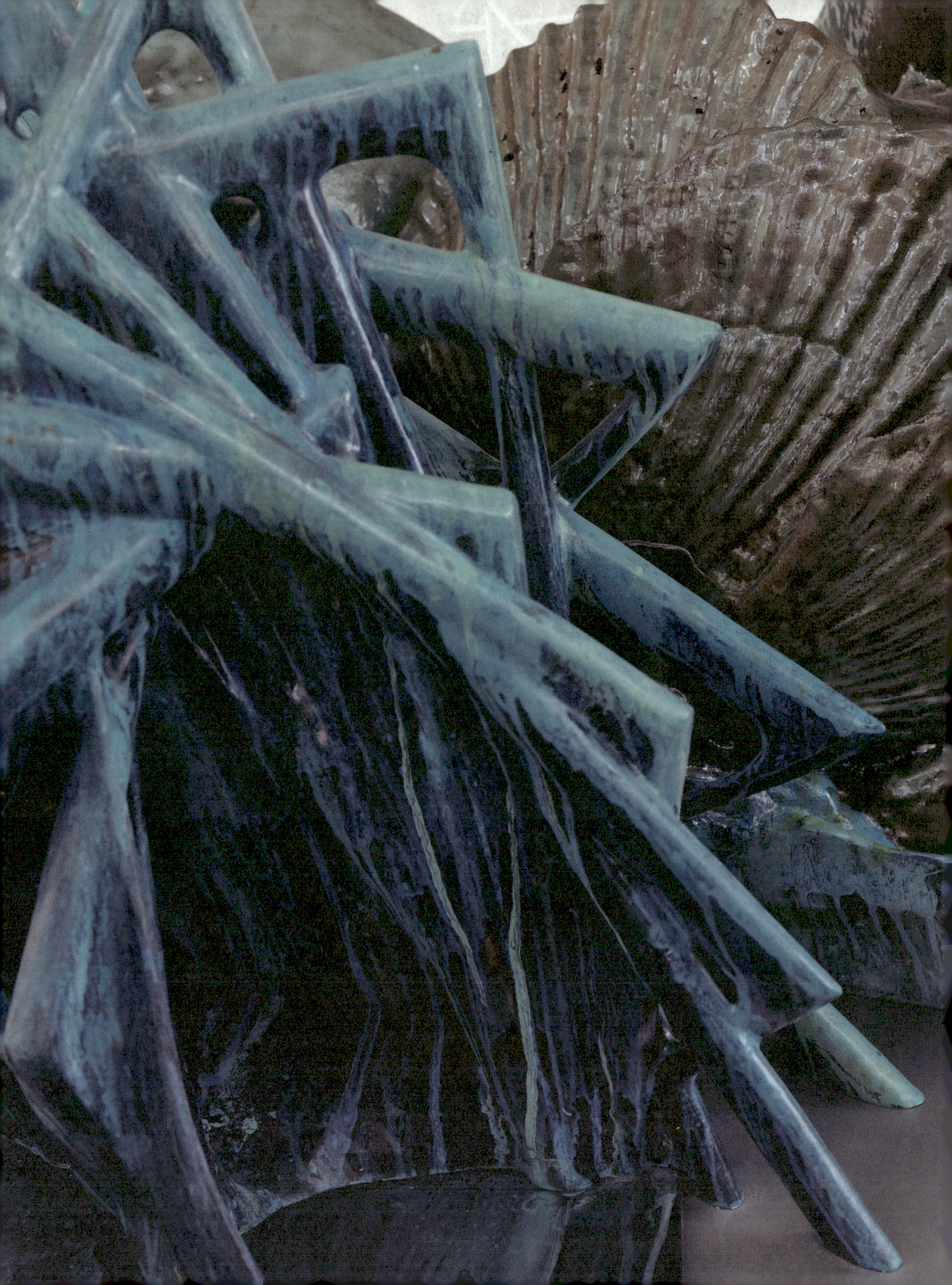

[08]

[08] [09] *Symbiosis – Tact*, 2023. Aluminum, brass, red copper. 210 × 210 × 185 cm

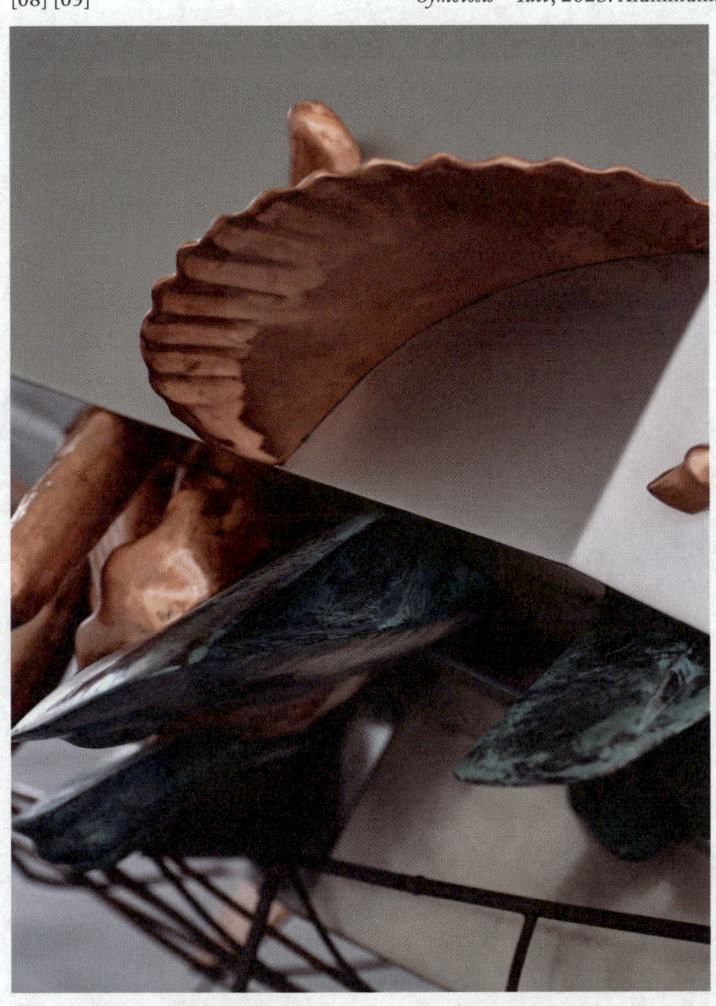

[09]

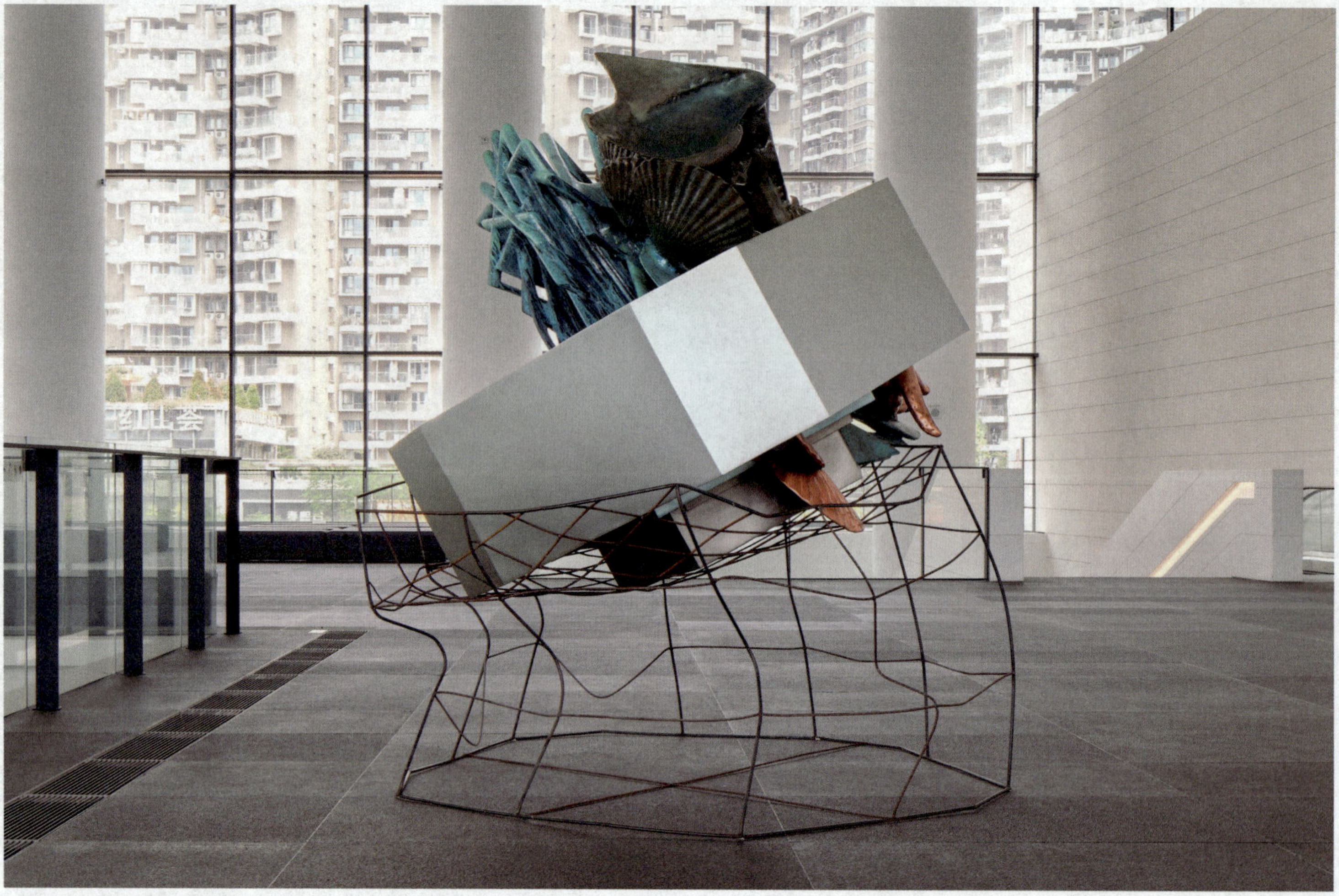

[10]

[10] [11, 12]

Symbiosis – Tact, 2023. Aluminum, brass, red copper. 210 × 210 × 185 cm

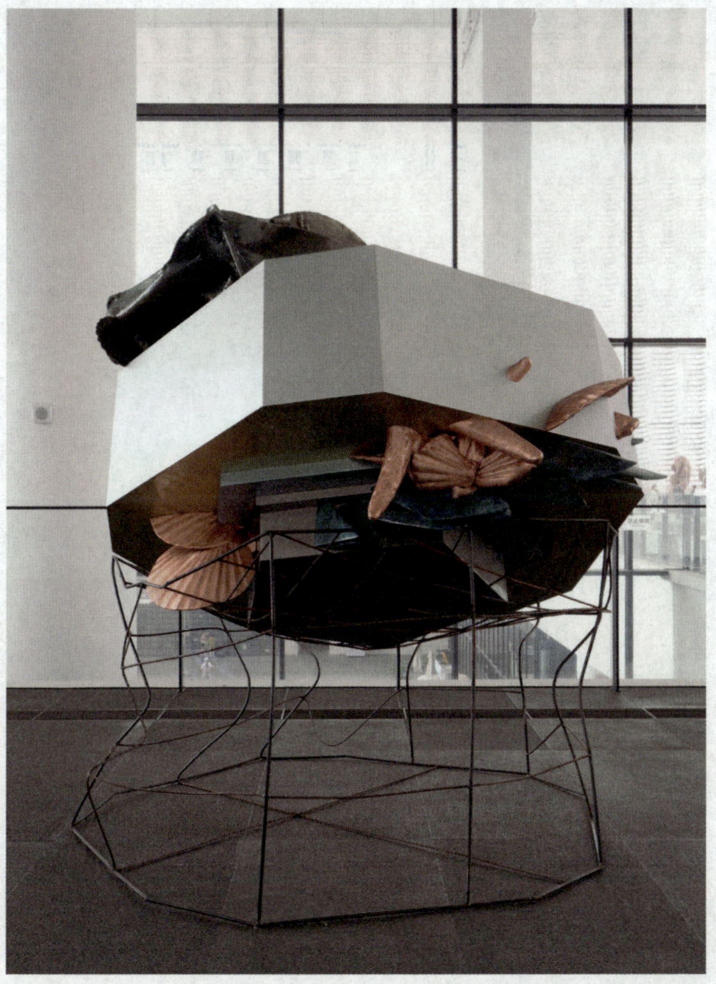

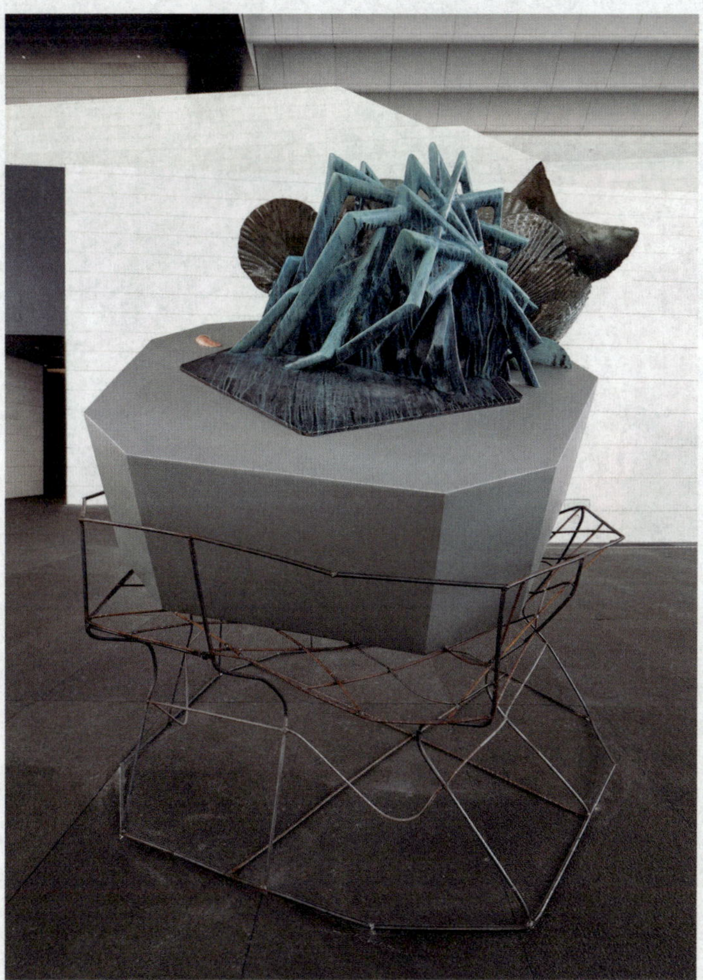

[11]
[12]

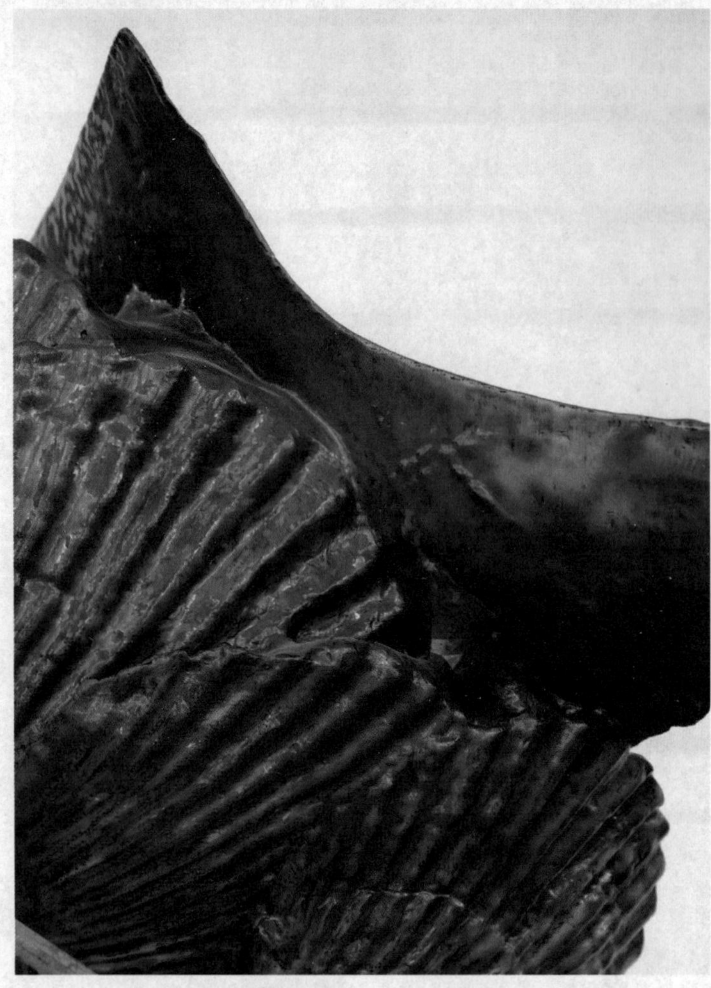

[13]

[14]

[13] [14] *Symbiosis – Tact*, 2023. Aluminum, brass, red copper. 210 × 210 × 185 cm

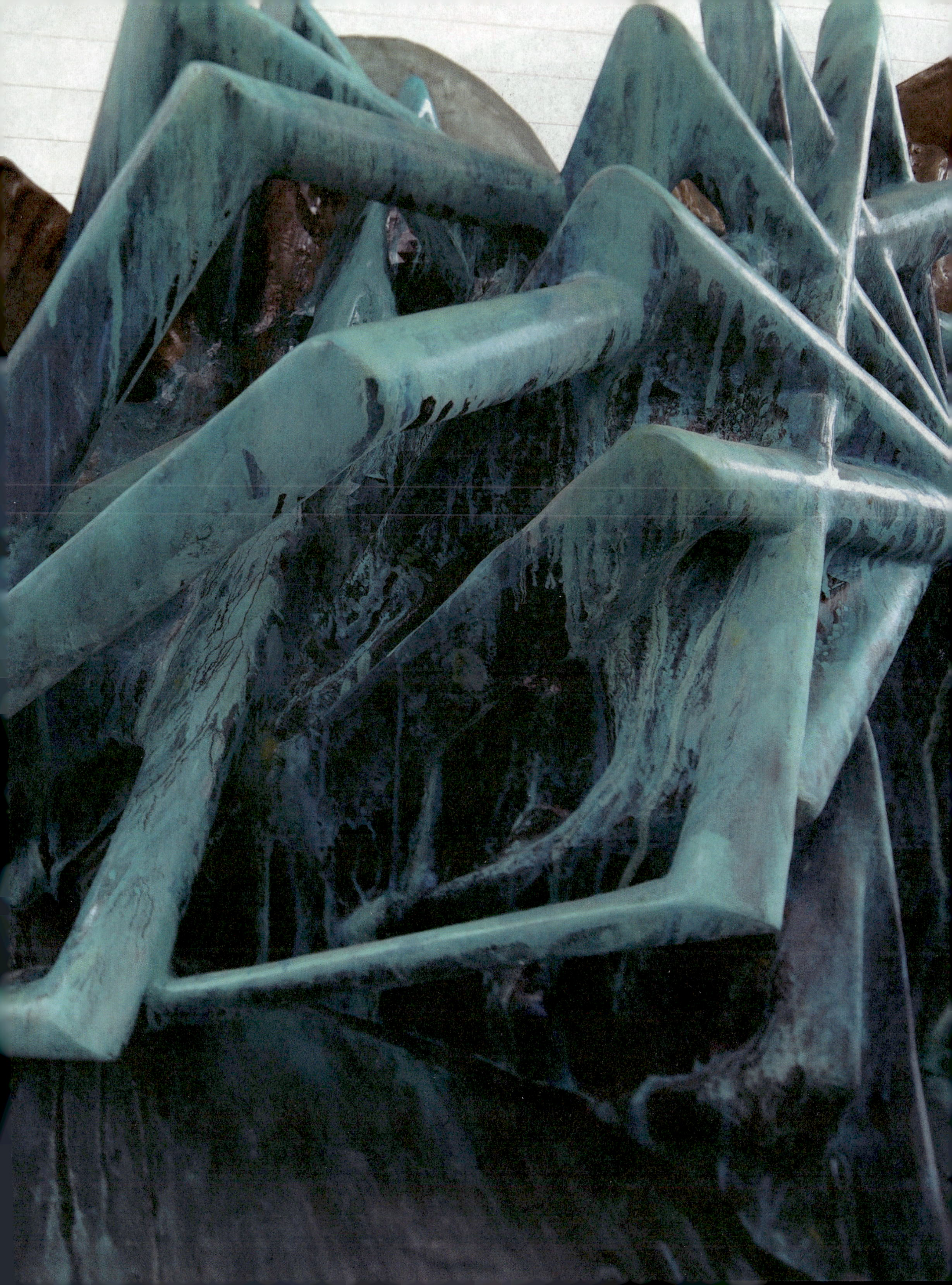

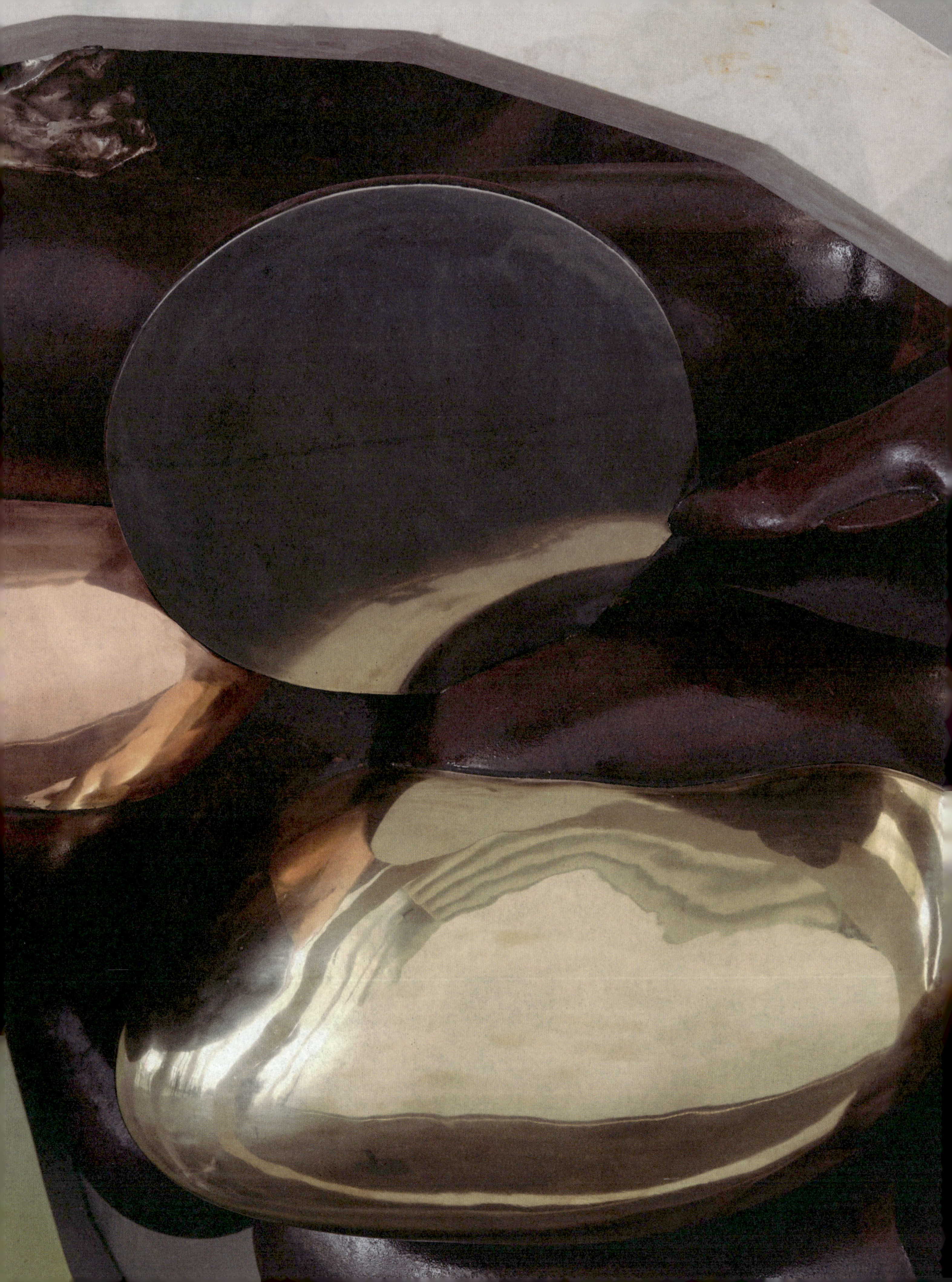

[15]

[16]

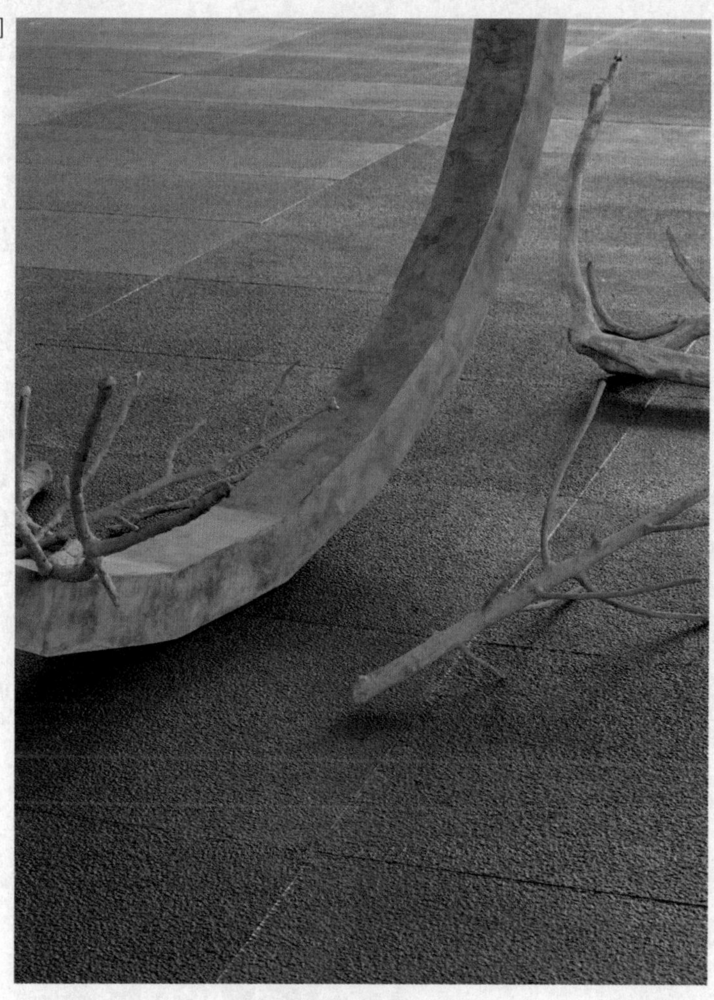

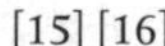

[15] [16] *Symbiosis – Meticulousness*, 2023. Iron, stainless steel, brass, red copper, plaster, wood. 340 × 400 × 125 cm

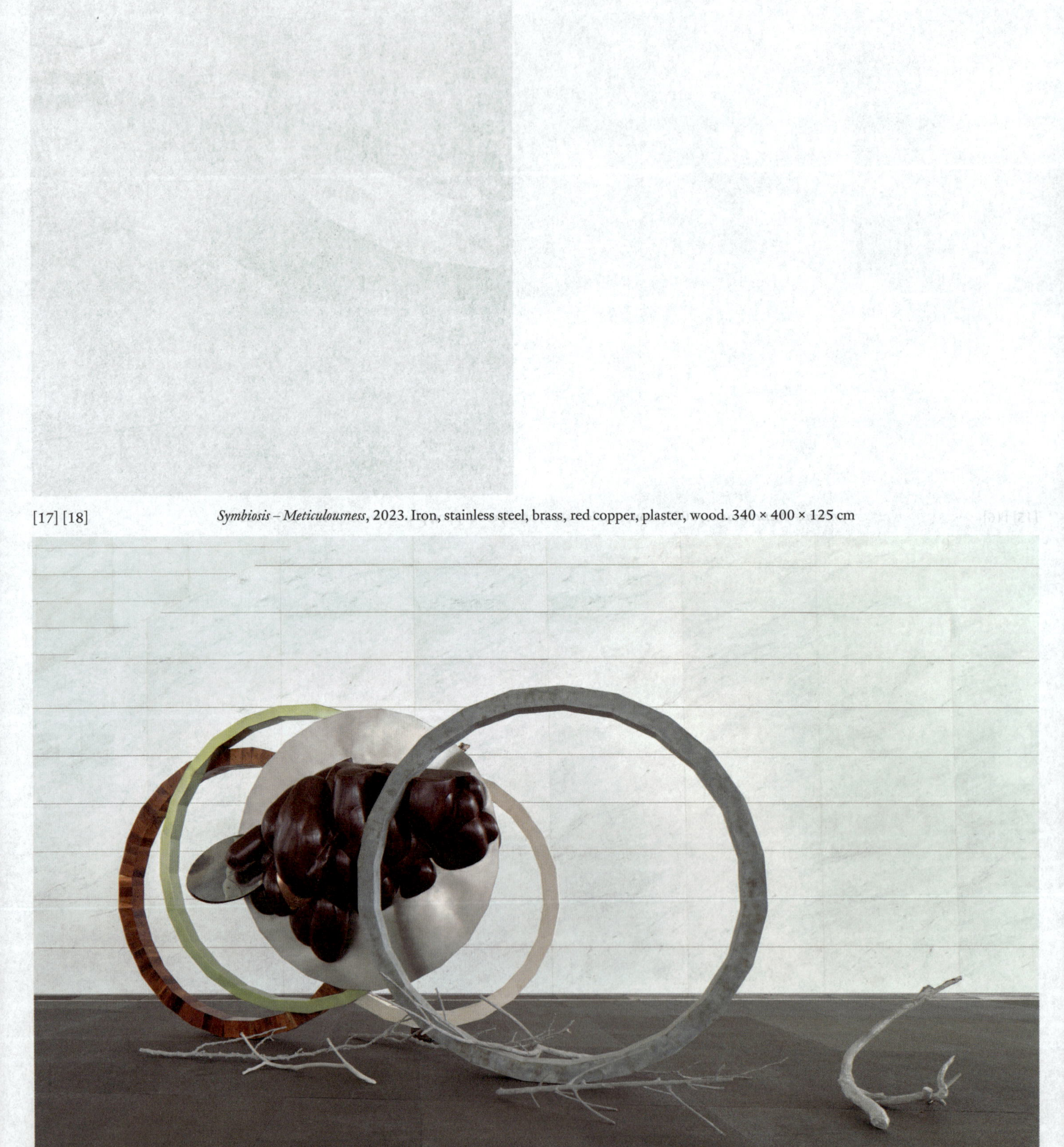

[17] [18] *Symbiosis – Meticulousness*, 2023. Iron, stainless steel, brass, red copper, plaster, wood. 340 × 400 × 125 cm

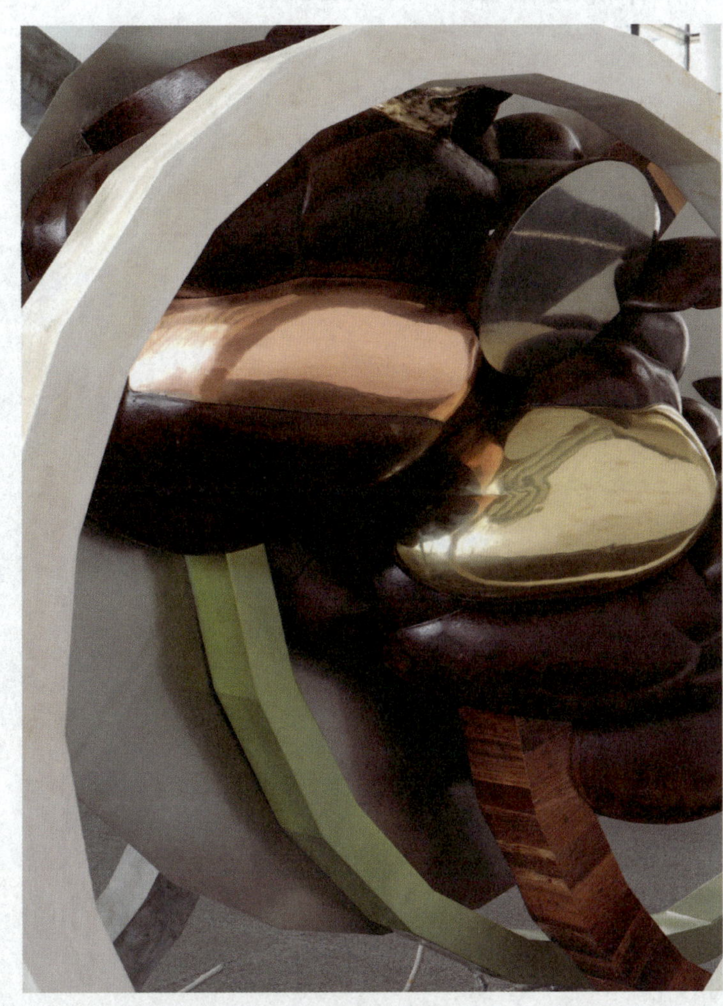

[18]

[19]

[20]

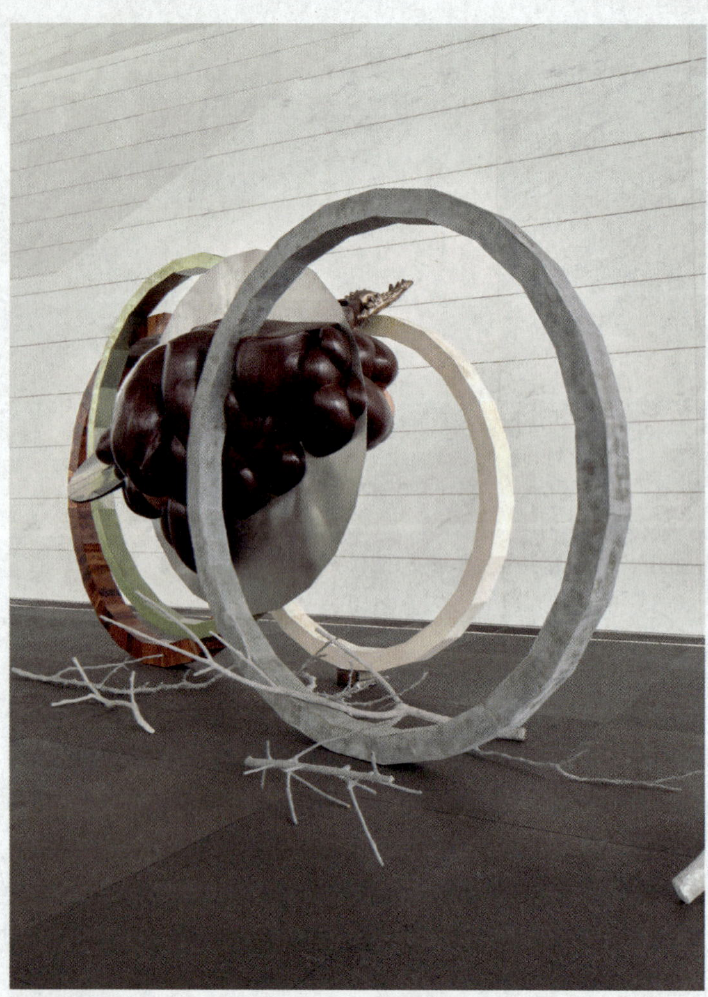

[19] [20] *Symbiosis – Meticulousness*, 2023. Iron, stainless steel, brass, red copper, plaster, wood. 340 × 400 × 125 cm

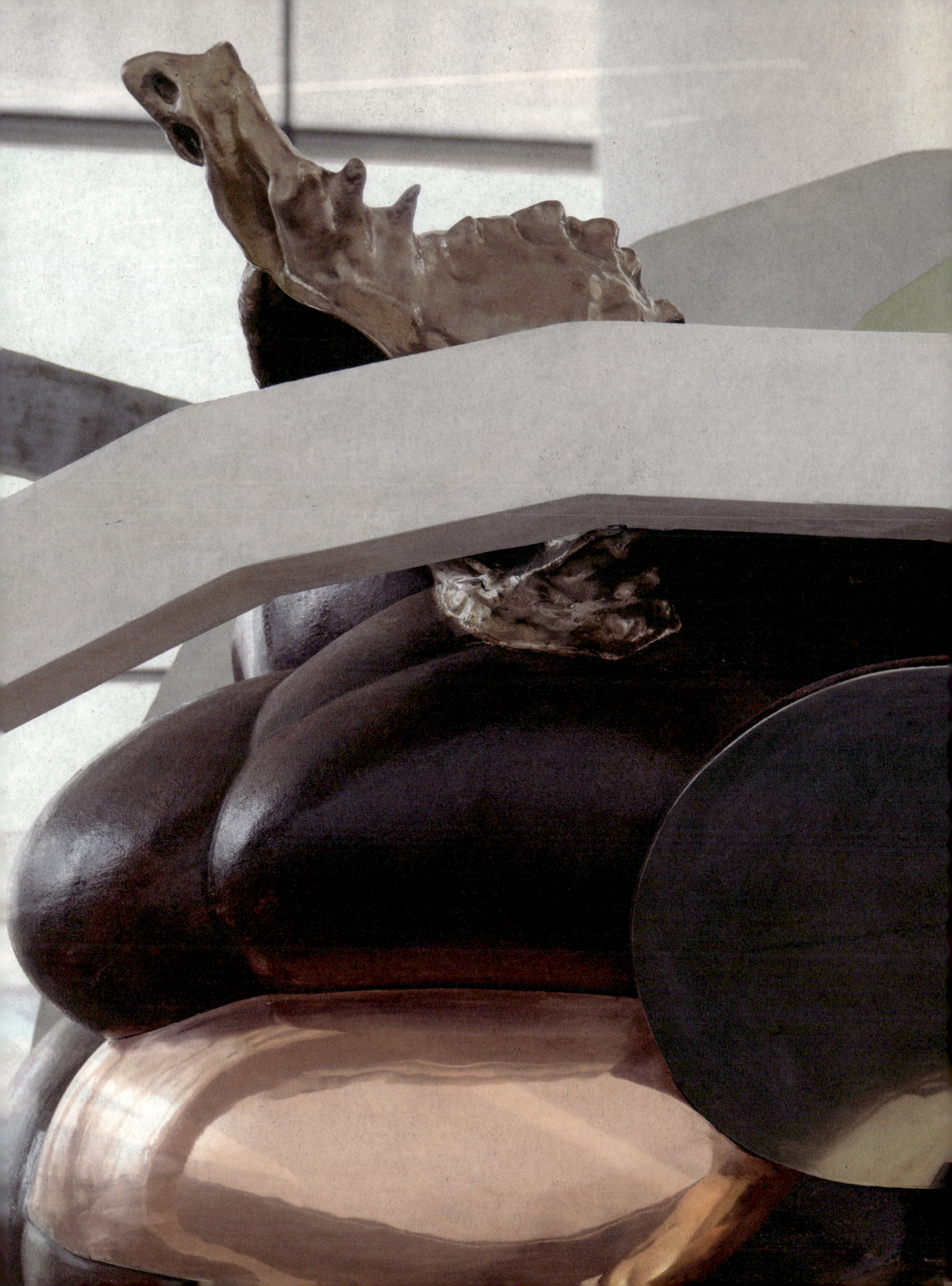

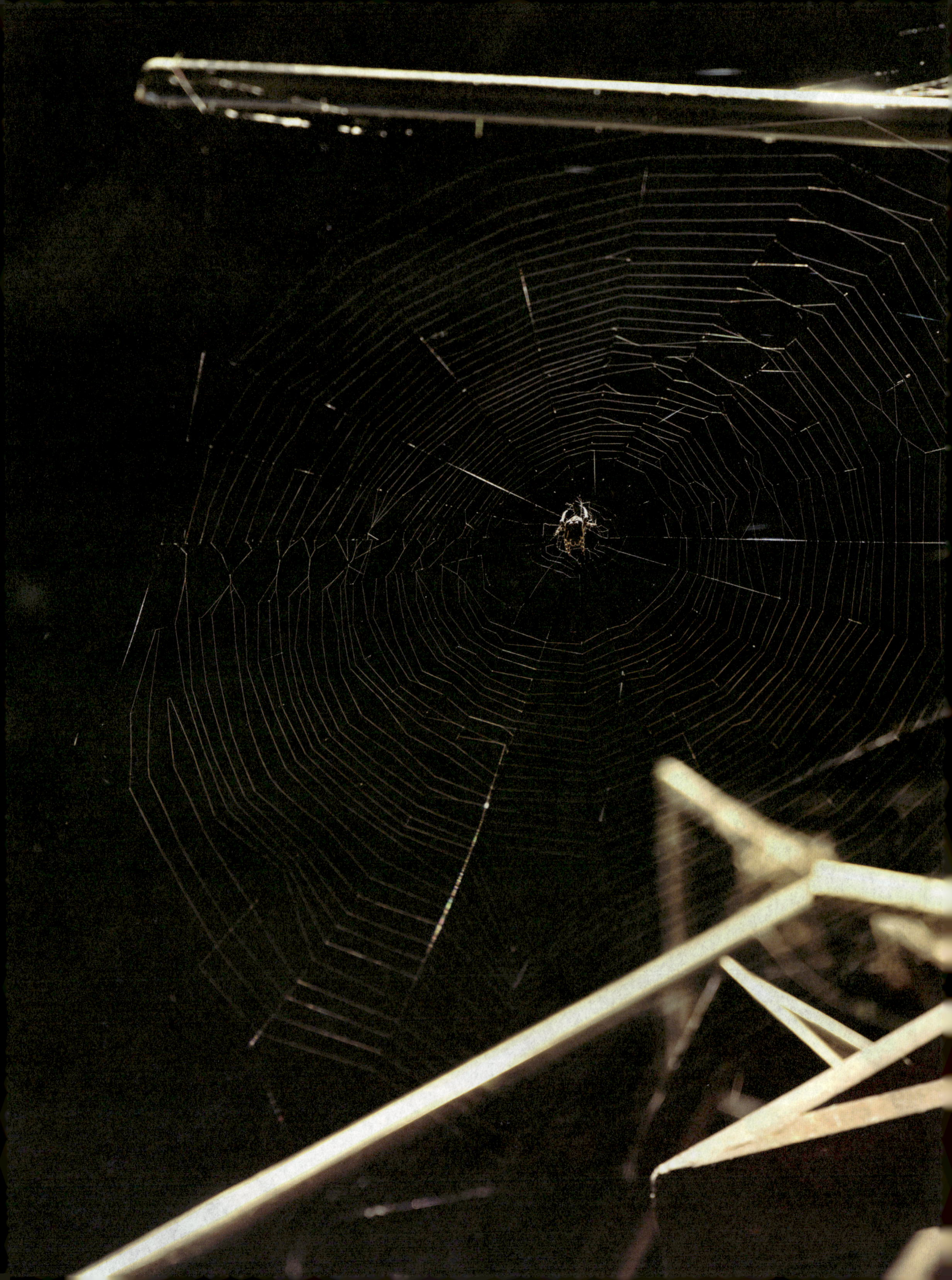

[21] [22] *The Dubious of Entanglement by Plants*, 2012–24. Iron, stainless steel, brass, red copper, wood, plants. 490 × 450 × 400 cm

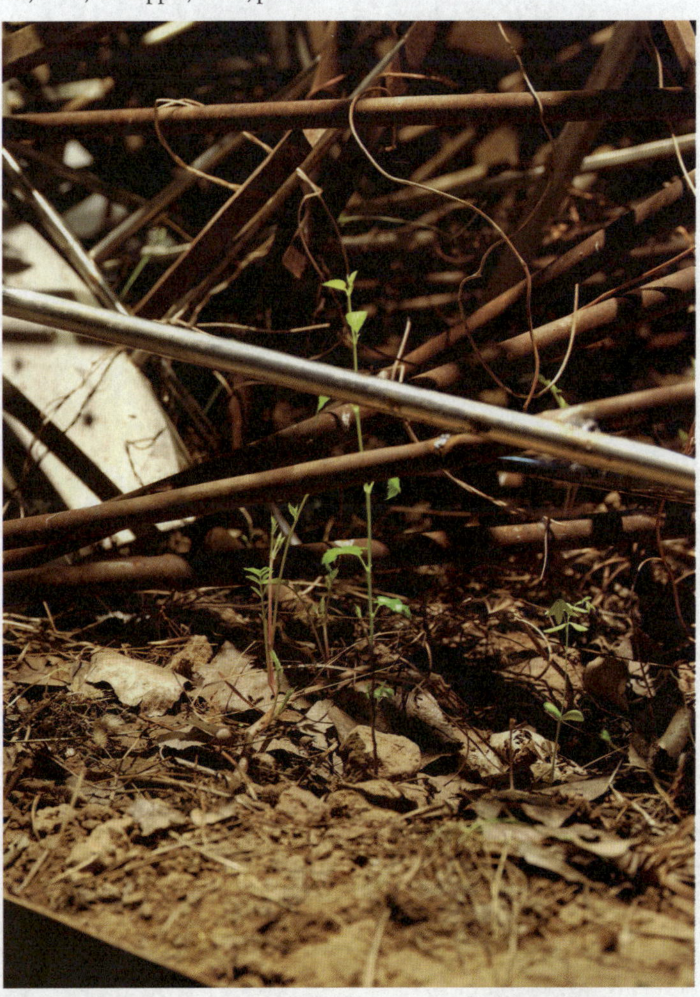

[21]

[22]

[23]

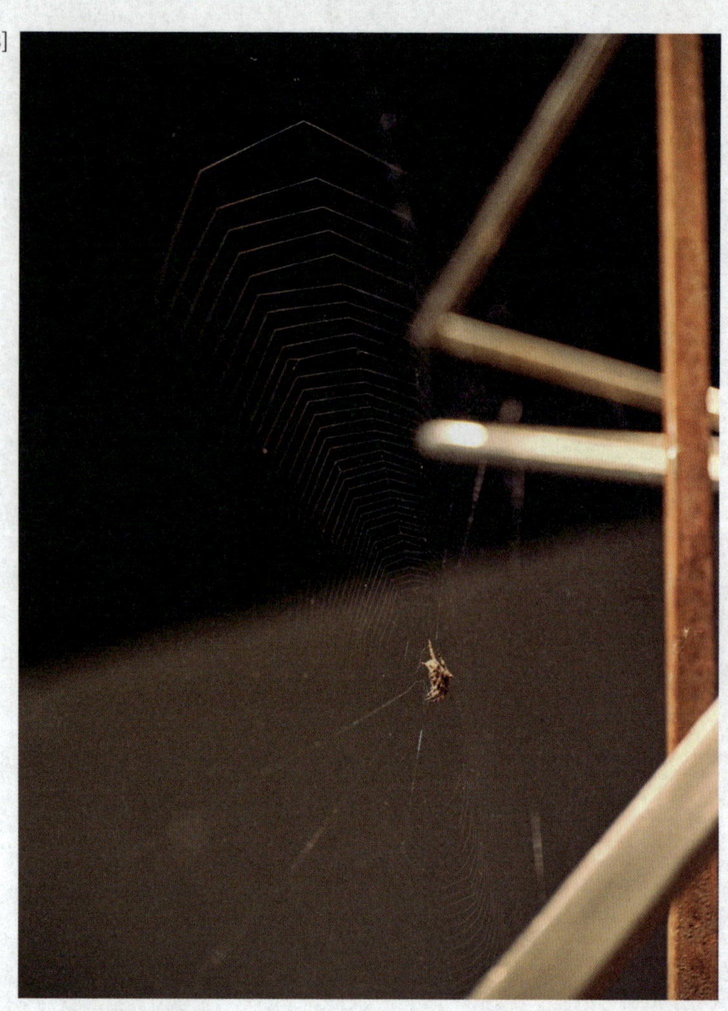

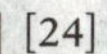

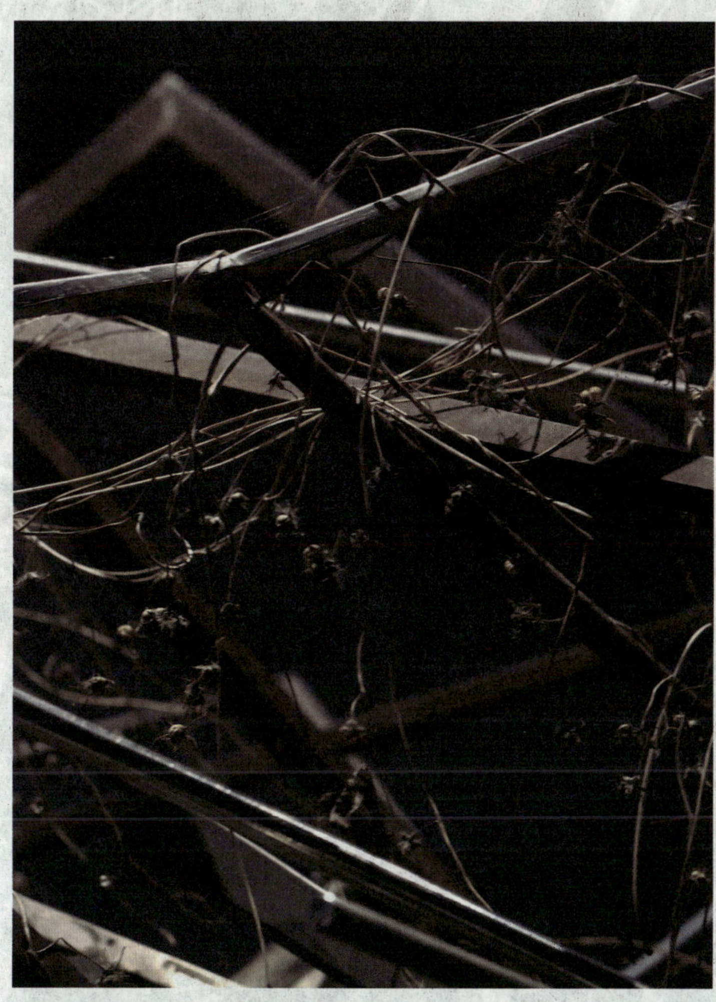

[24]

[23] [24, 25] *The Dubious of Entanglement by Plants*, 2012–24. Iron, stainless steel, brass, red copper, wood, plants. 490 × 450 × 400 cm

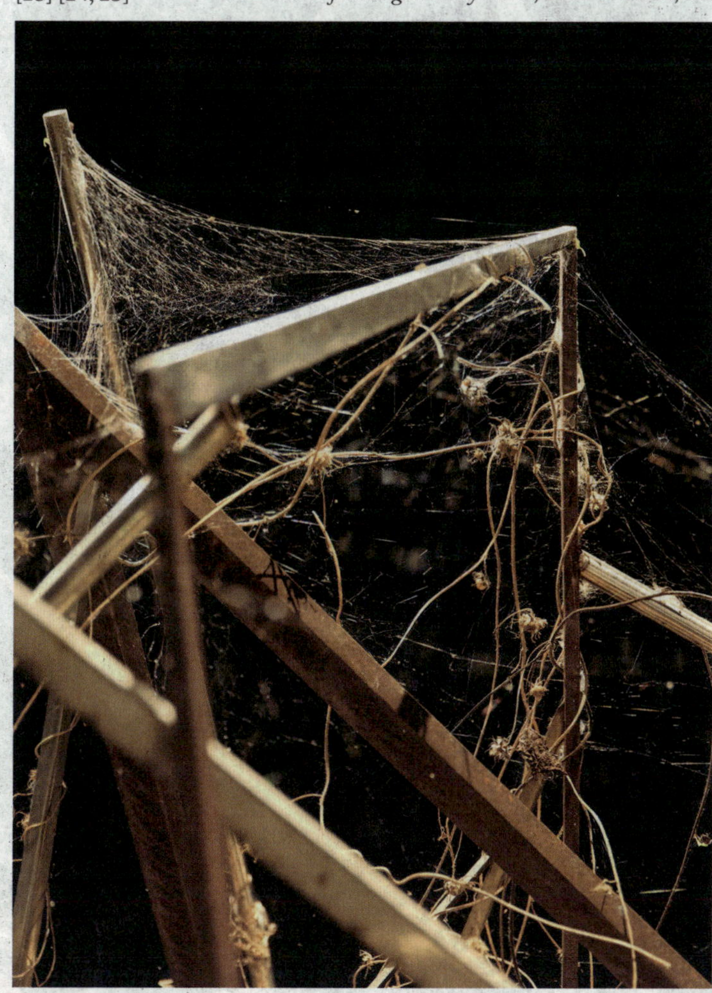

[25]

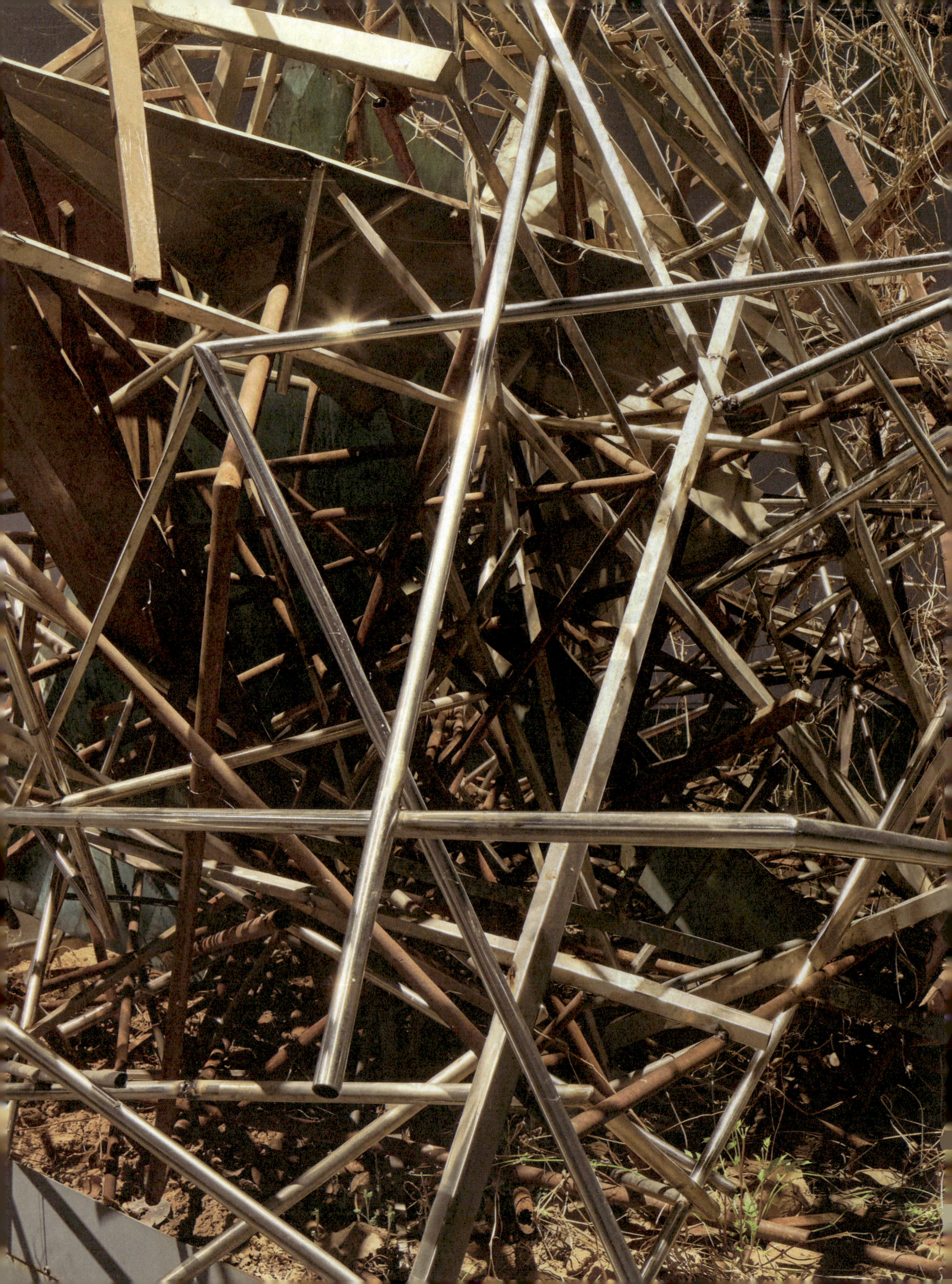

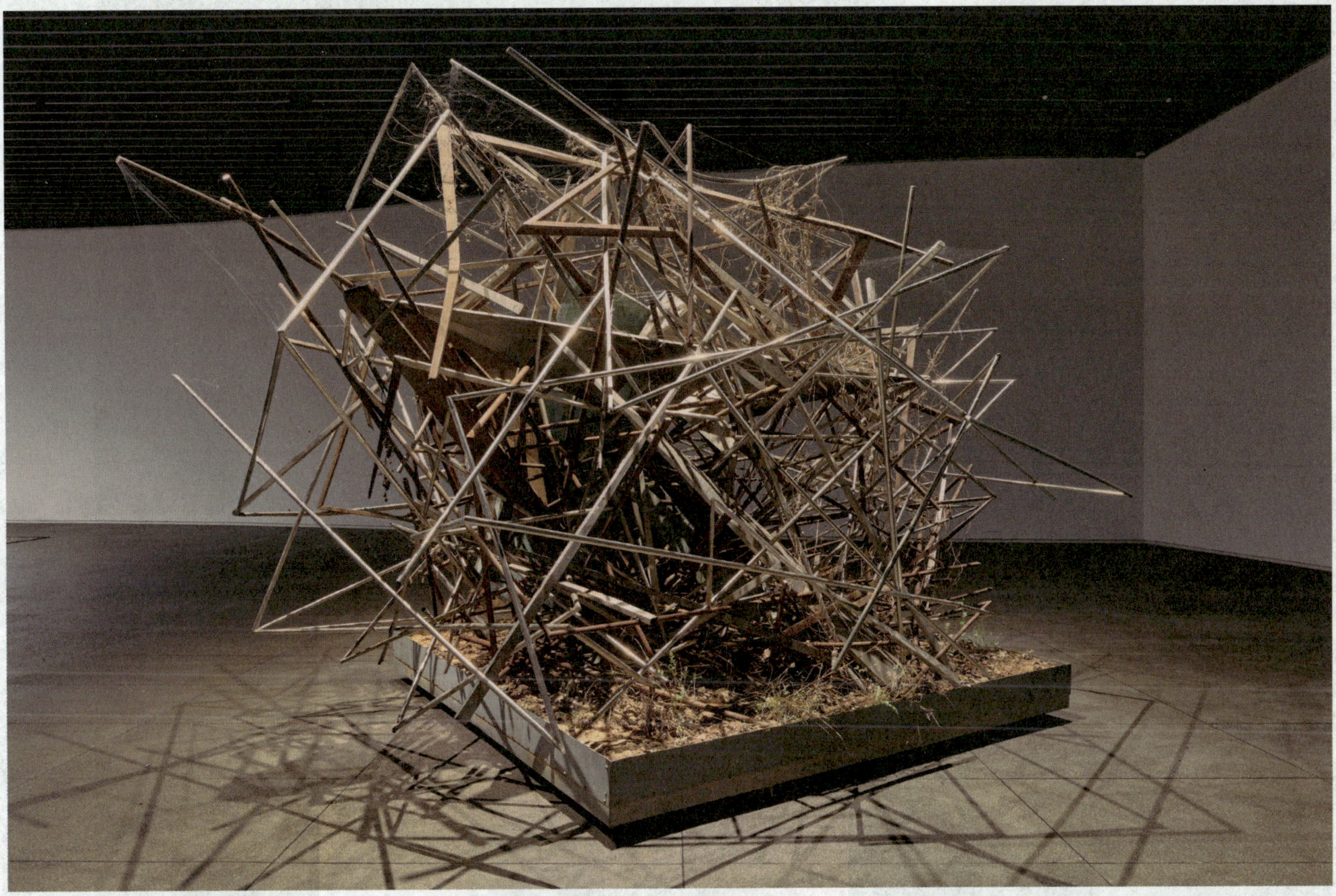

[26] [27, 28] *The Dubious of Entanglement by Plants*, 2012–24. Iron, stainless steel, brass, red copper, wood, plants. 490 × 450 × 400 cm

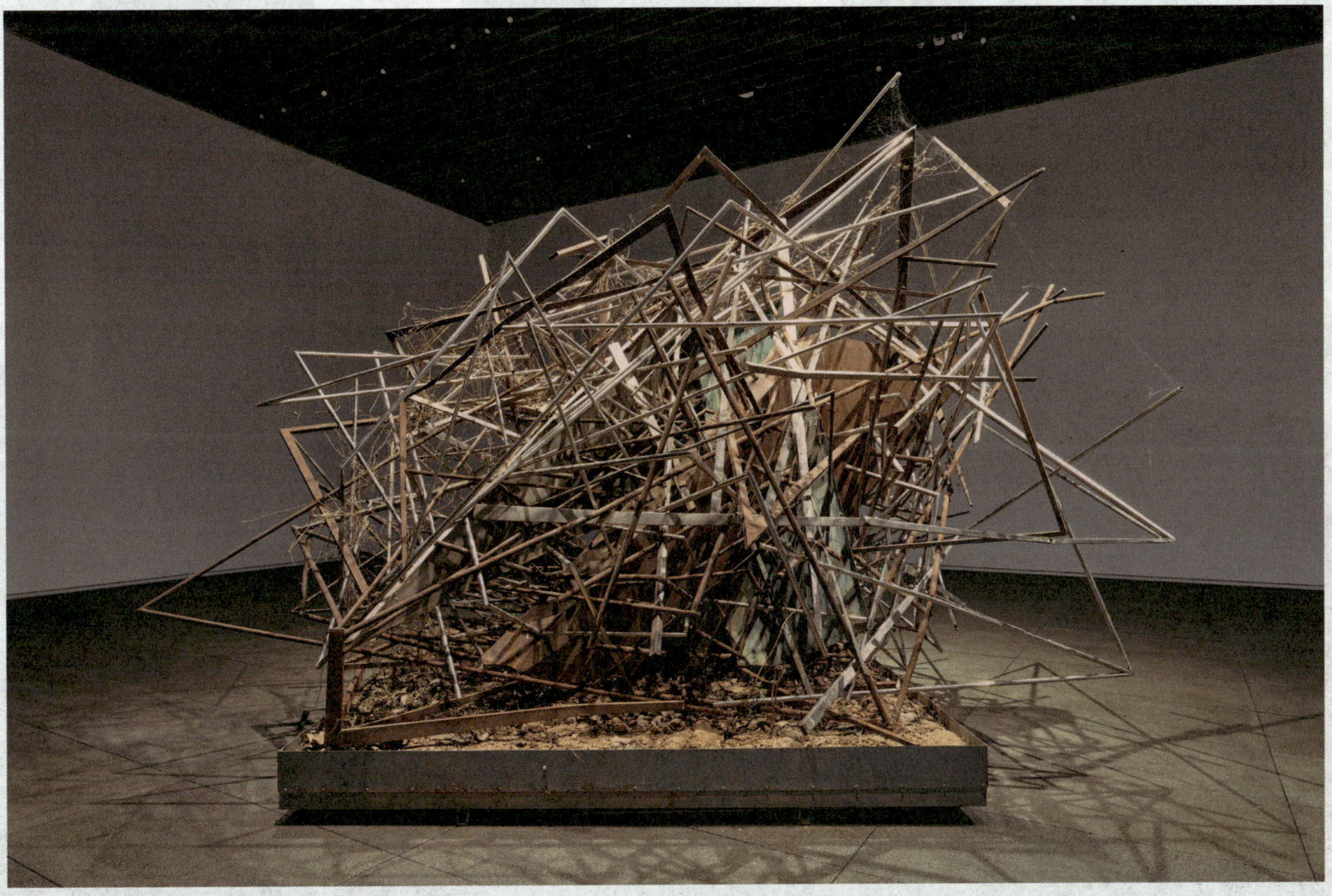

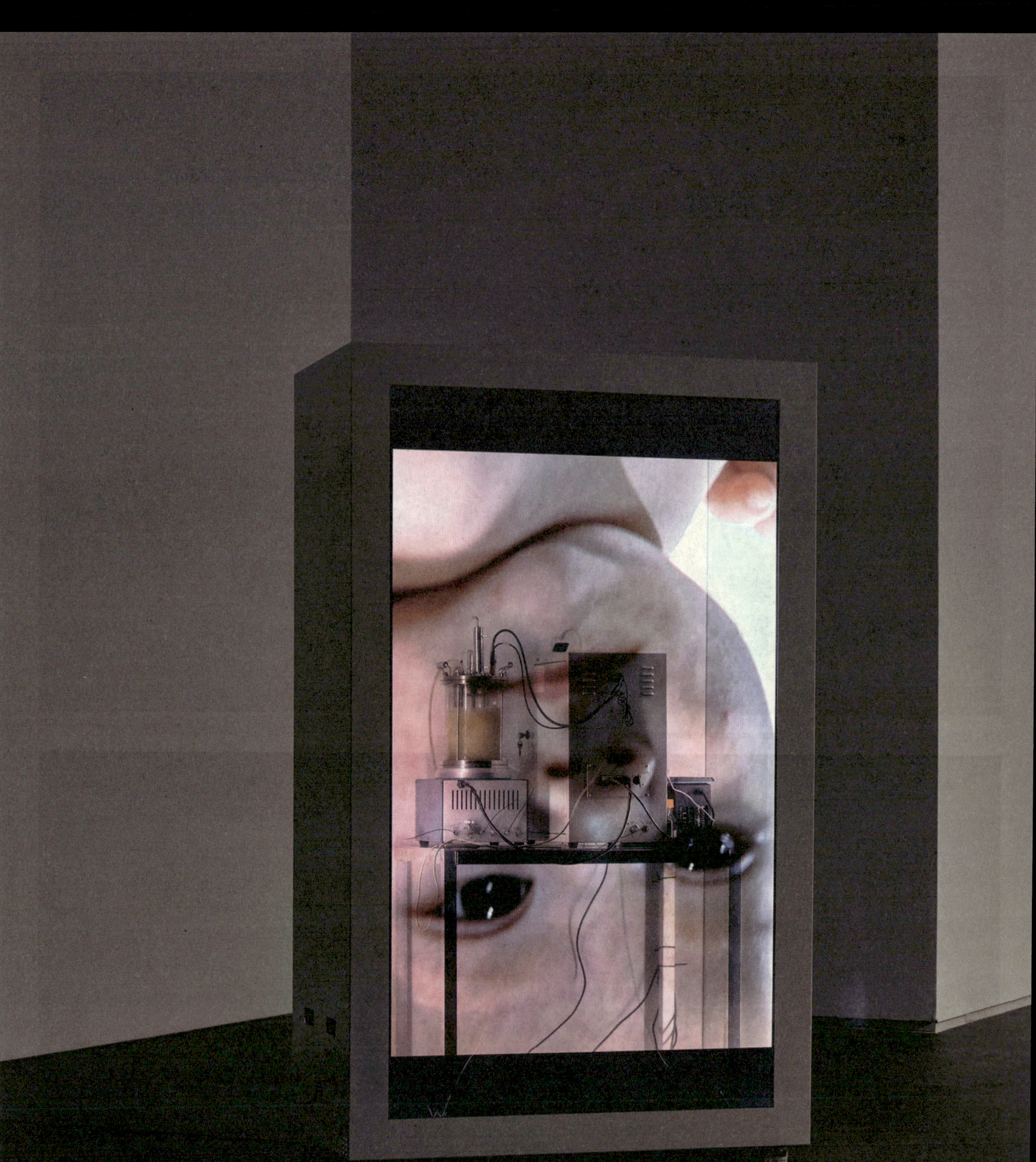

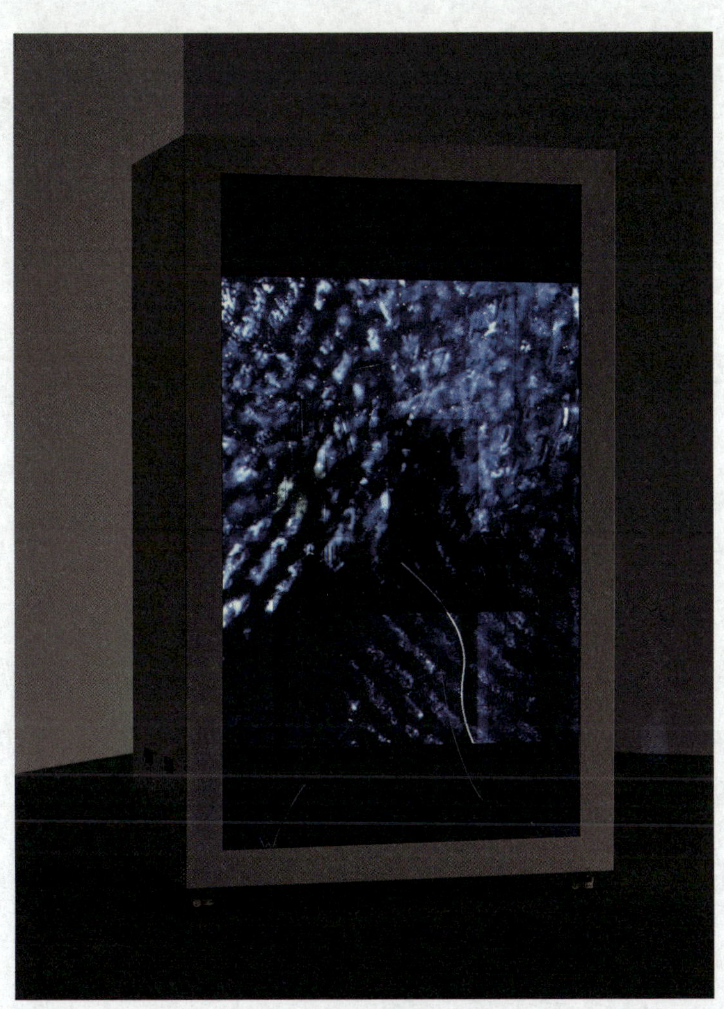

[30]

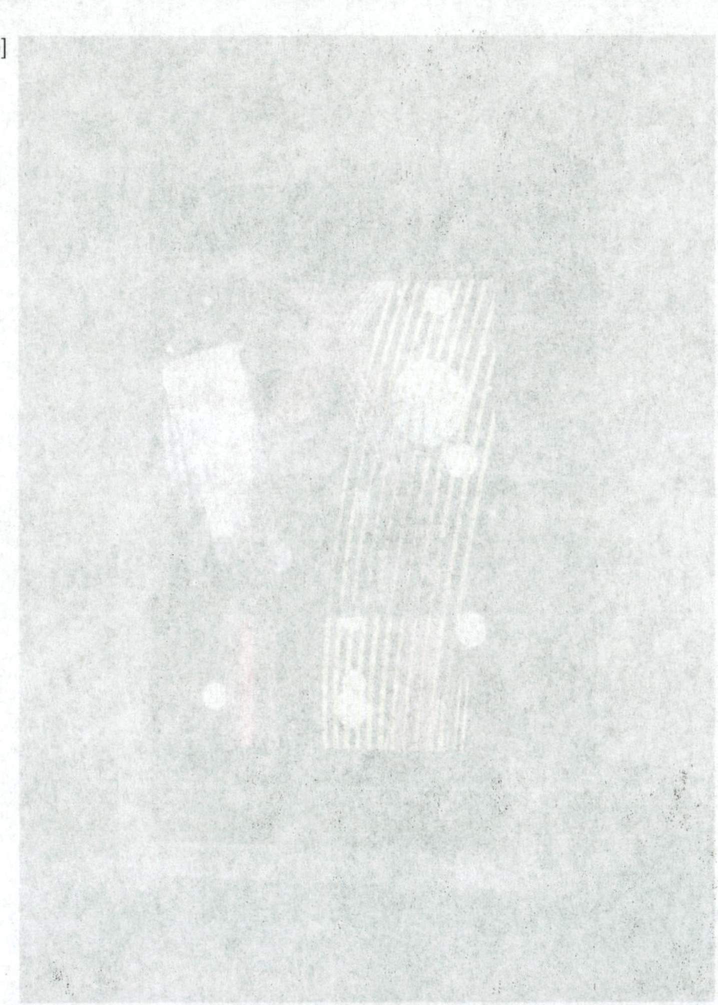

[29] [30, 31] *I Don't Know*, 2024. Fermenters, microorganisms, transparent screens, computers, cameras. 240 × 80 × 146 cm

[29]

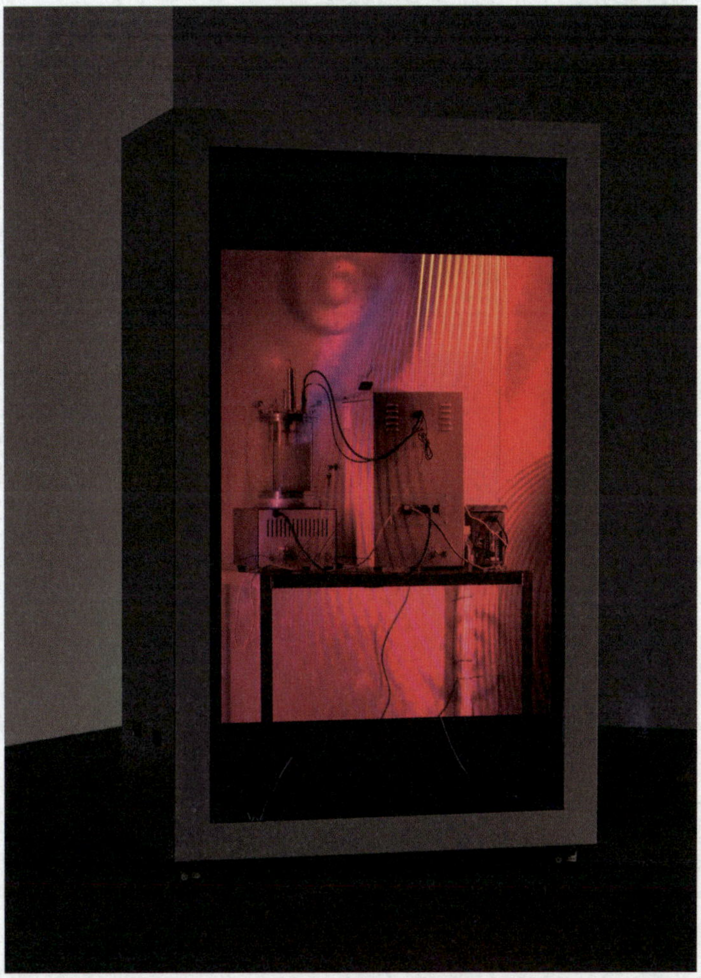

[31]

[32]

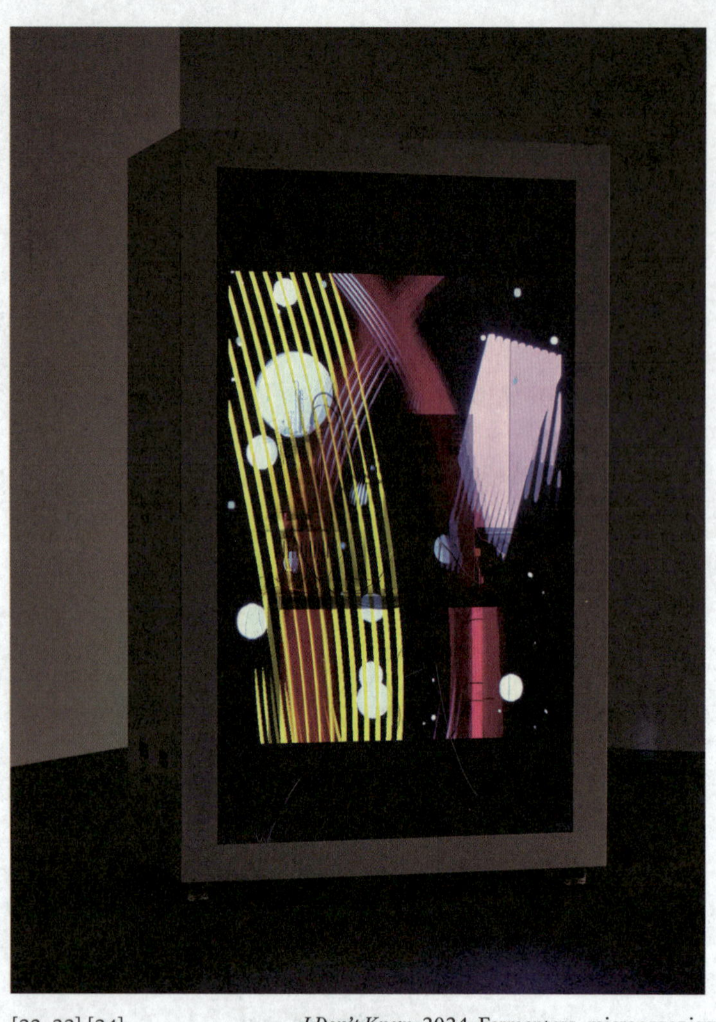

[34]

[32, 33] [34] *I Don't Know*, 2024. Fermenters, microorganisms, transparent screens, computers, cameras. 240 × 80 × 146 cm

[33]

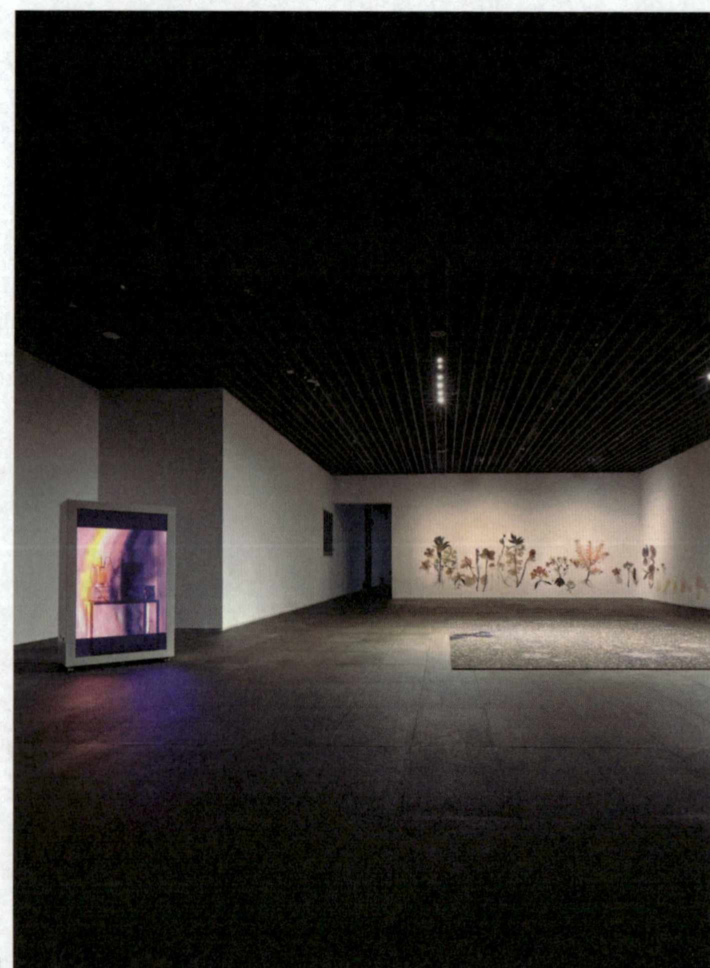

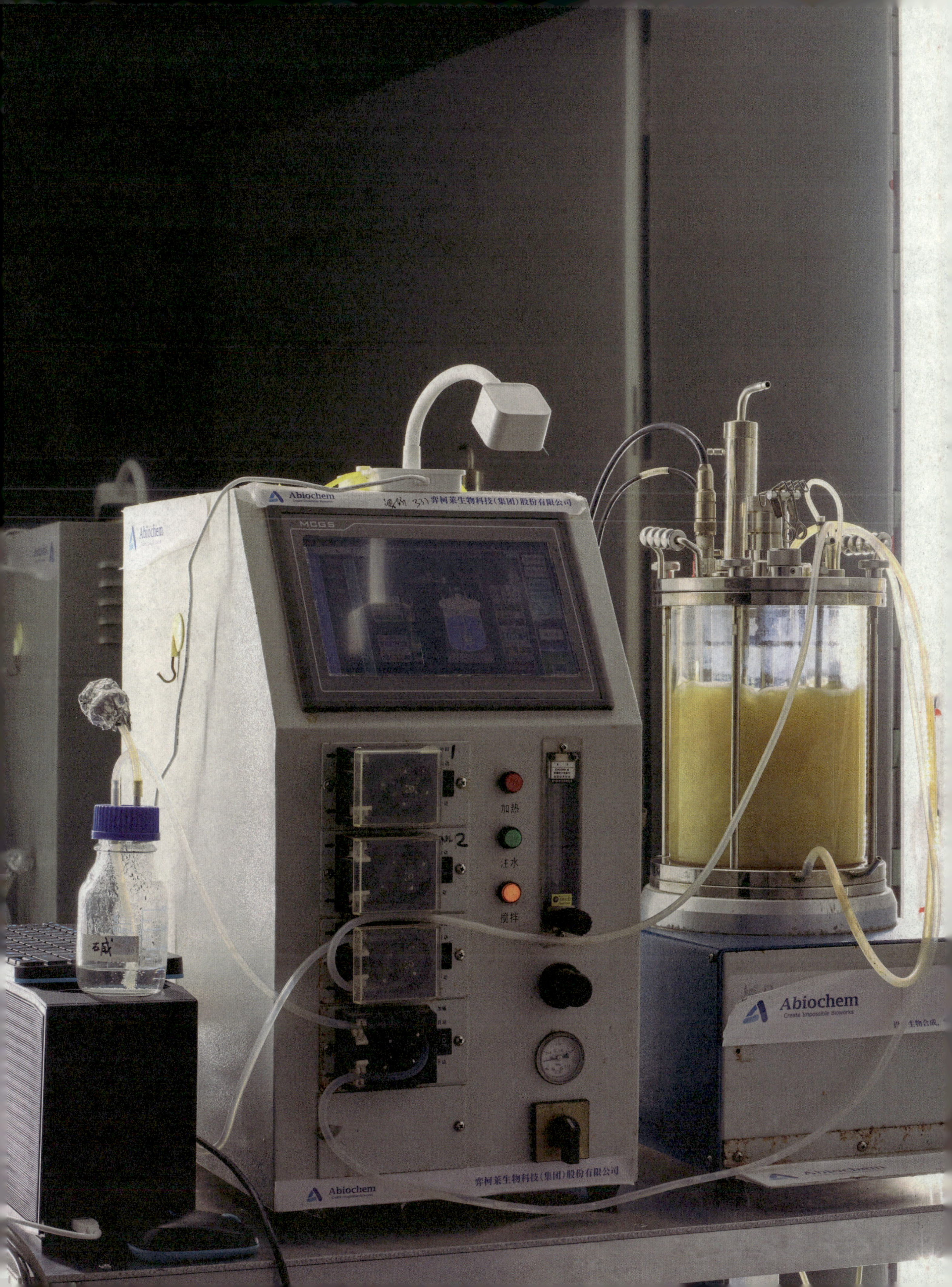
Abiochem
弈柯莱生物科技(集团)股份有限公司
MCGS
加热
注水
搅拌
Abiochem
Create Impossible Bioworks
Abiochem
弈柯莱生物科技(集团)股份有限公司

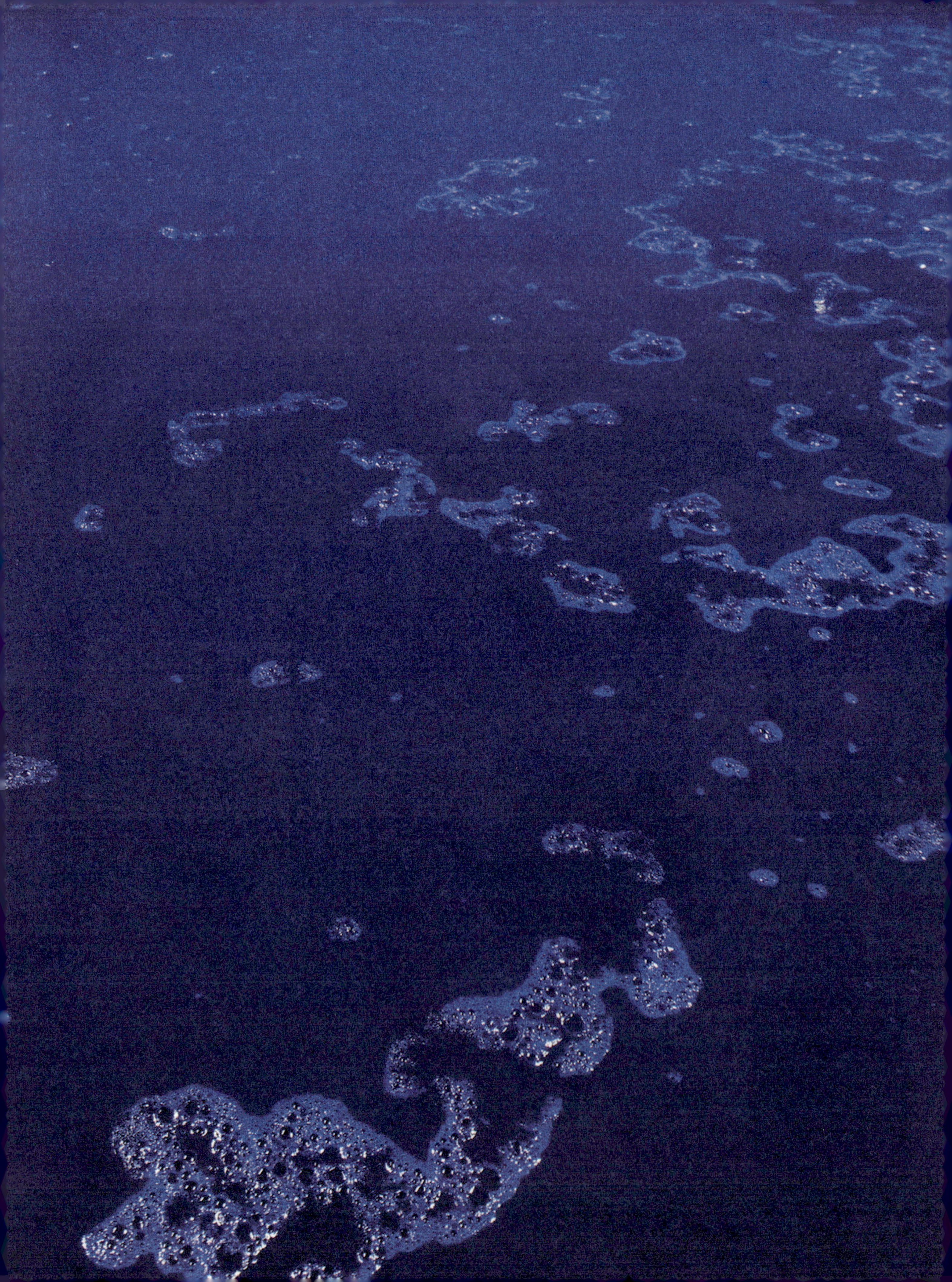

[35]

[35] [36] *Biological Klein Blue*, 2022. Microorganisms. 5 × 699 × 527 cm

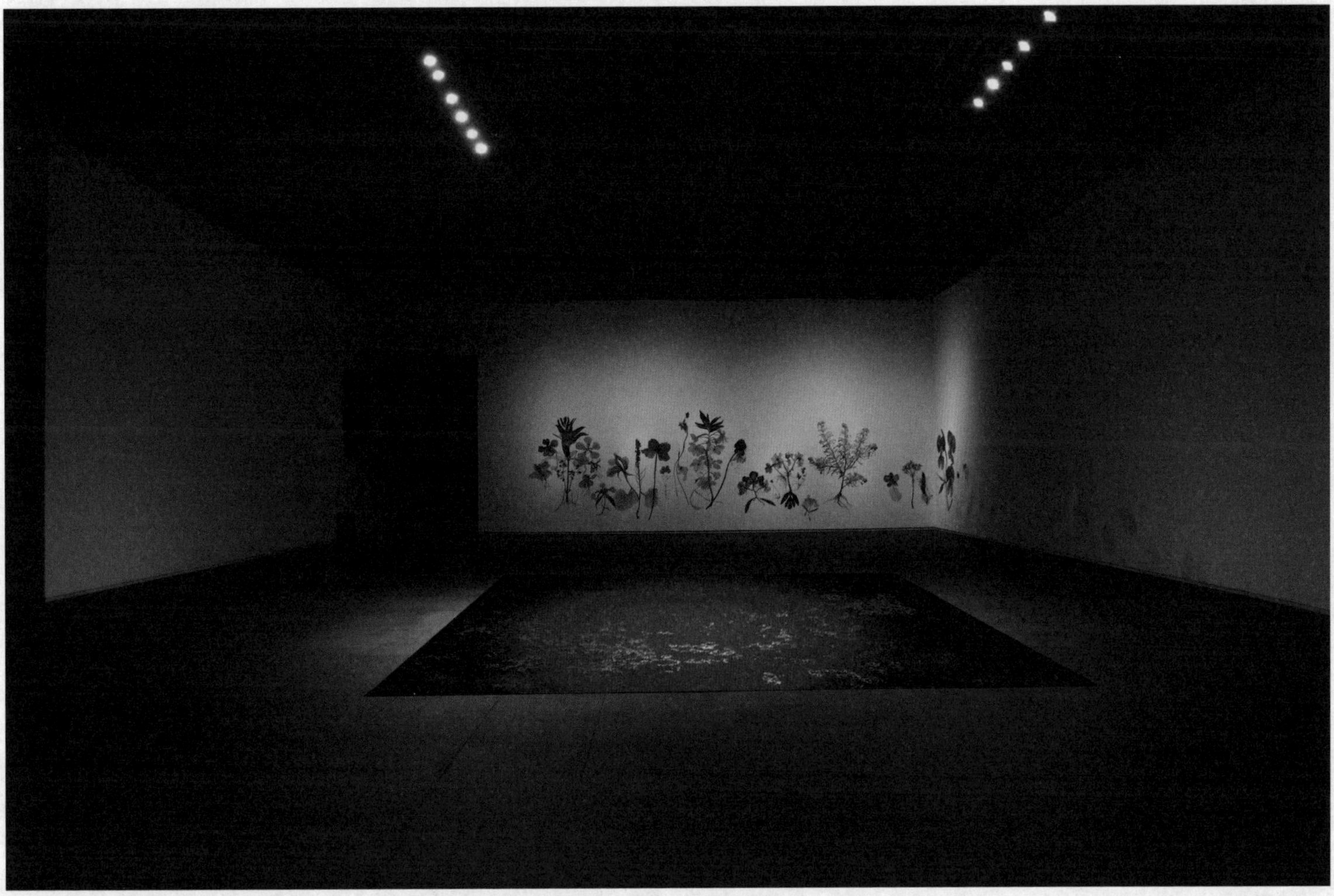

[37]
[38]

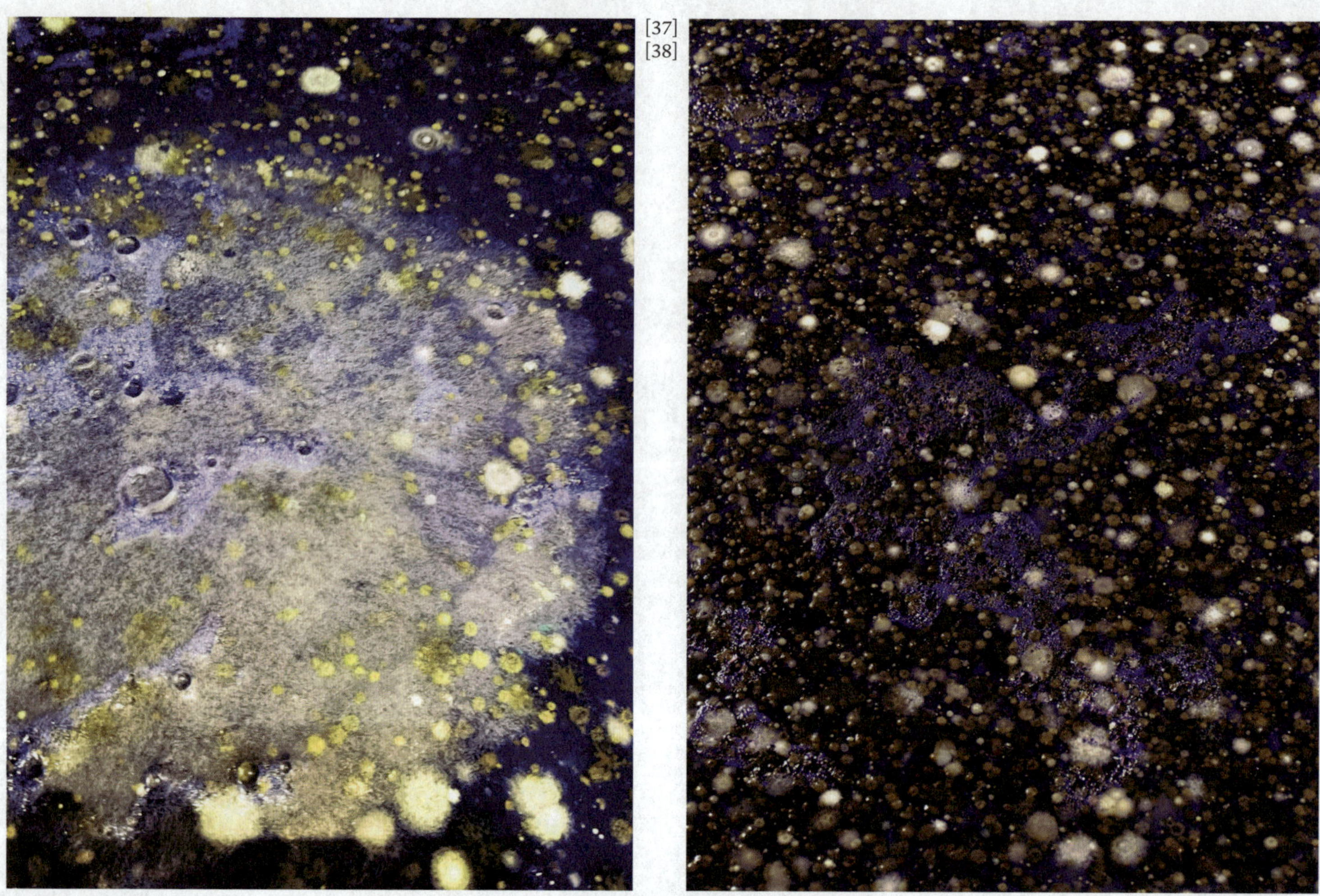

[37, 38] [39] *Biological Klein Blue*, 2022. Microorganisms. 5 × 699 × 527 cm

[39]

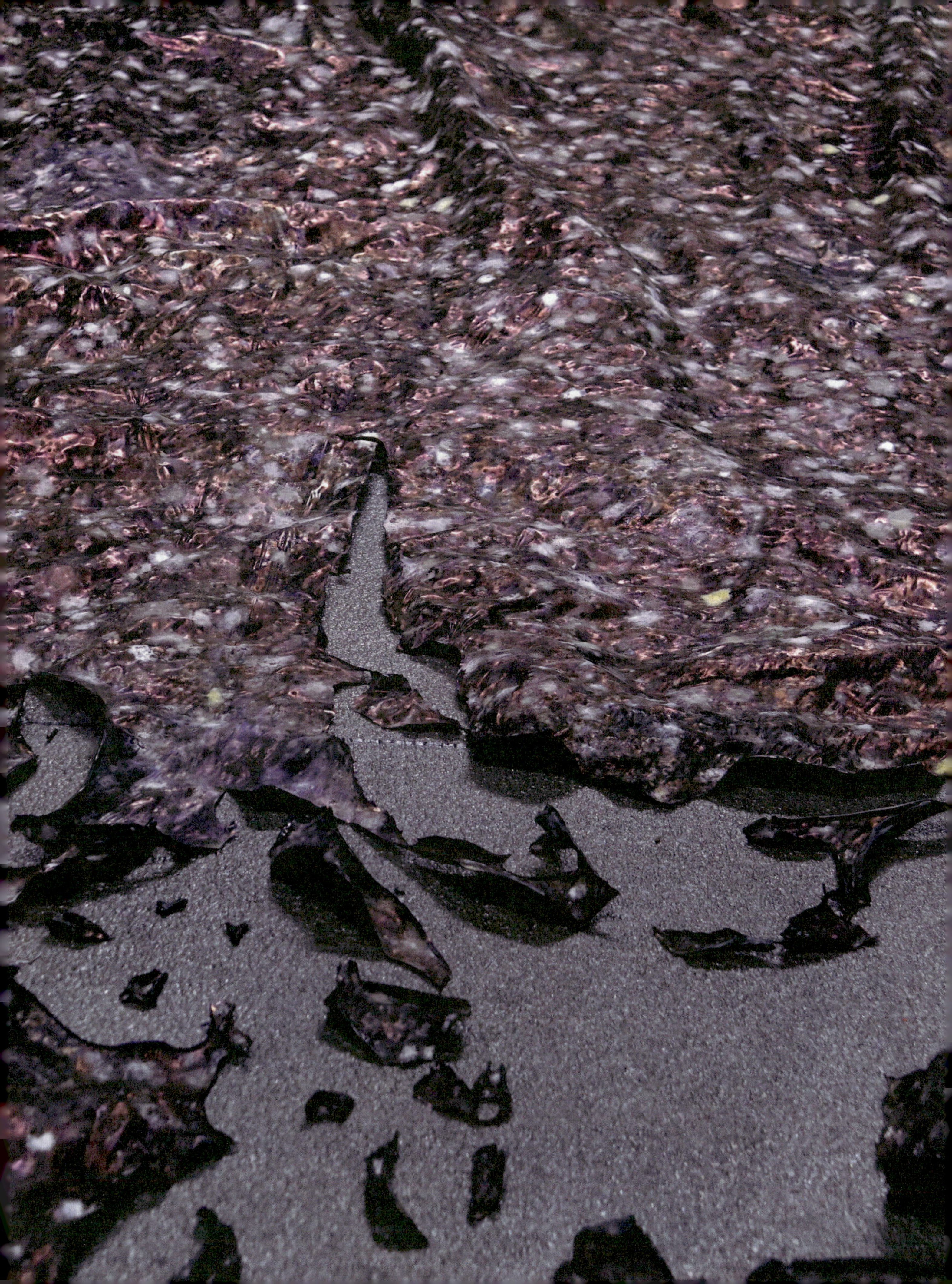

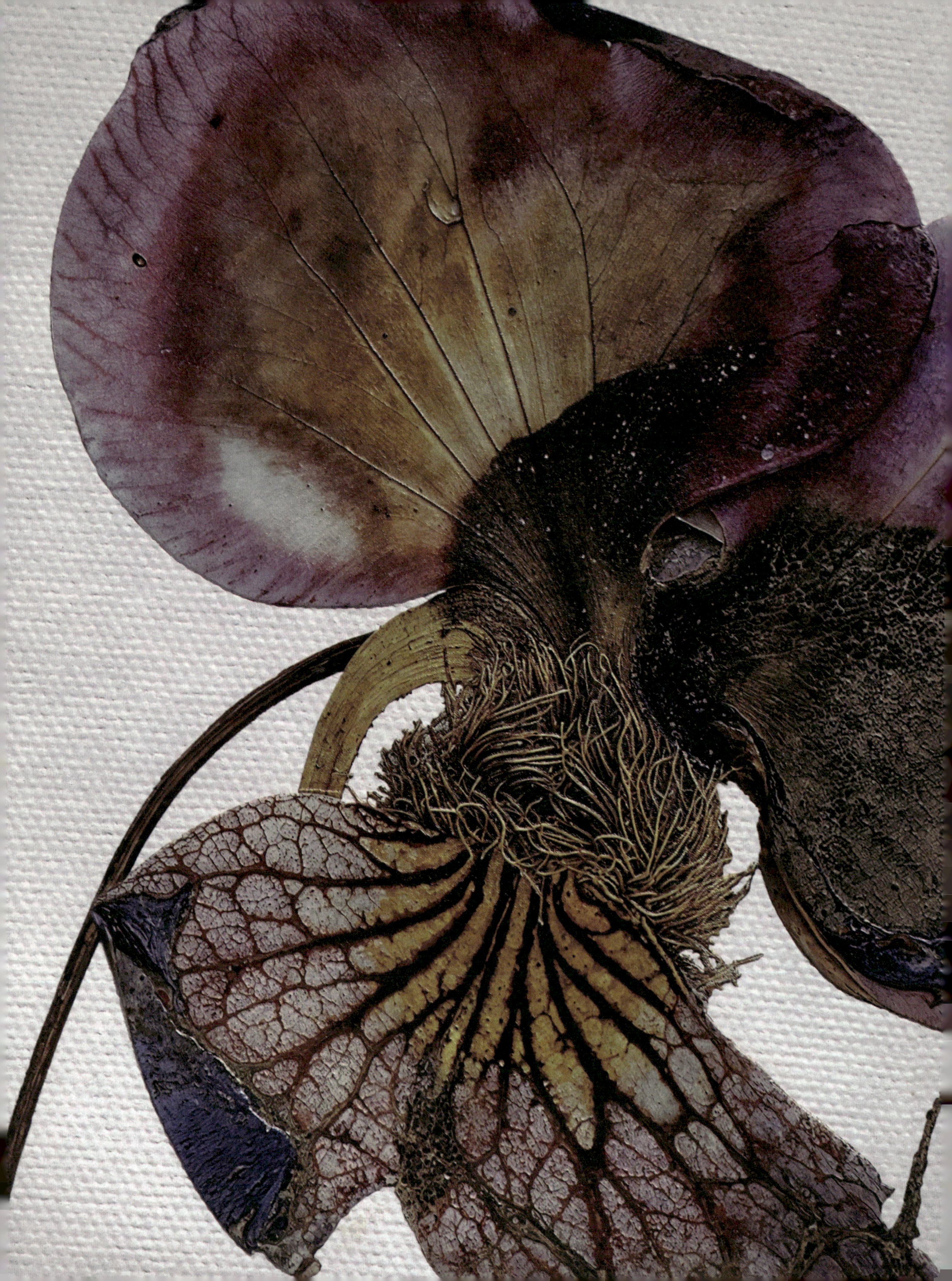

[41]
[42]

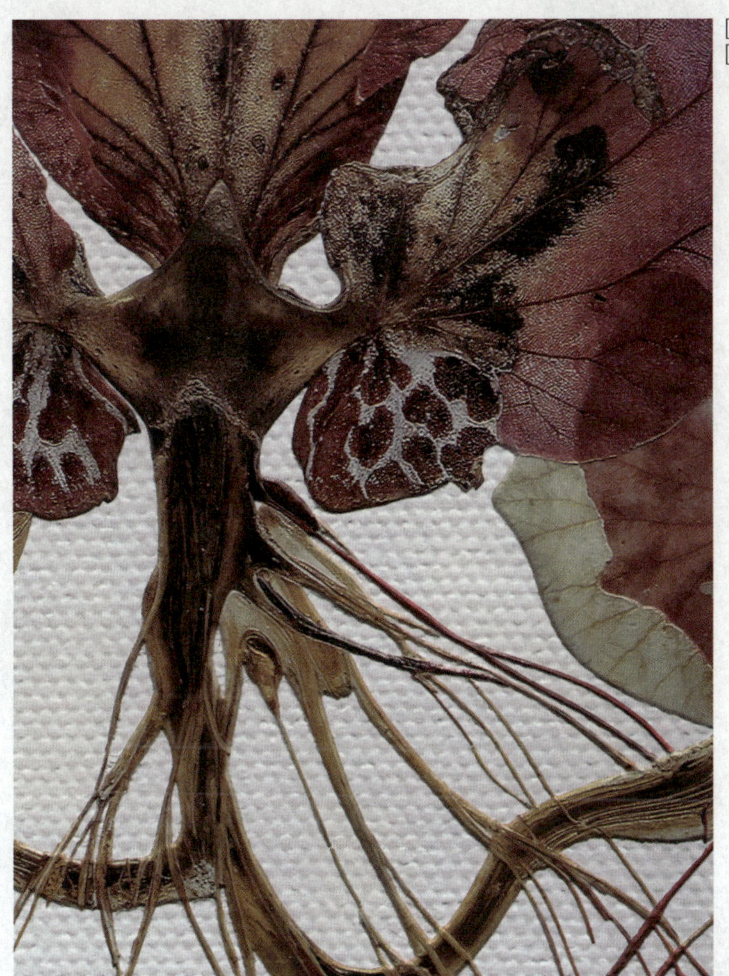

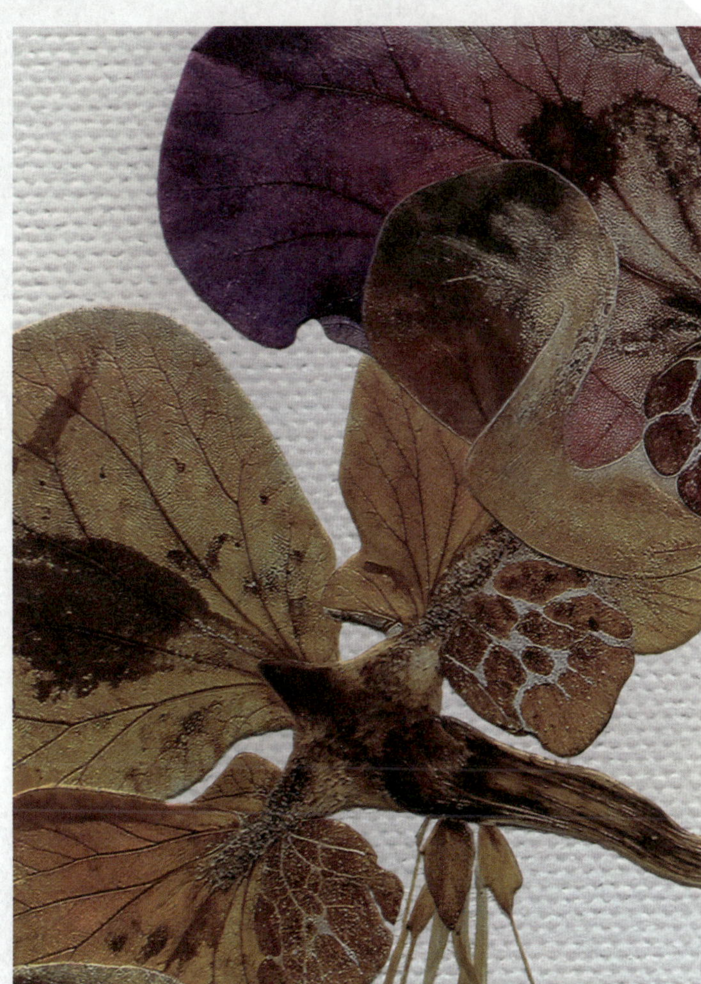

[40] [41, 42] *Plant*, 2024. Acetate. 560 × 1135 cm

[40]

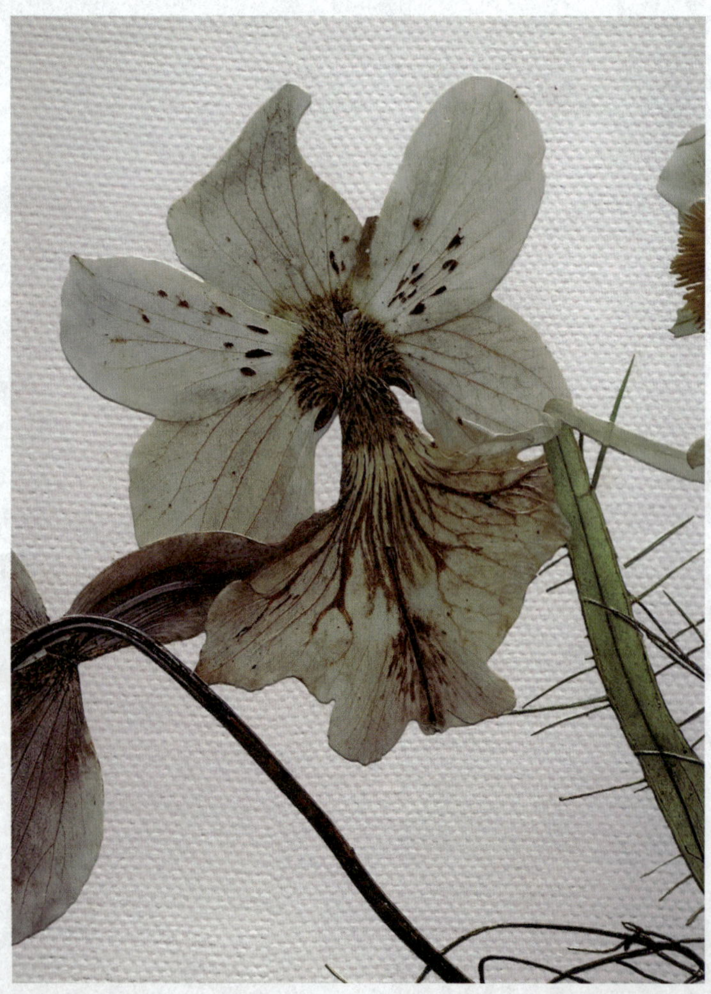

[43]
[44]

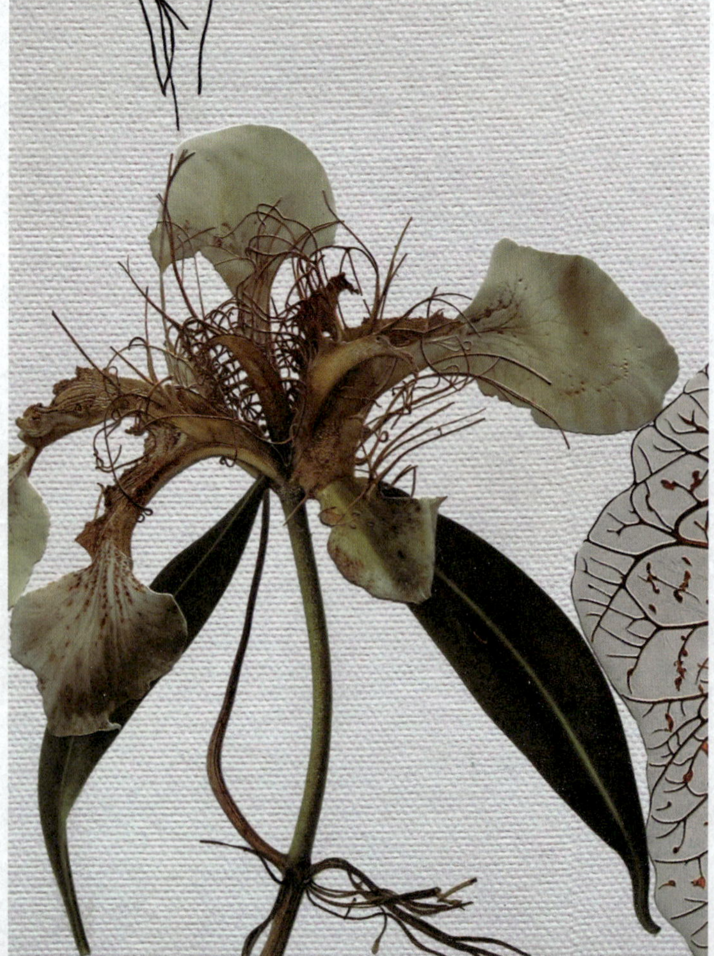

[45]

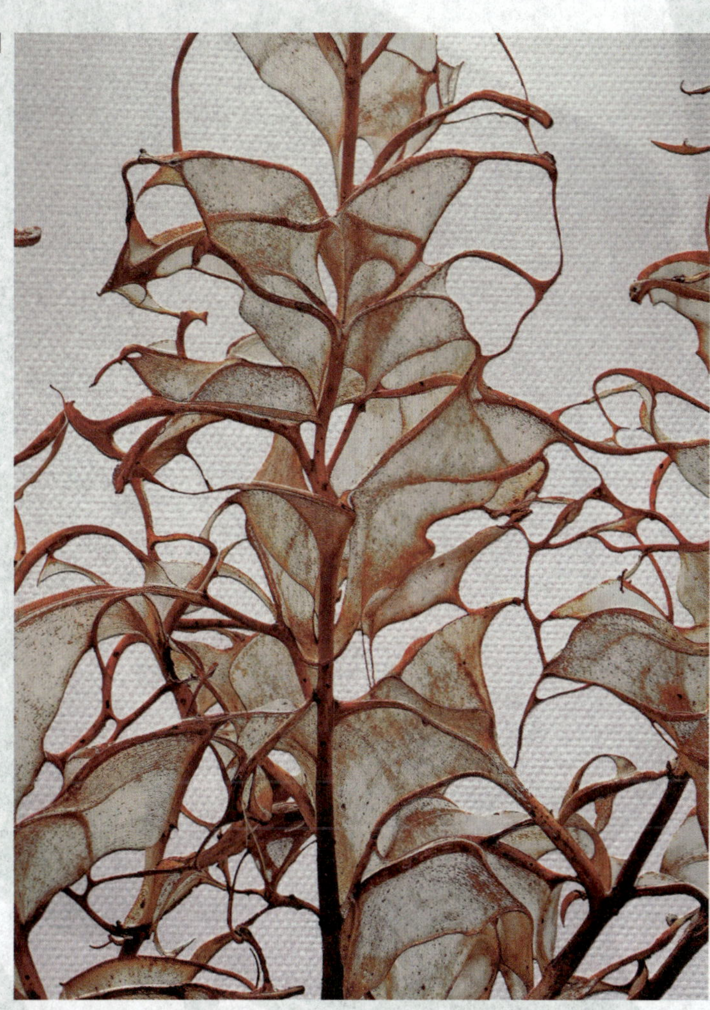

[43, 44] [45]

Plant, 2024. Acetate. 560 × 1135 cm

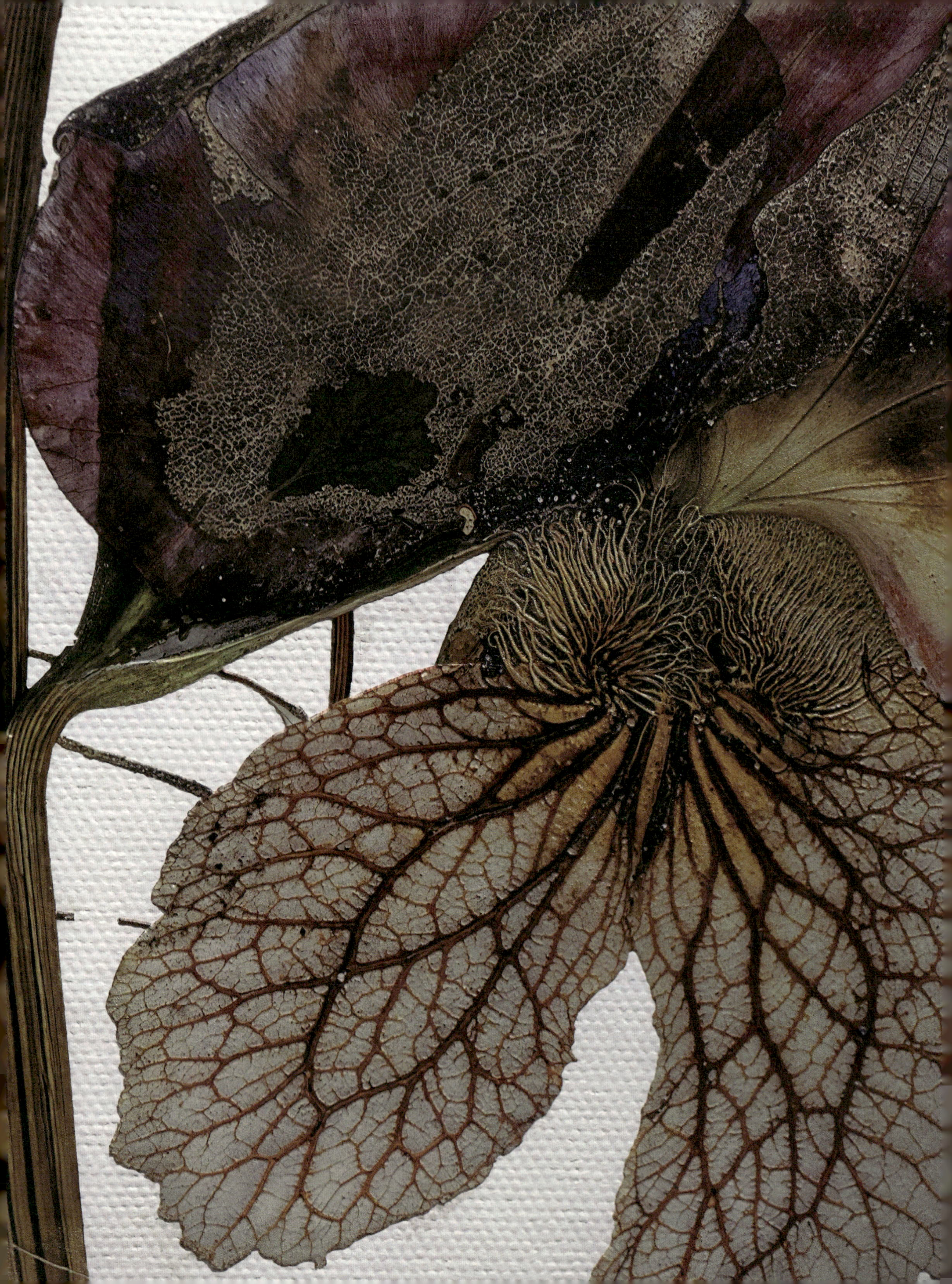

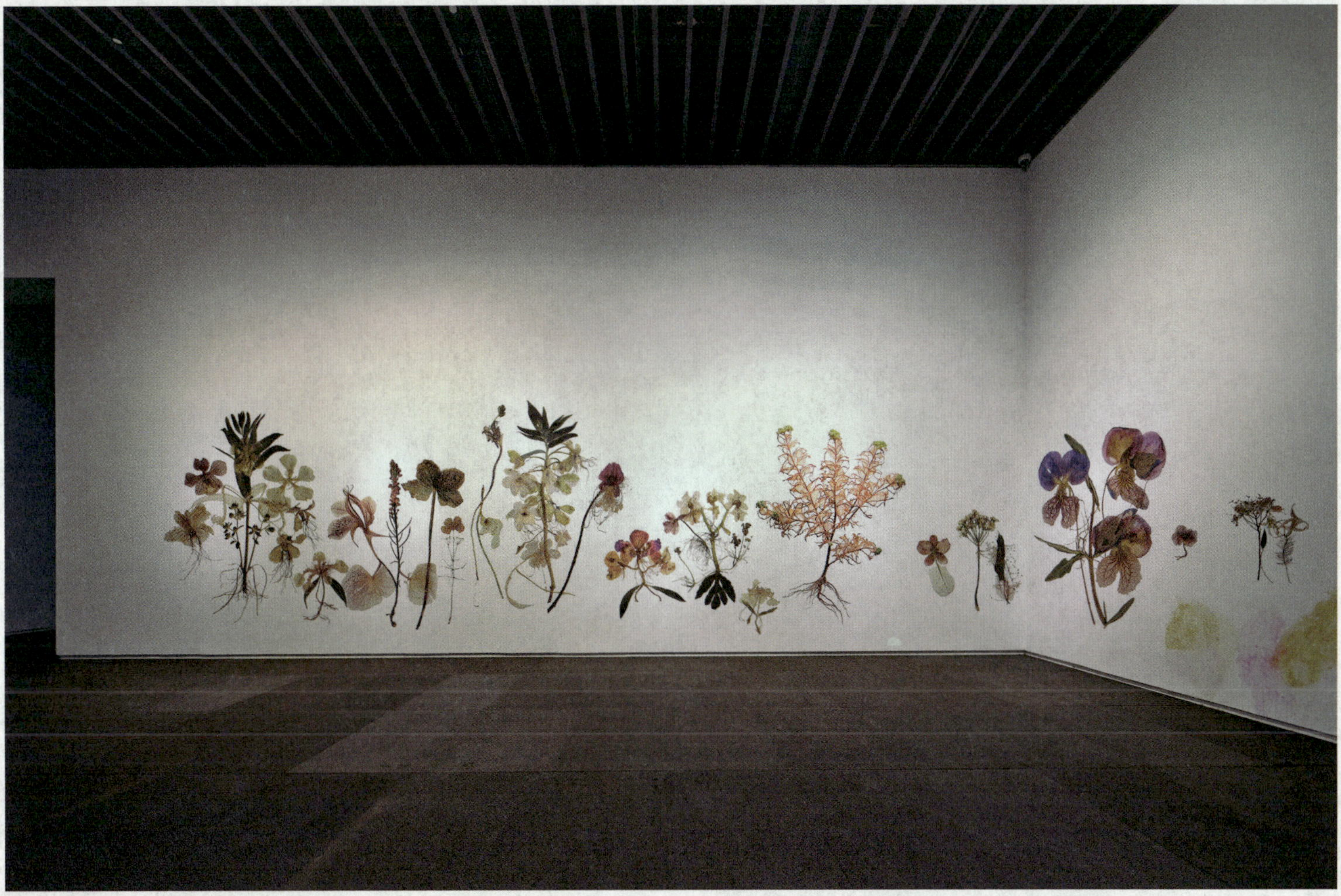

[46] [47, 48]

Plant, 2024. Acetate. 560 × 1135 cm

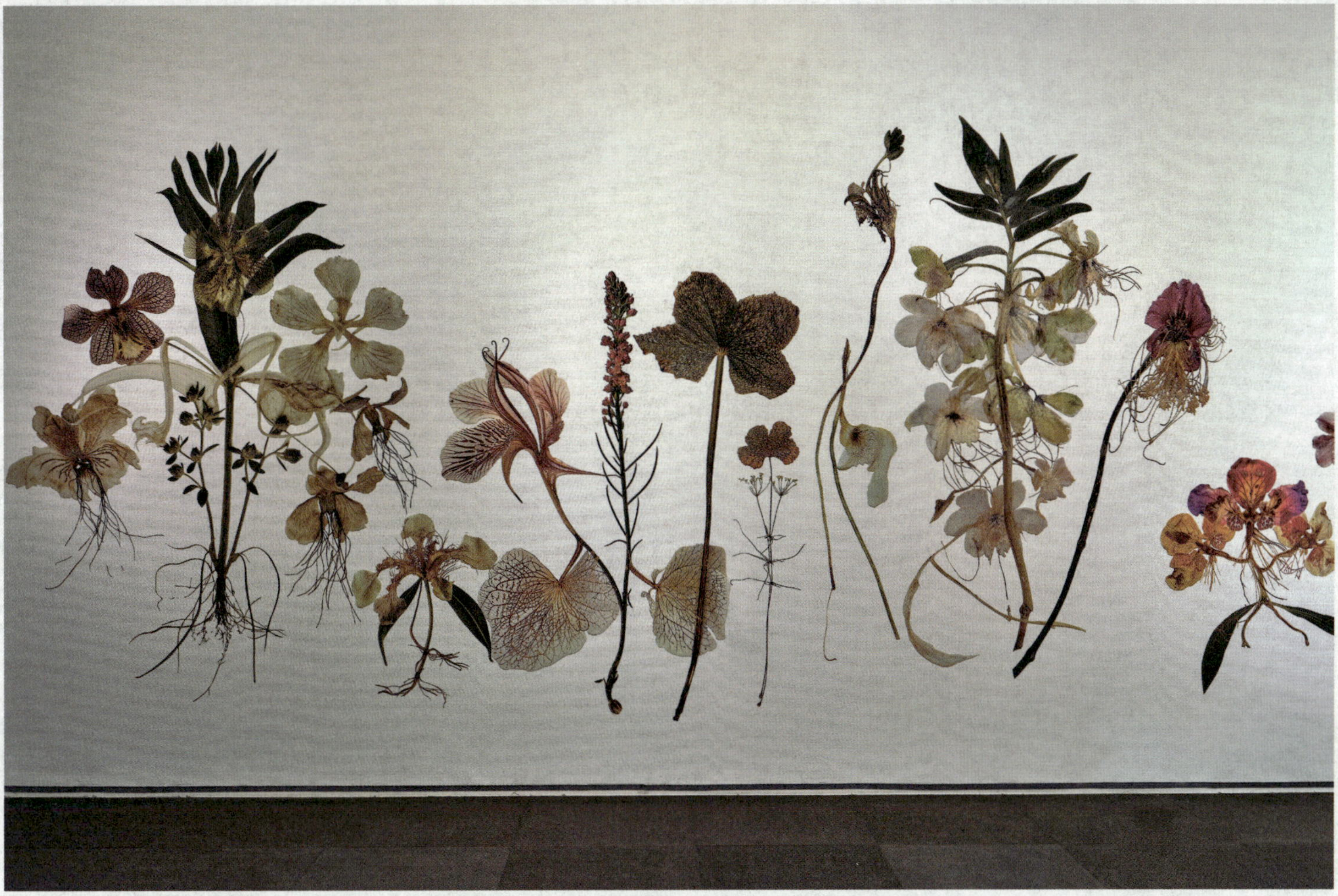

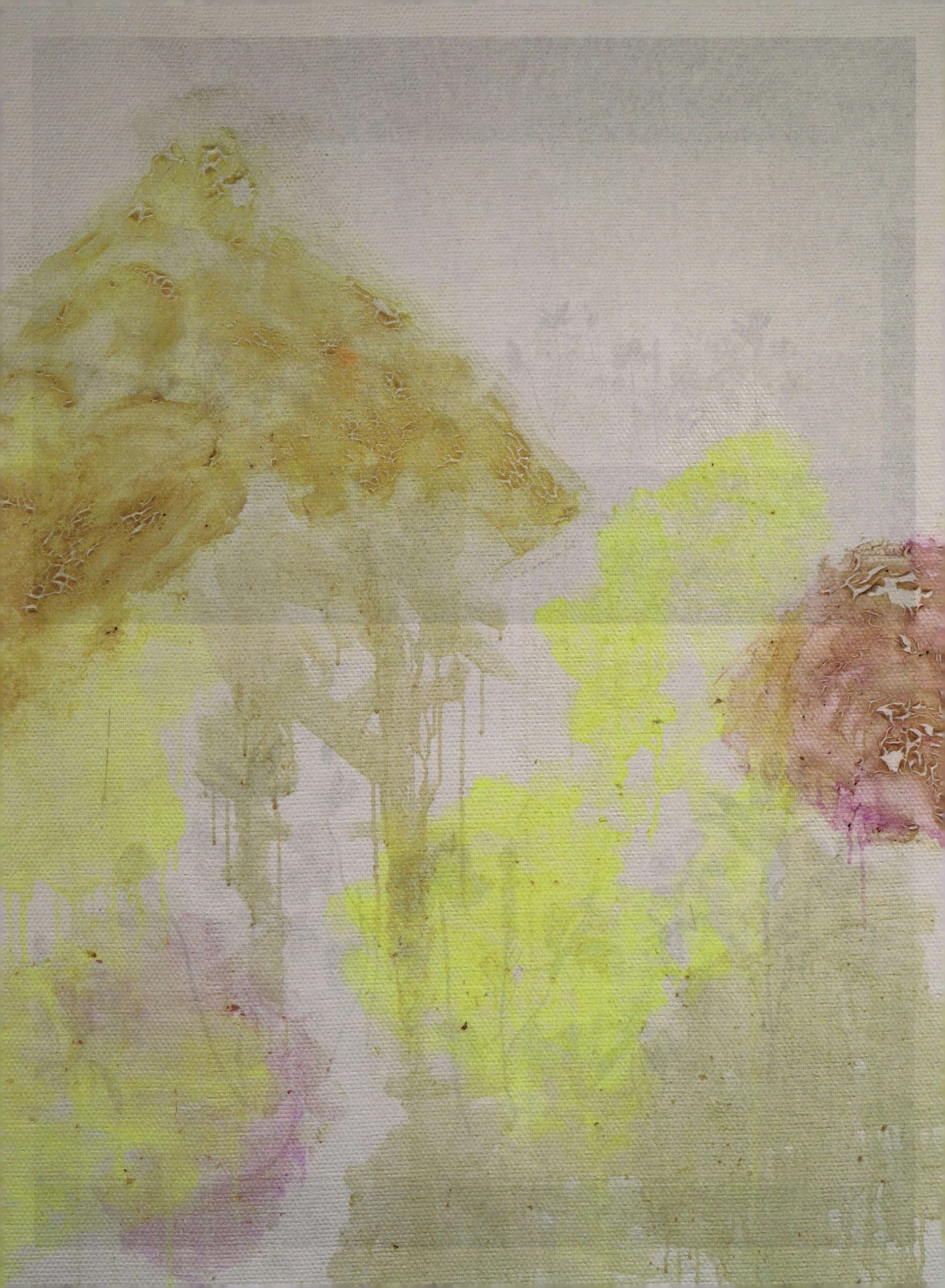

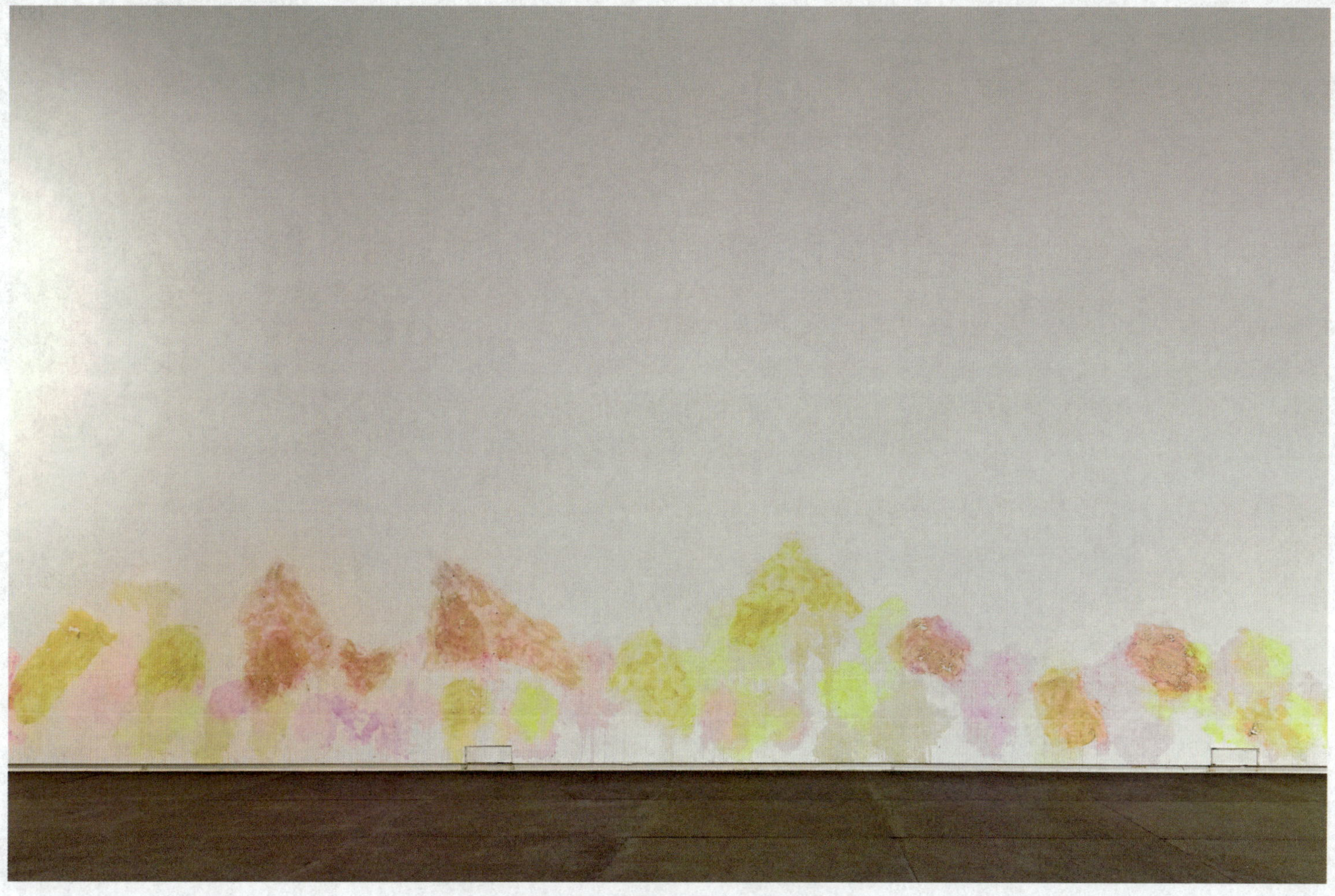

[49] [50] *Define*, 2022. Microorganisms. Variable dimensions

[51] [52] *Define*, 2022. Microorganisms. Variable dimensions

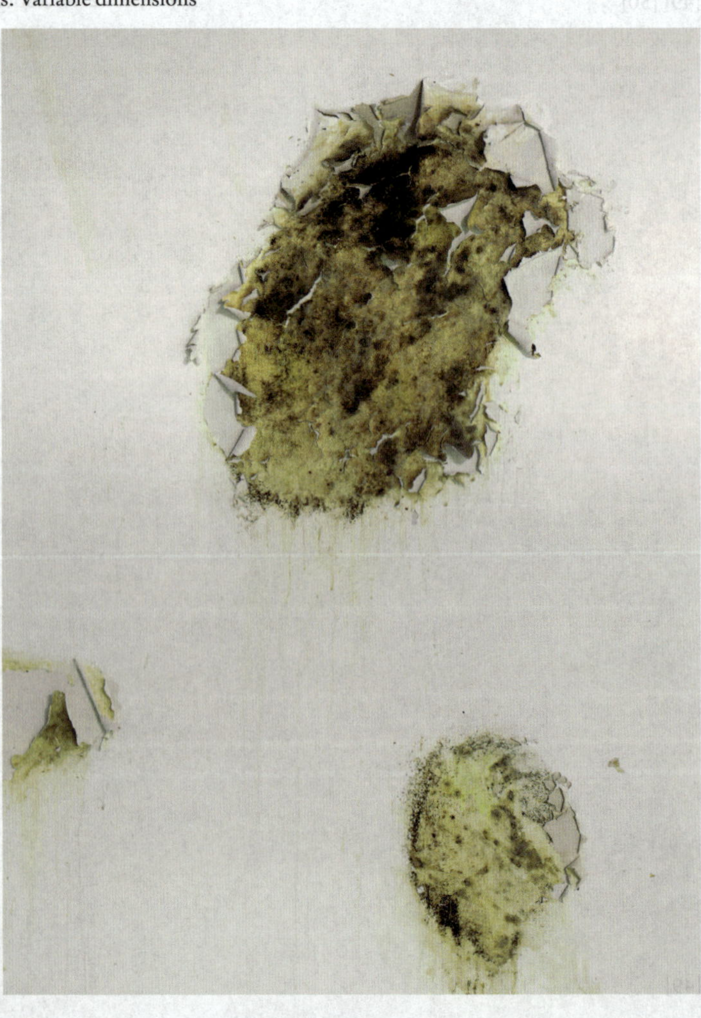

[51]

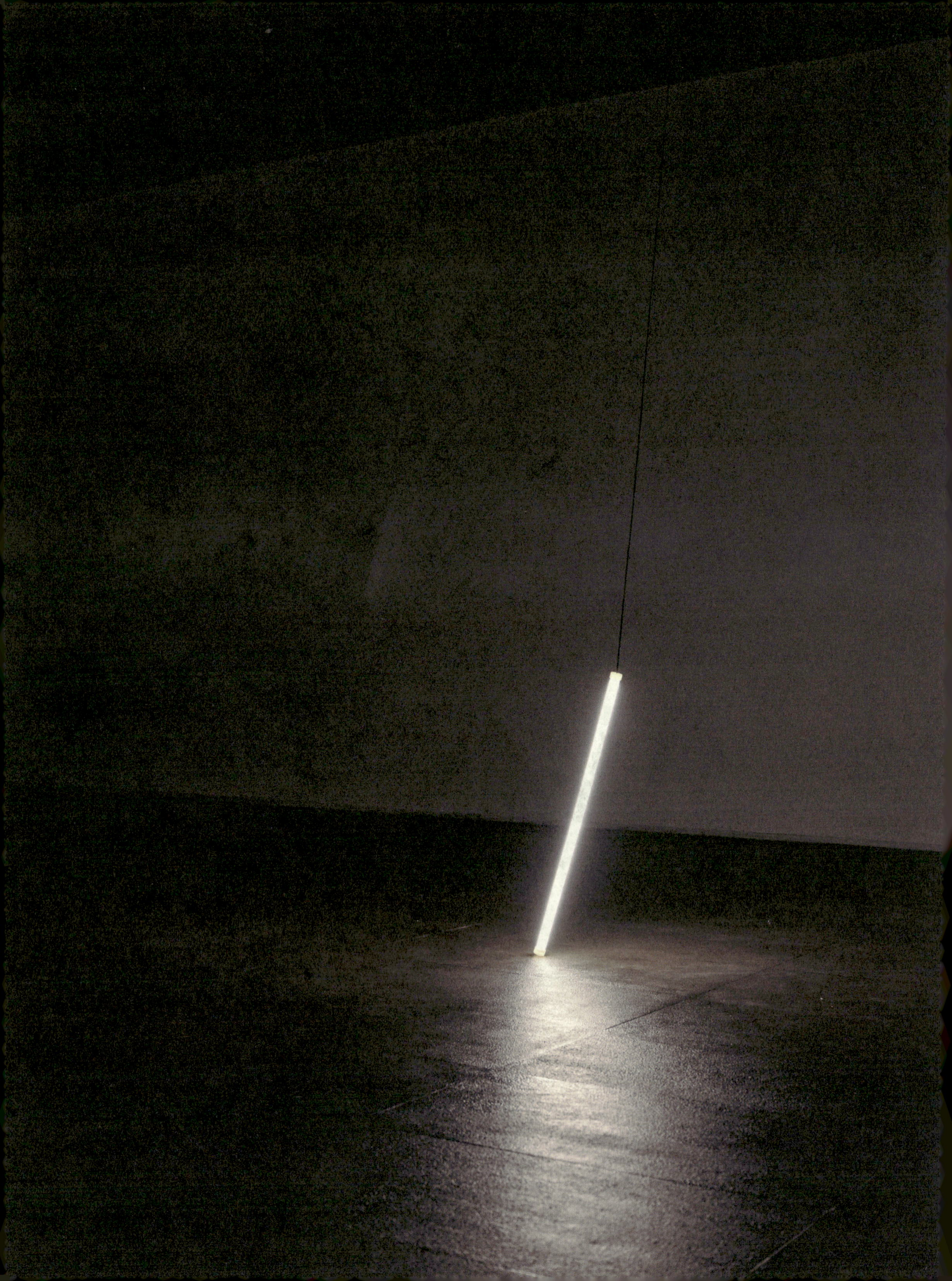

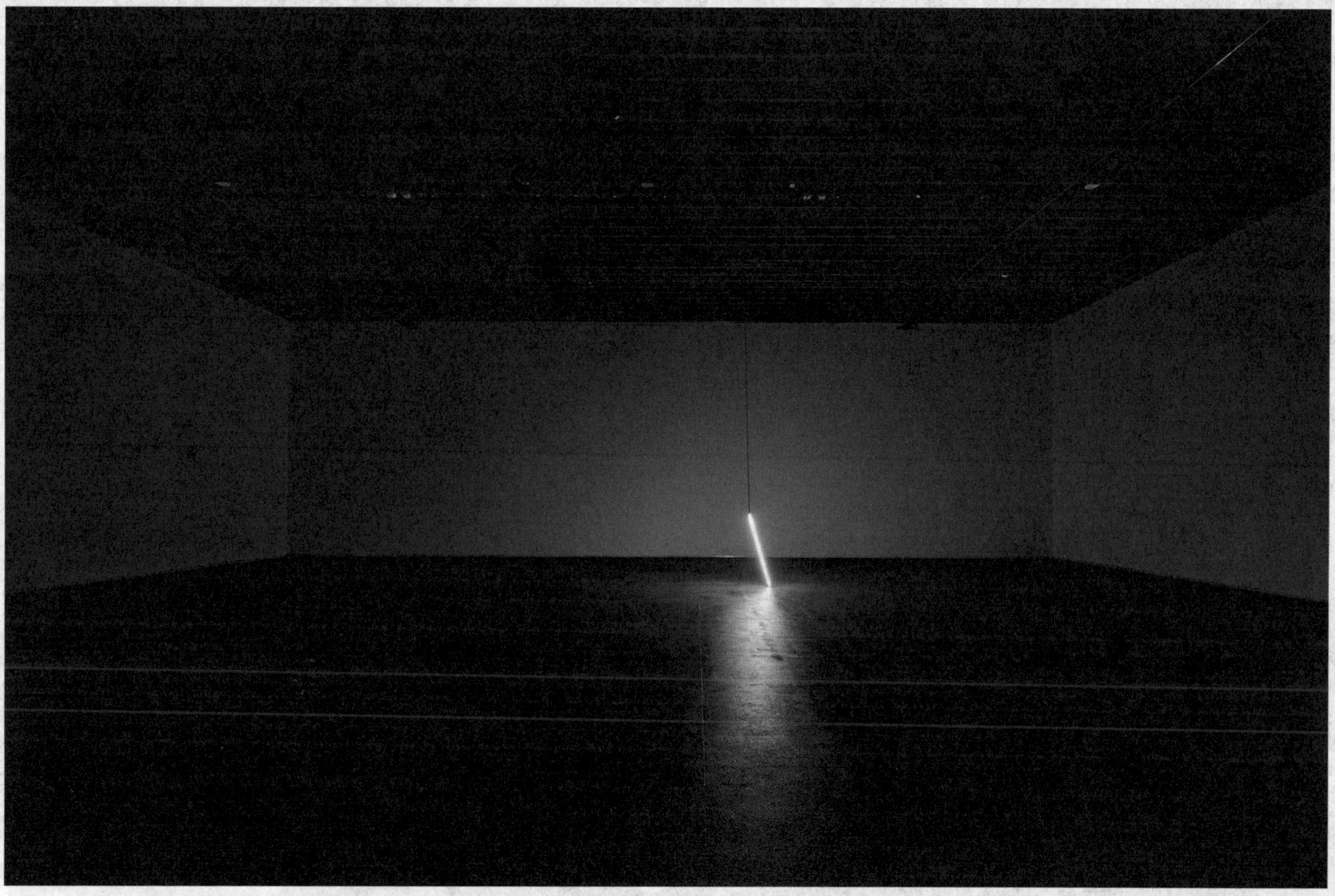

[53] [54, 55]

Meandering, 2019–24. Steel, LED lamp tube, micro-computer, micro-motor. 700 × 1000 × 1000 cm

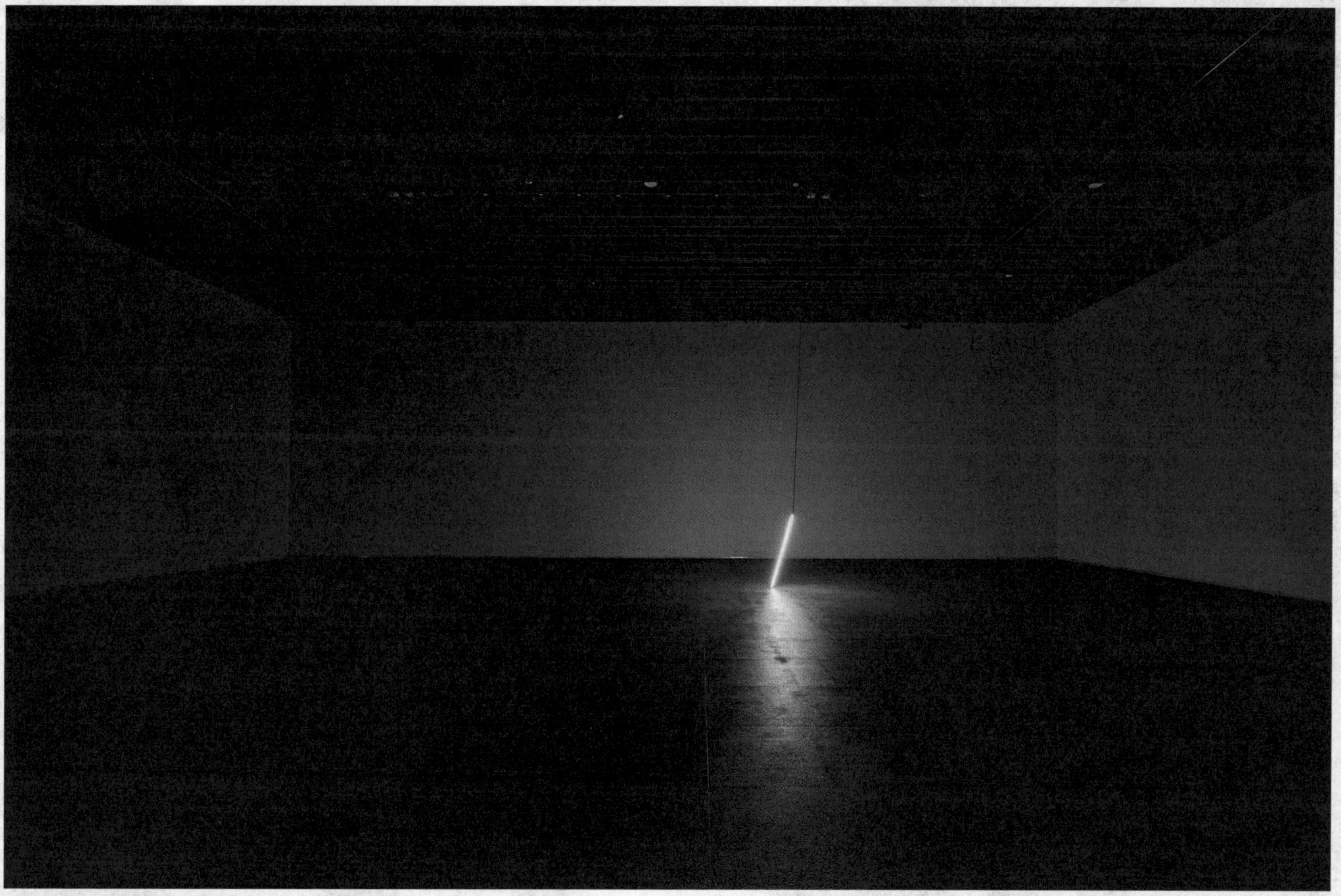

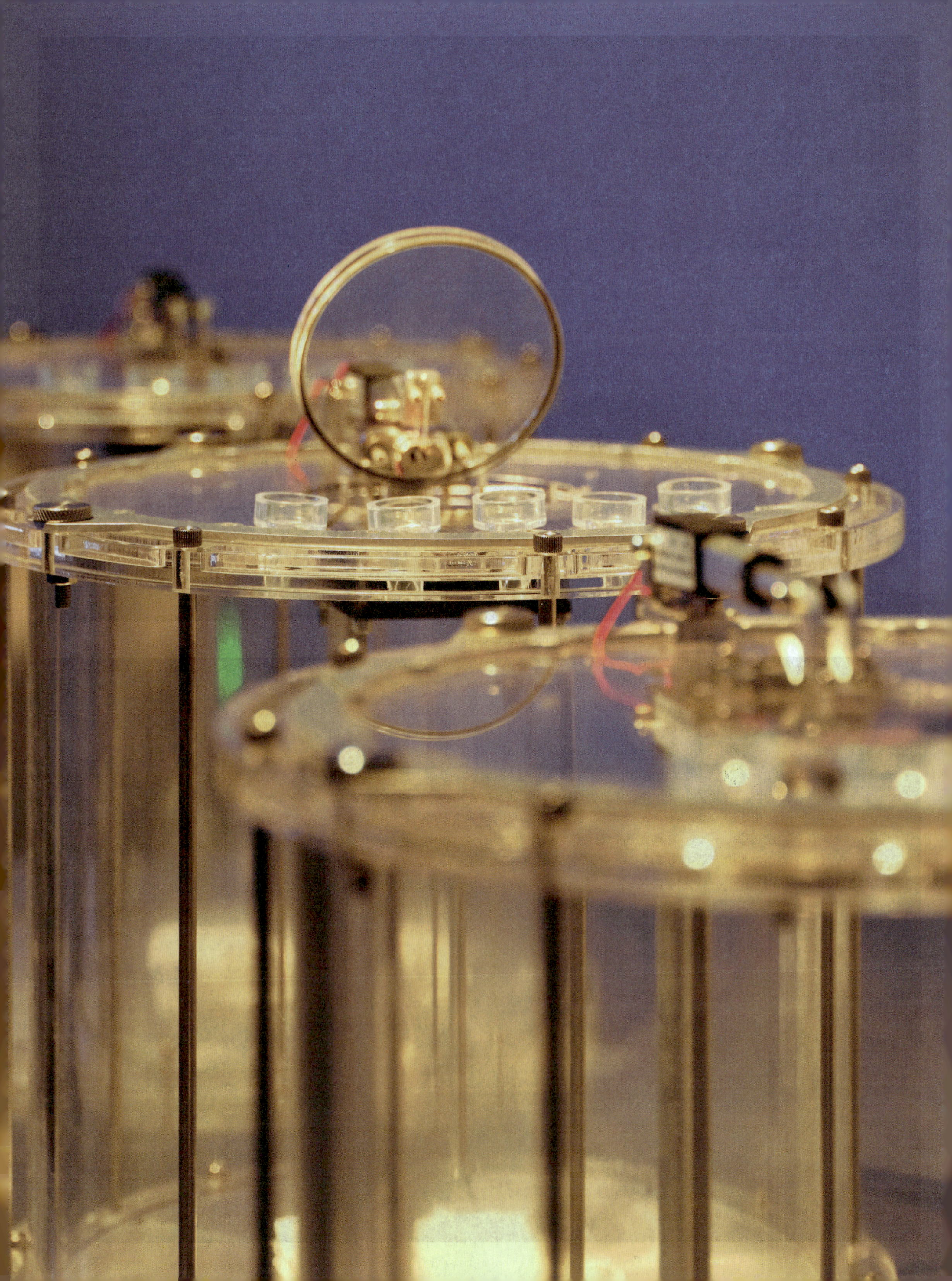

[56]

[57]

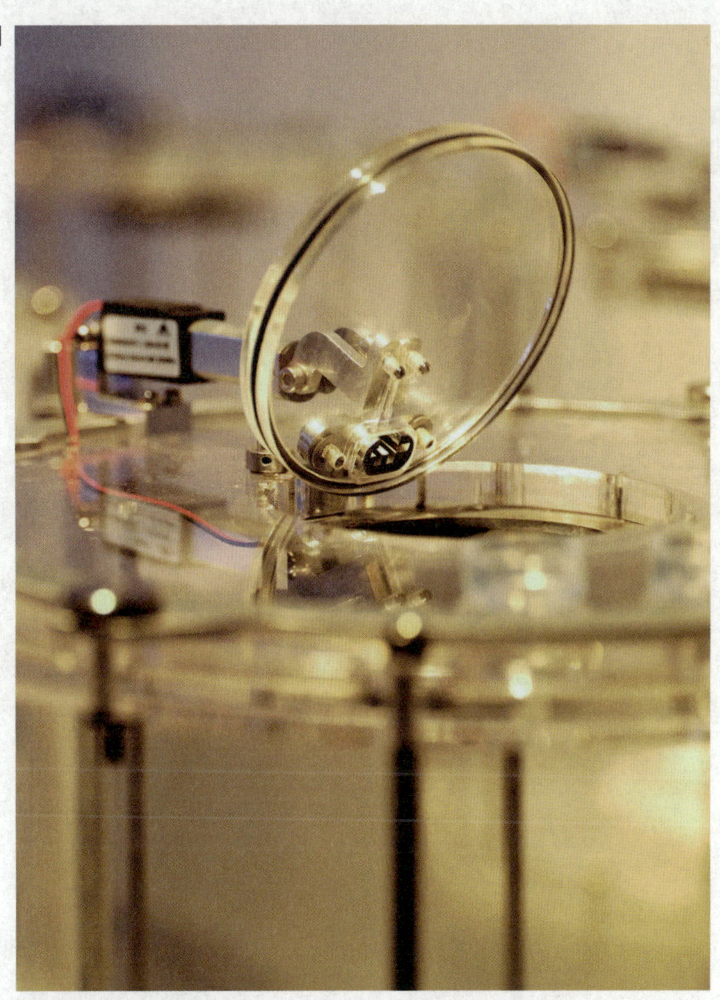

[56] [57, 58] *I'm Not Sure About the Ones I Gave*, 2024. Medical gauze swab, aluminum, PMMA, micro-computer, micro-motor. 135 × 168 × 110 cm

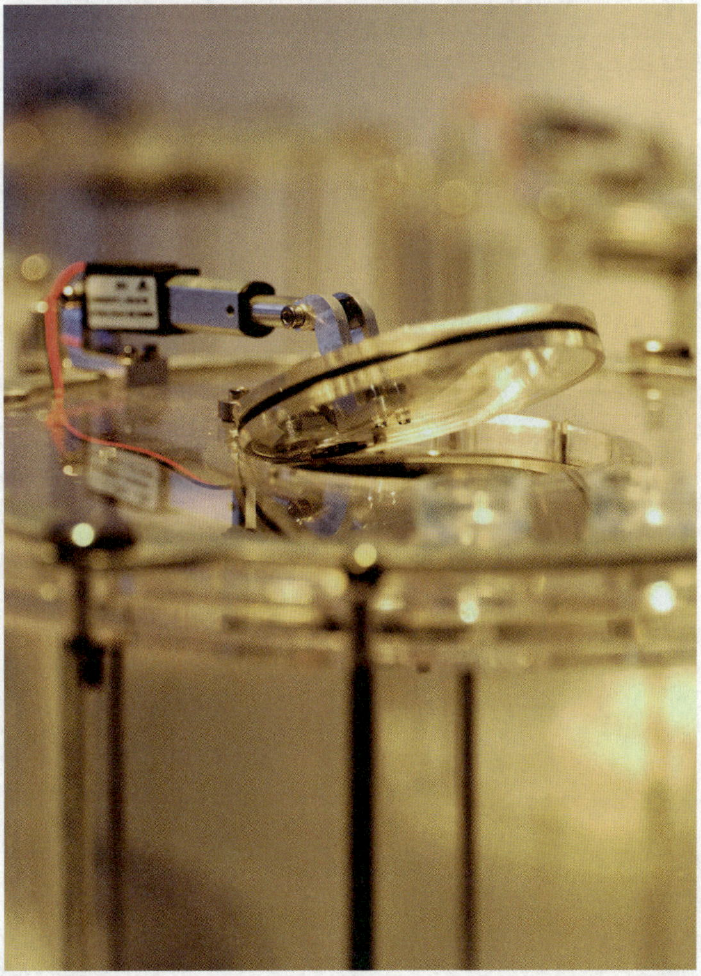

[58]

[59]

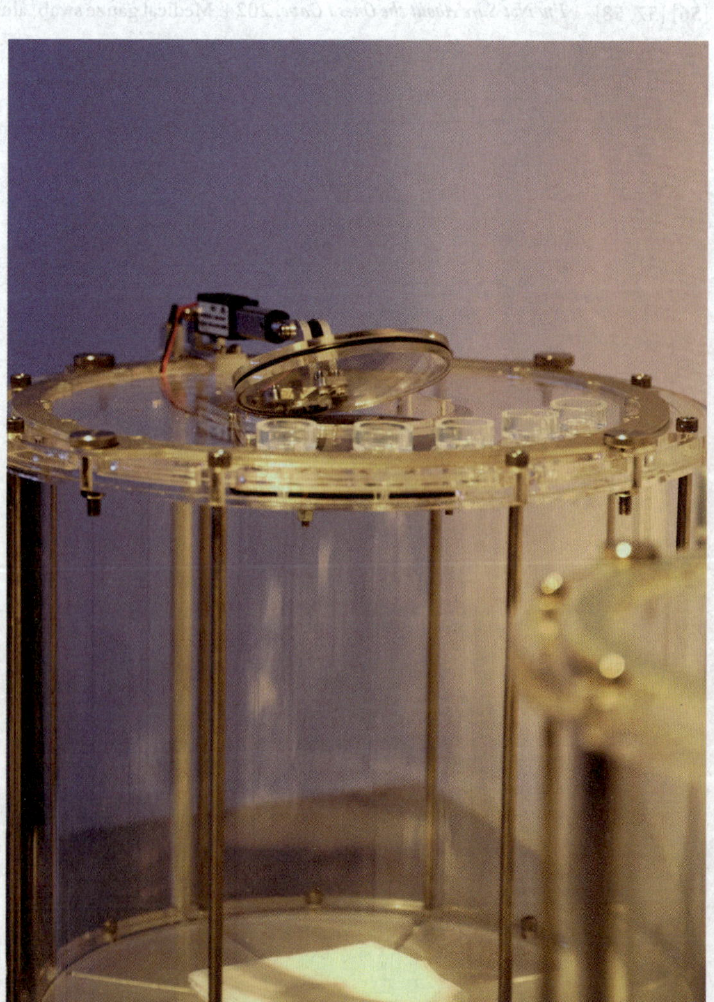

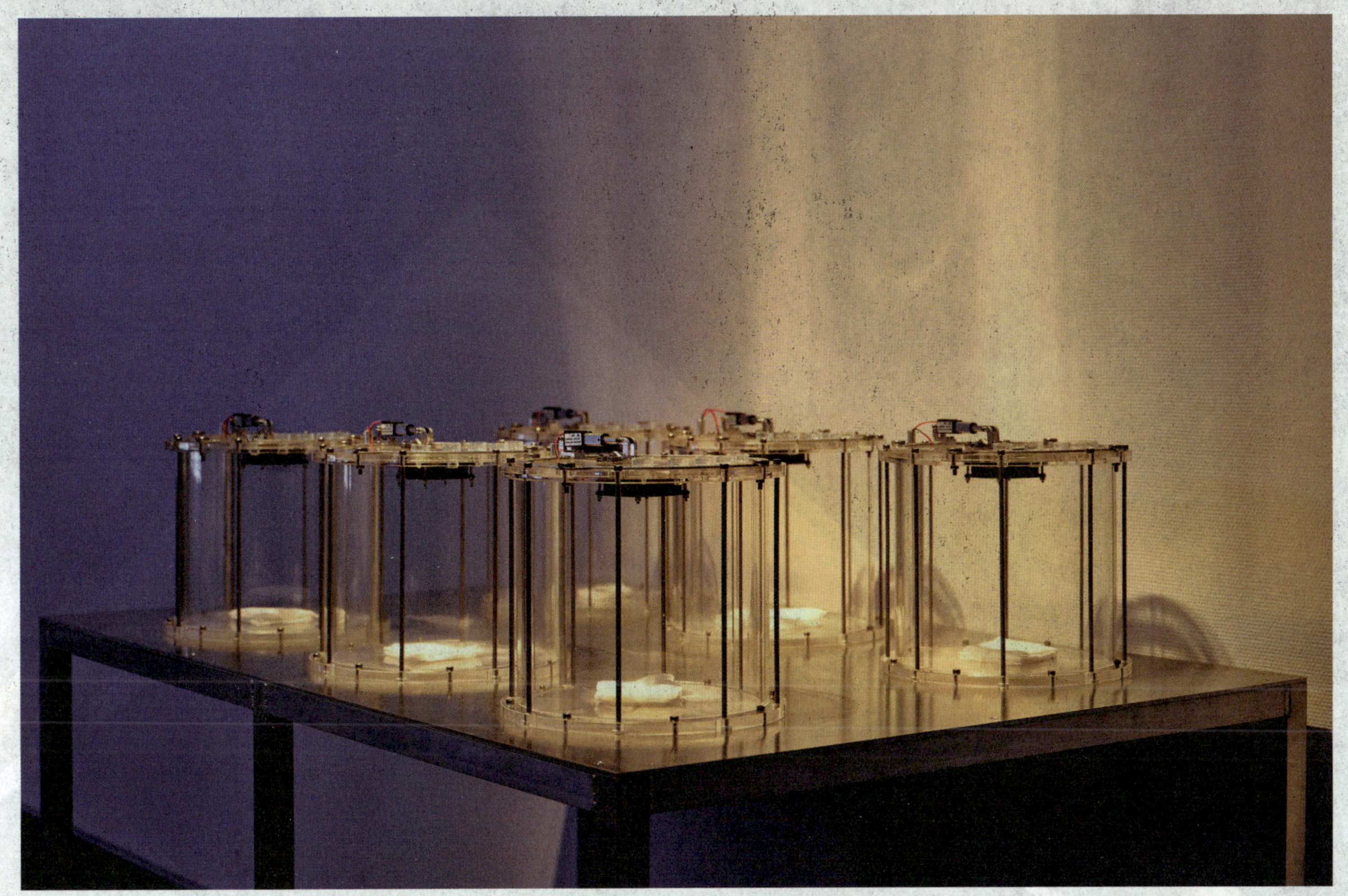

[59] [60] *I'm Not Sure About the Ones I Gave*, 2024. Medical gauze swab, aluminum, PMMA, micro-computer, micro-motor. 135 × 168 × 110 cm

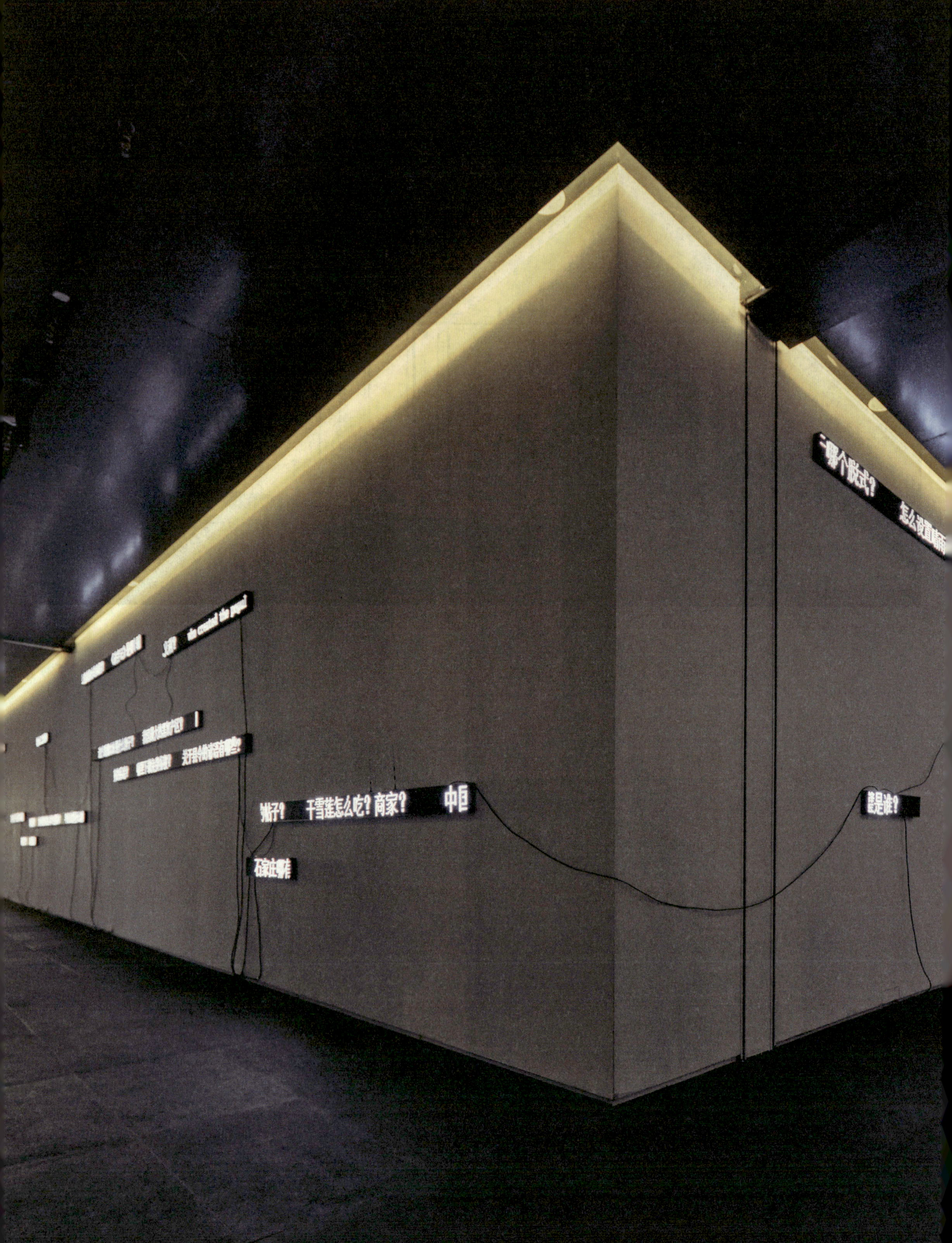
干雪莲怎么吃？商家？

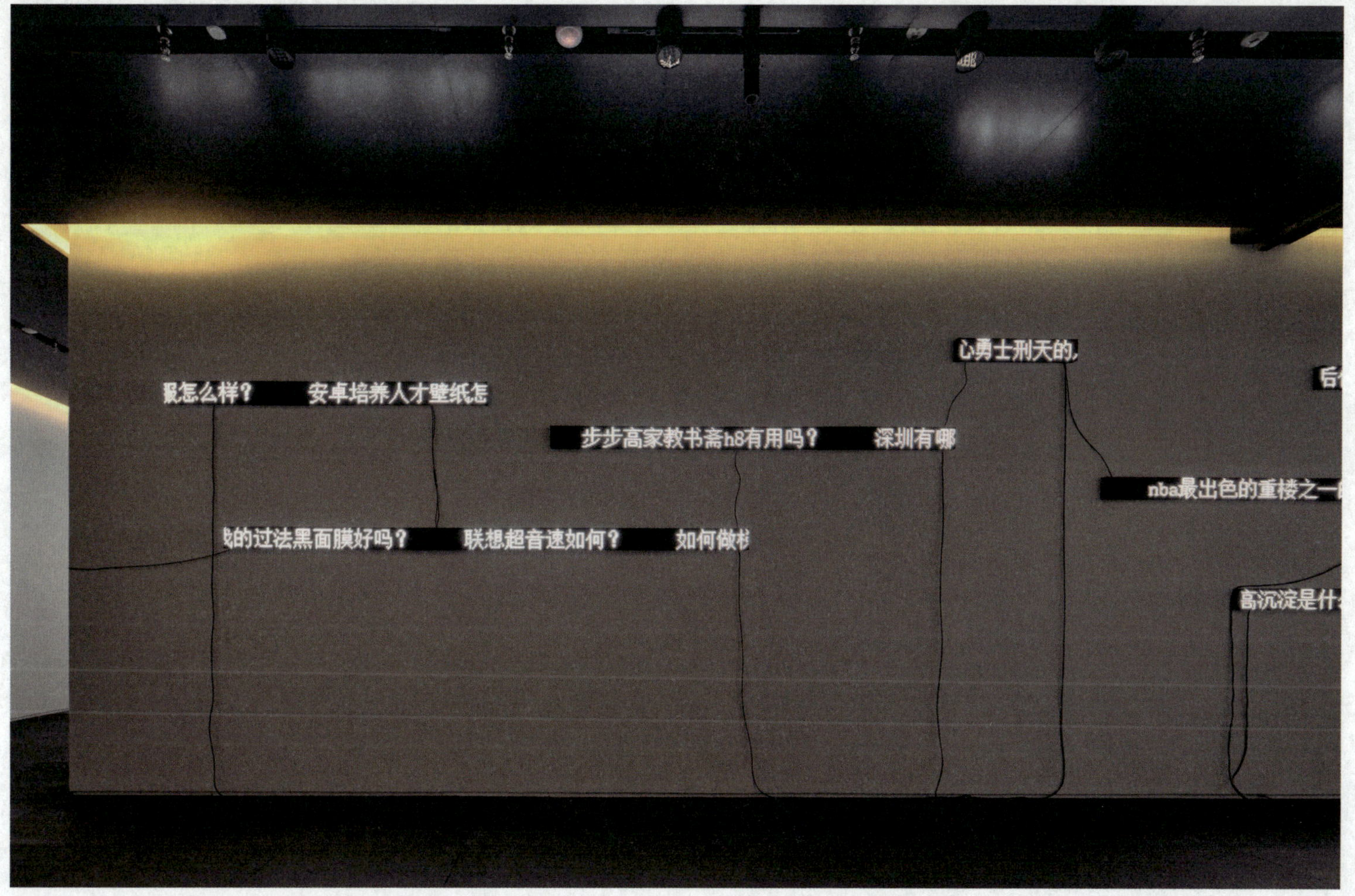

[61] [62] *Questions for Us*, 2024. LED screen, computer. Variable dimensions

[61]

传什么时候出
安卓培养人才壁纸怎么下载？
书斋h8有用吗？
深圳有哪些光区公司？
的重楼之一的文斯.卡特，他
子吗？
联想超音速如何？
如何做梯形芽好吃？
色？

[63] [64] *Questions for Us*, 2024. LED screen, computer. Variable dimensions

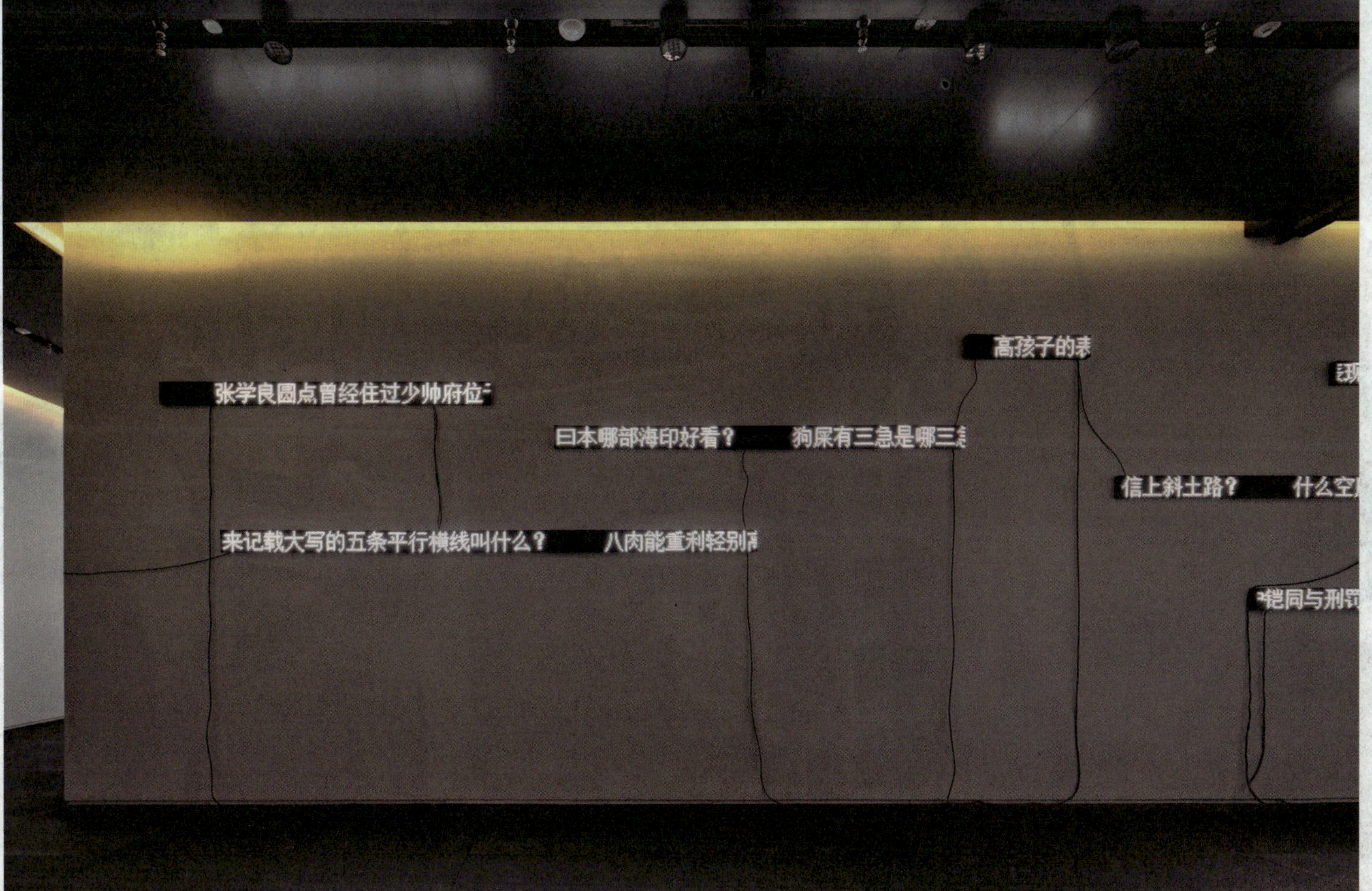

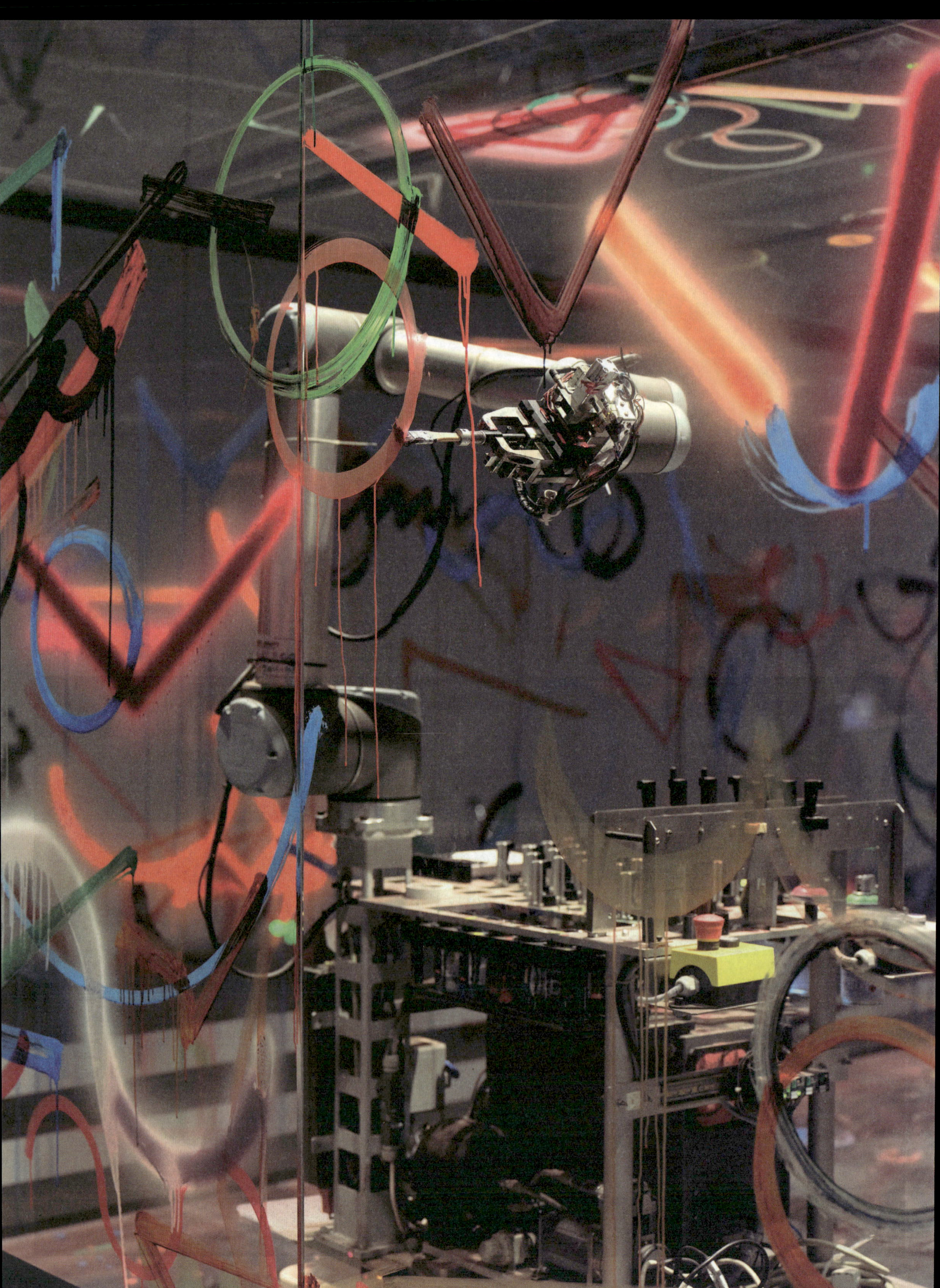

[65]

[66]

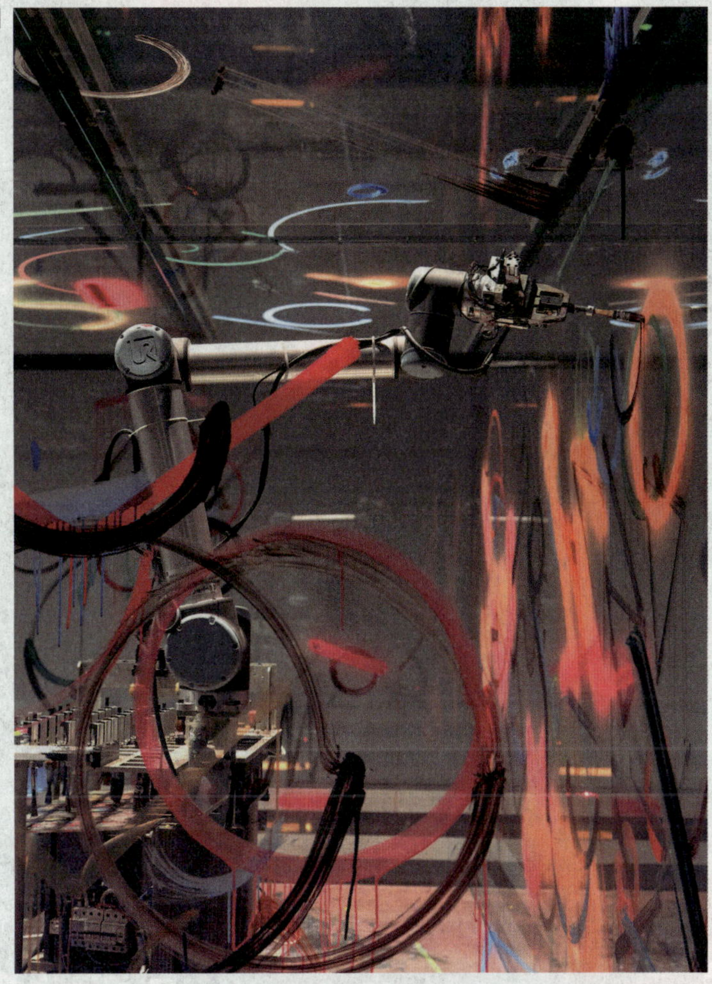

[65] [66, 67]

Dream, 2016–24. Glass, robot, automatic platform car. 289 × 616 × 438 cm

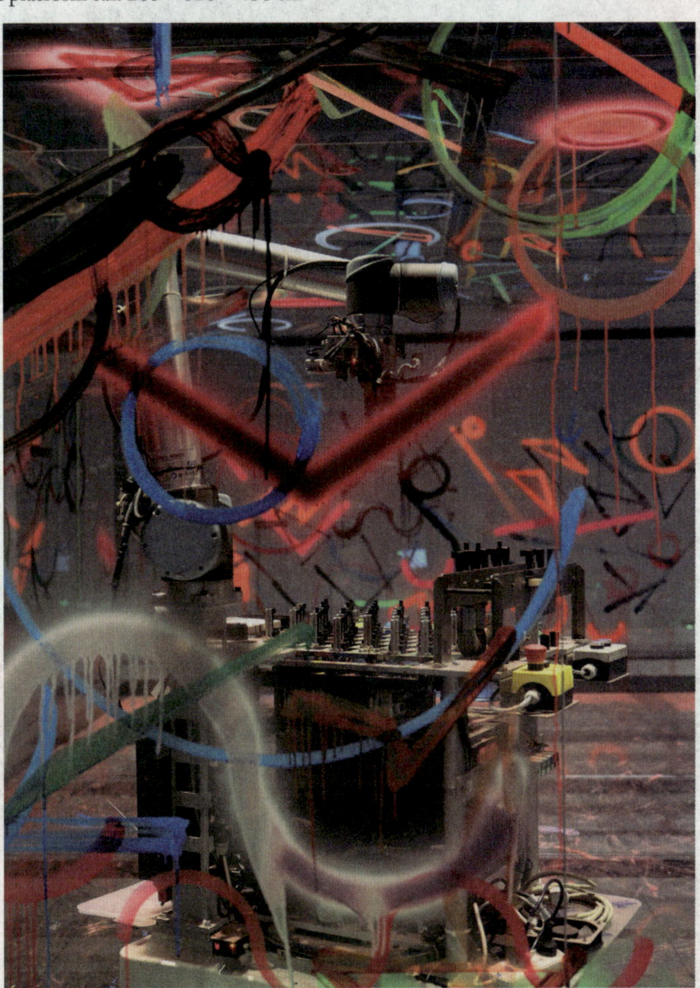

[67]

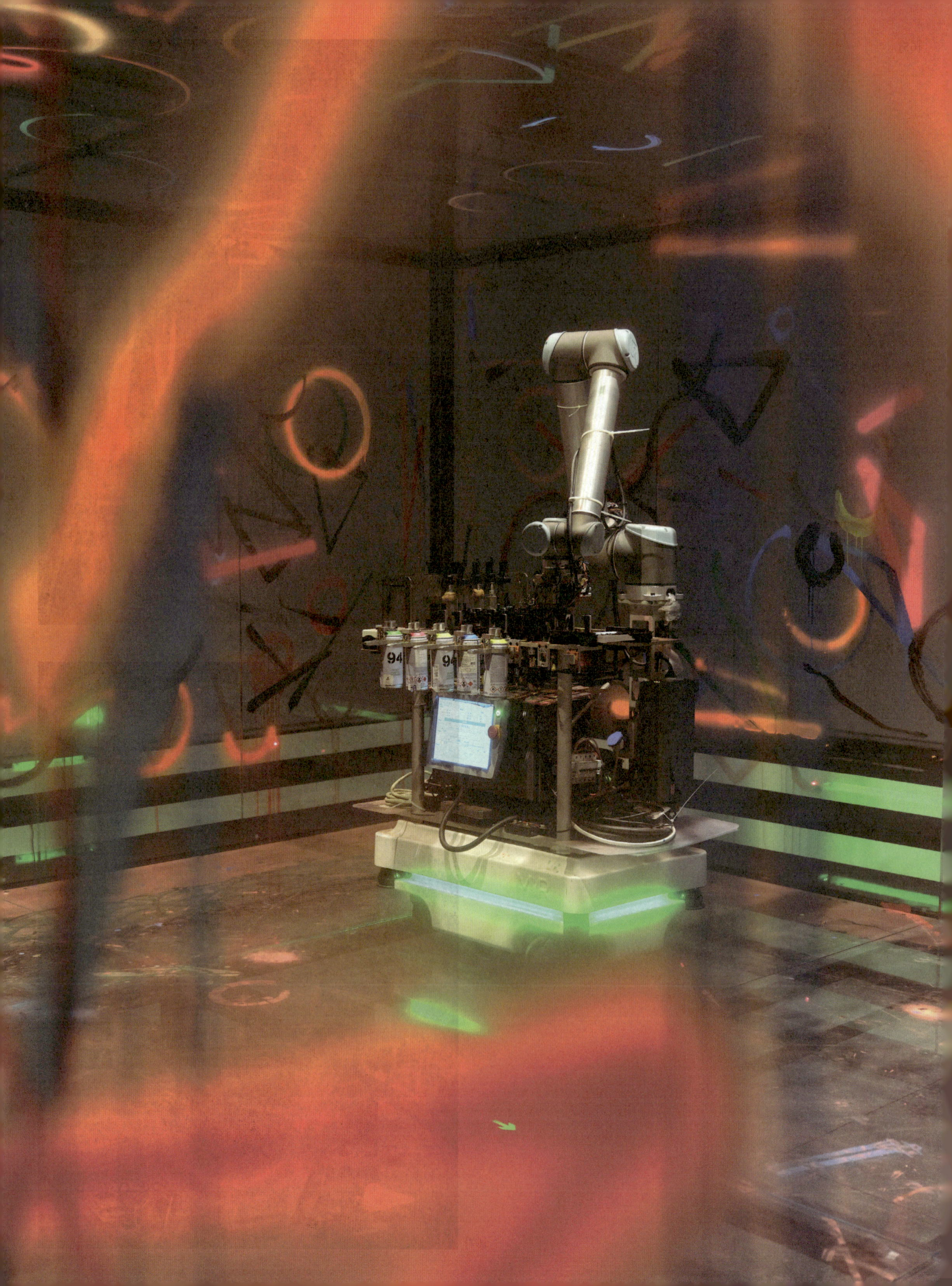
94
94

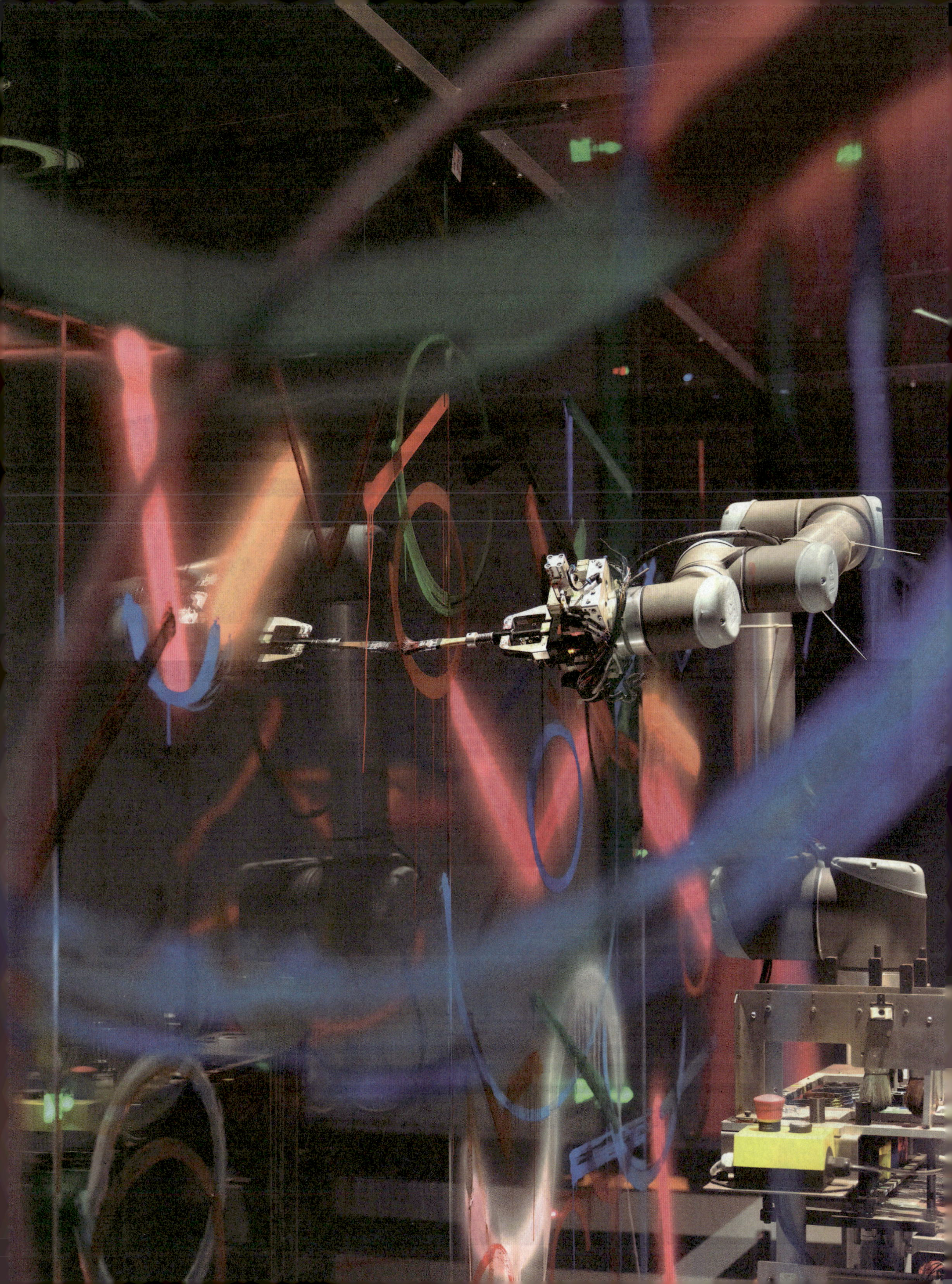

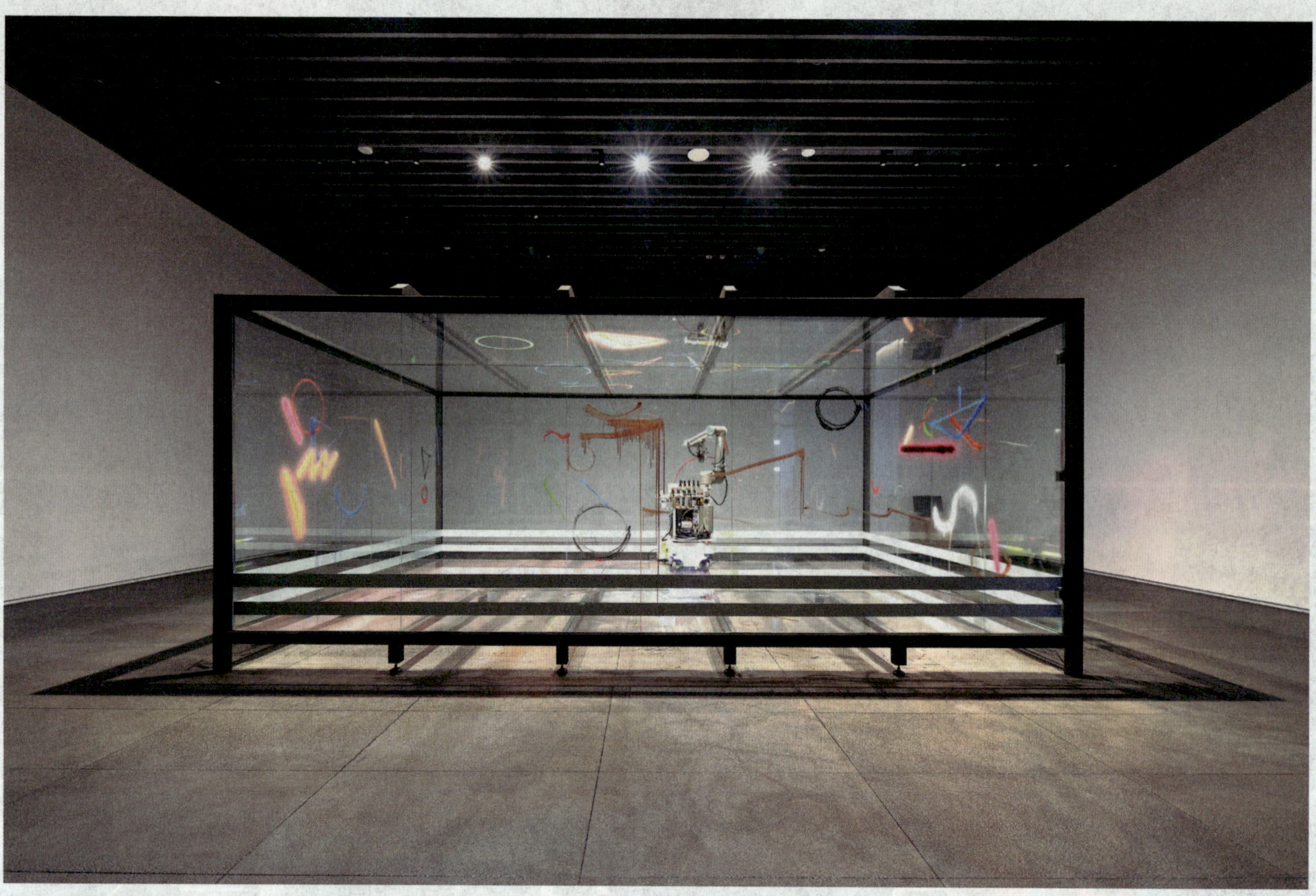

[70, 71] [72]

Dream, 2016–24. Glass, robot, automatic platform car. 289 × 616 × 438 cm

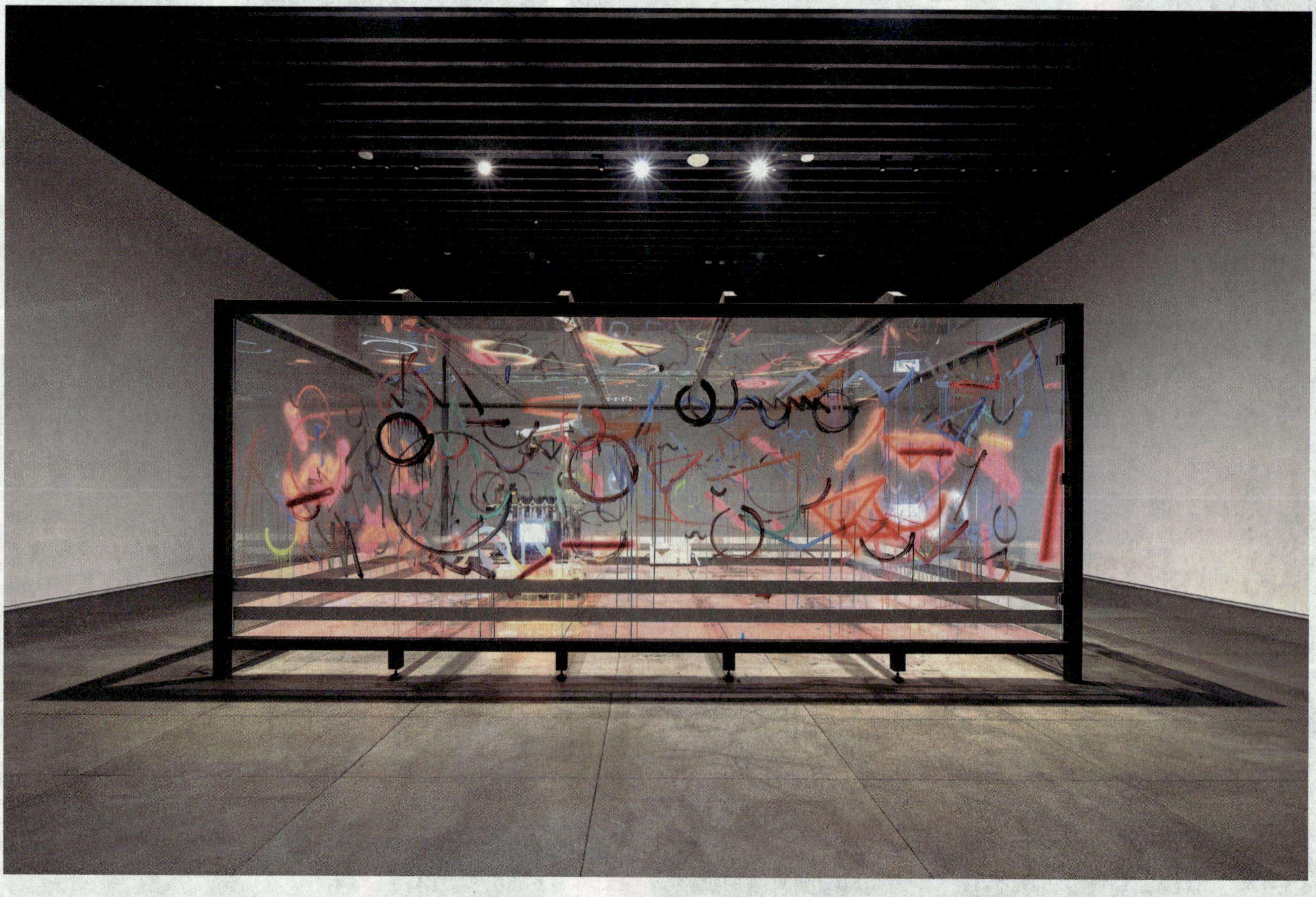

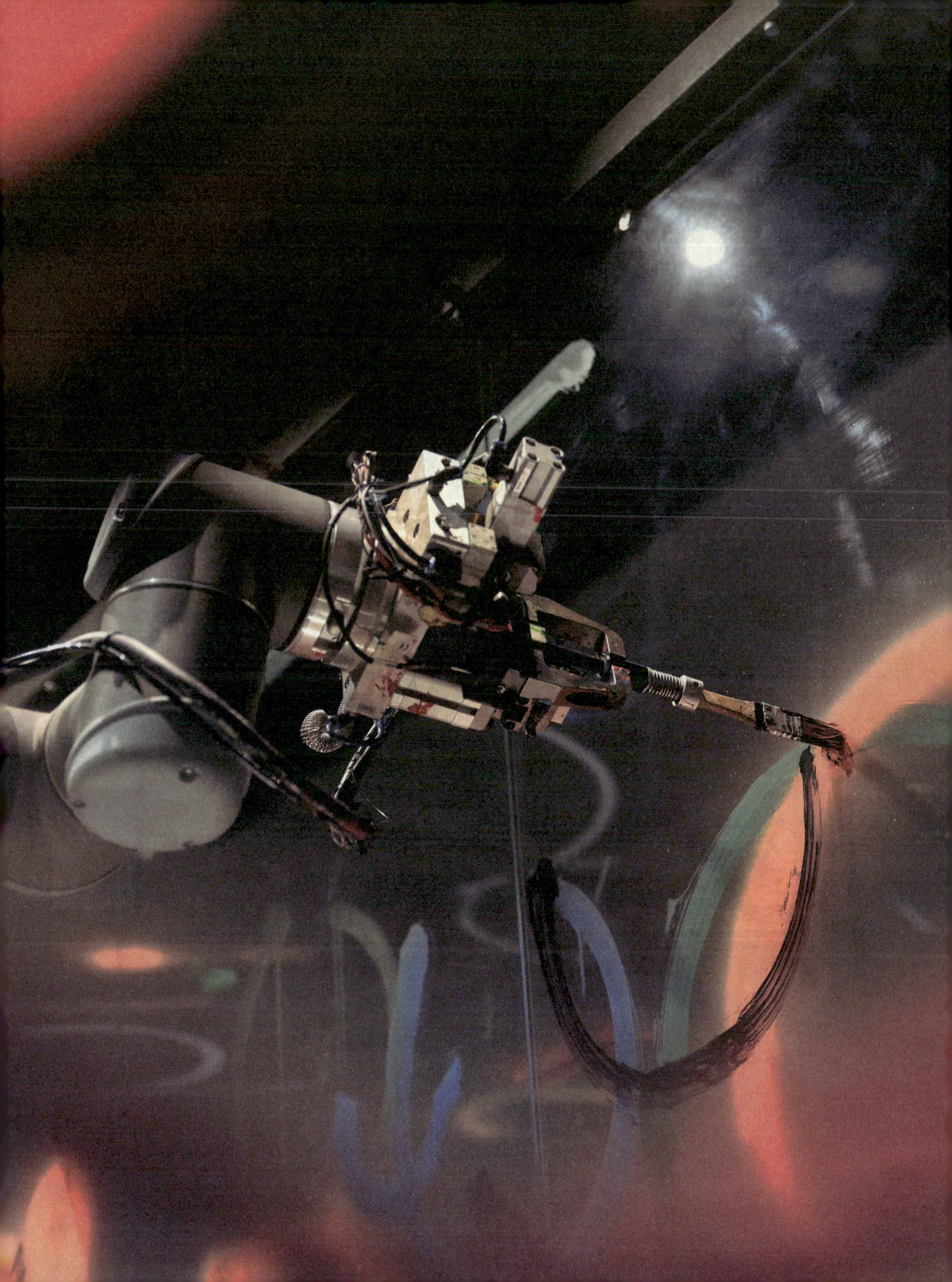

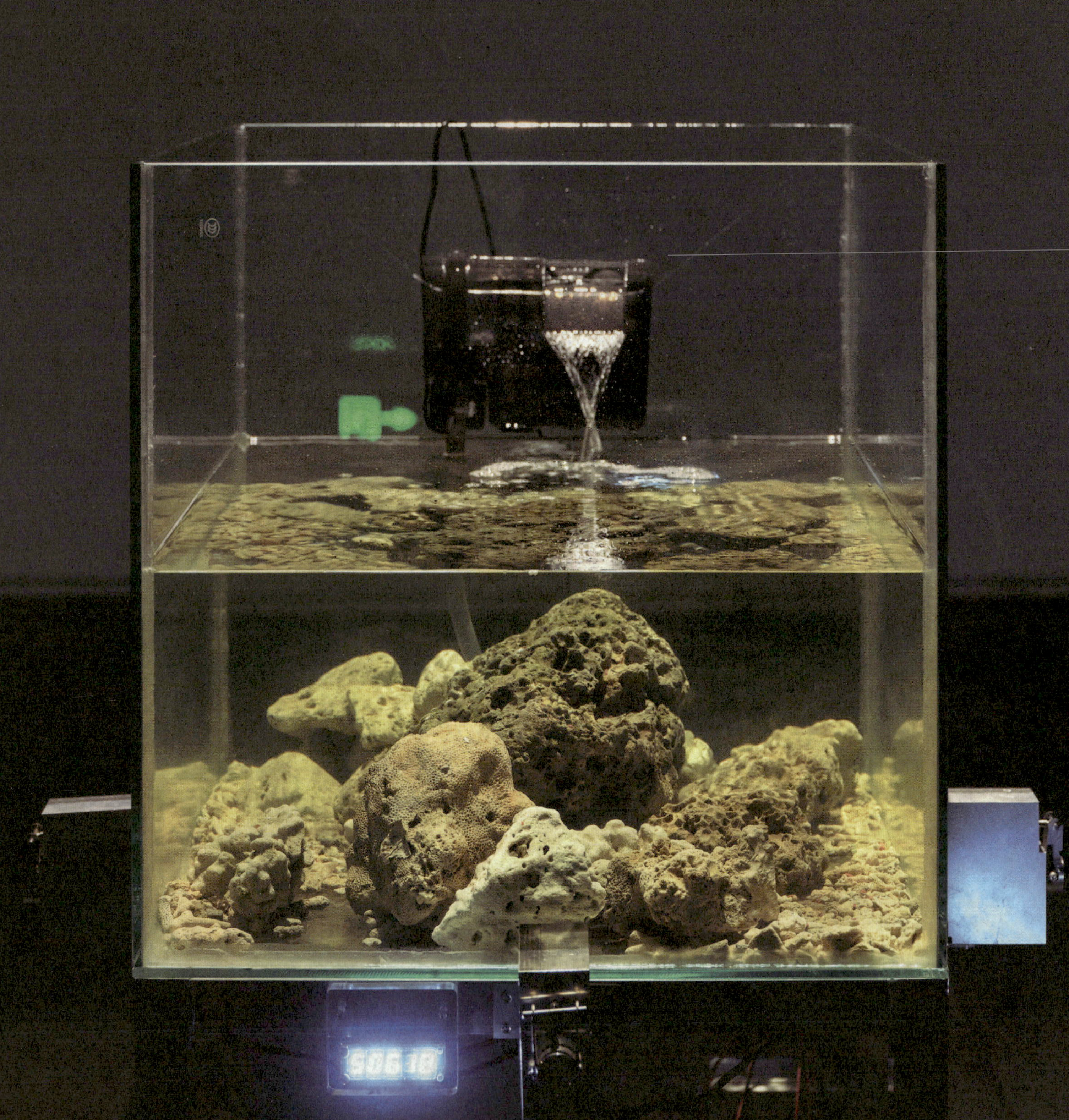

[73]

[73] [74] *Collapse*, 2024. Aluminum, glass, micro-computer, micro-motor, marine fish. 150 × 80 × 60 cm

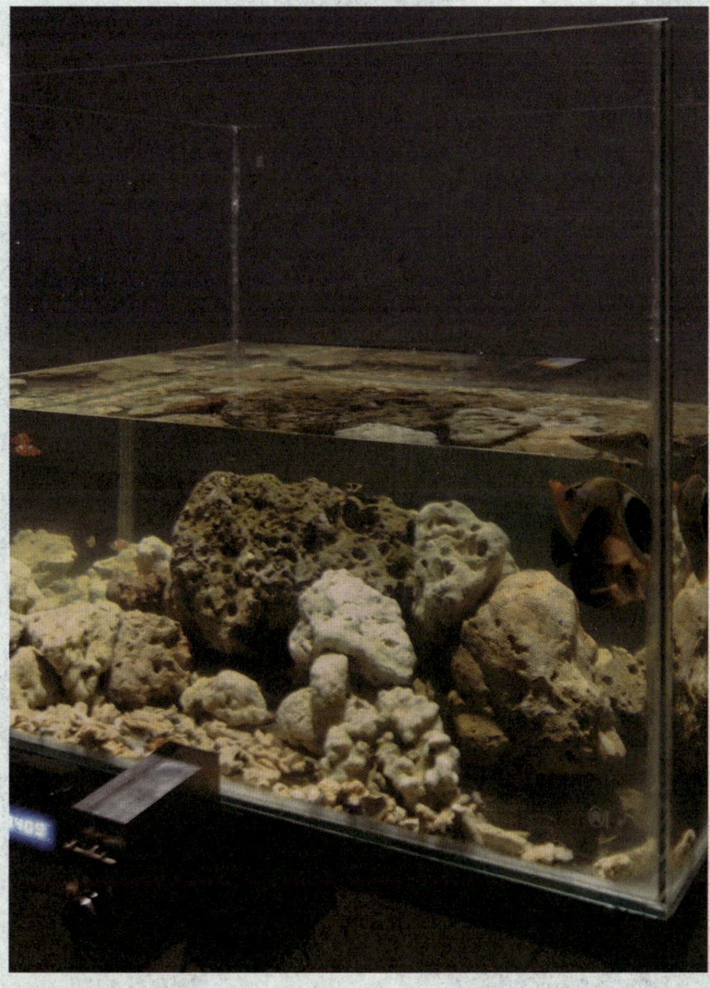

[74]

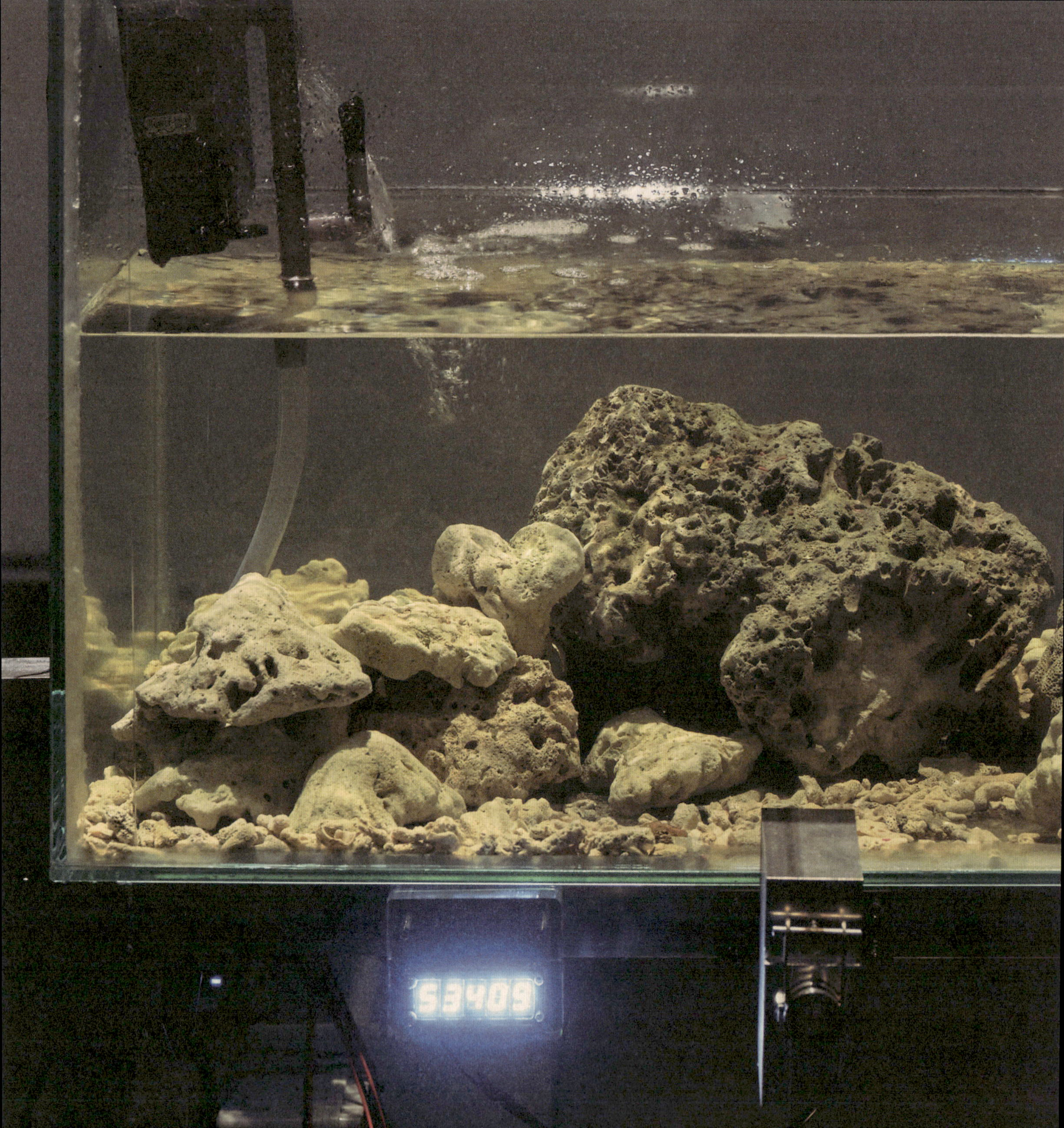
53409

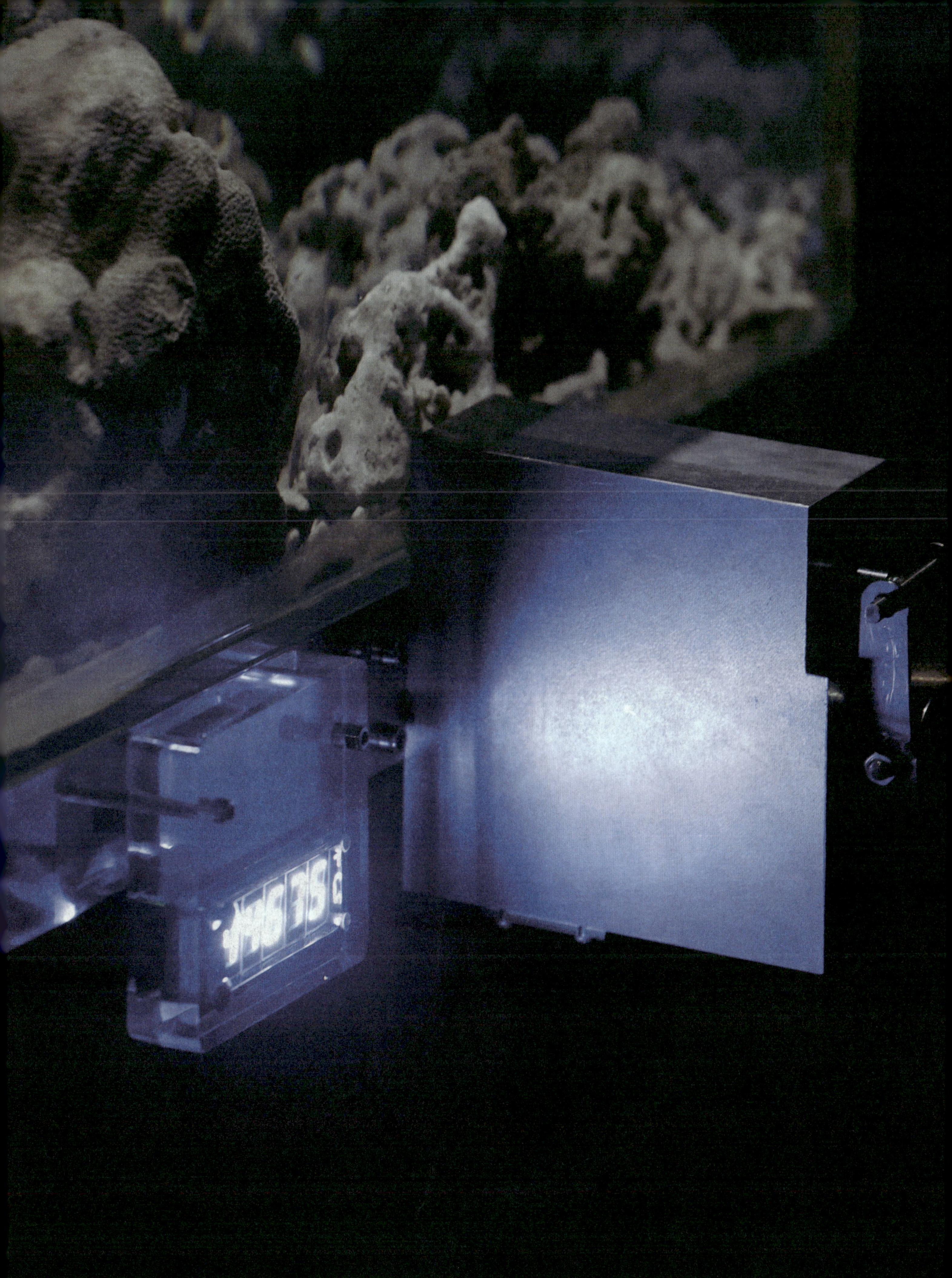

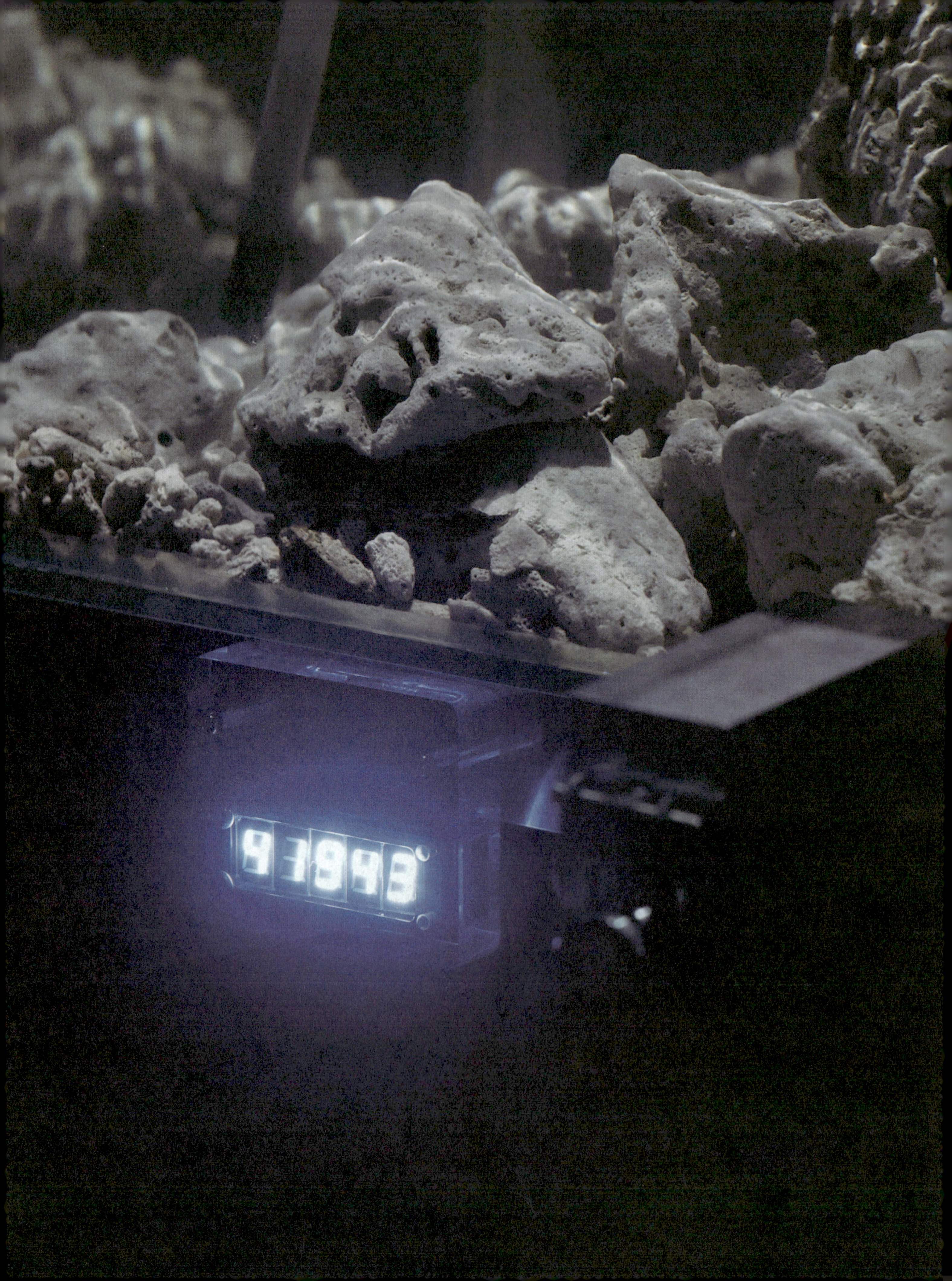

[78]
[79]

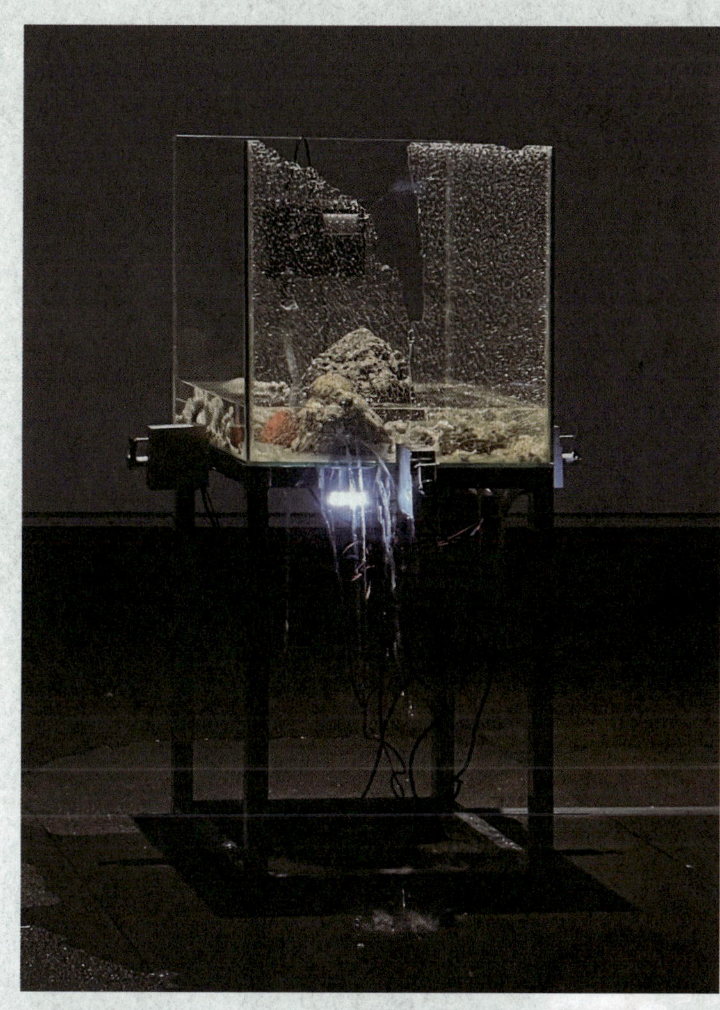

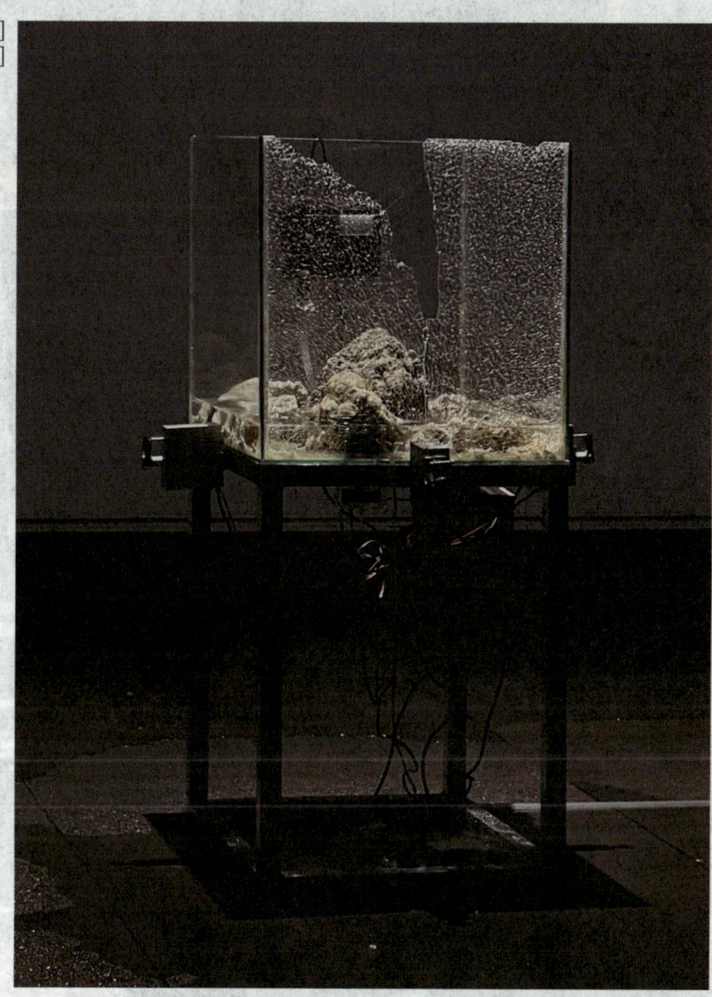

[77] [78, 79] *Collapse*, 2024. Aluminum, glass, micro-computer, micro-motor, marine fish. 150 × 80 × 60 cm

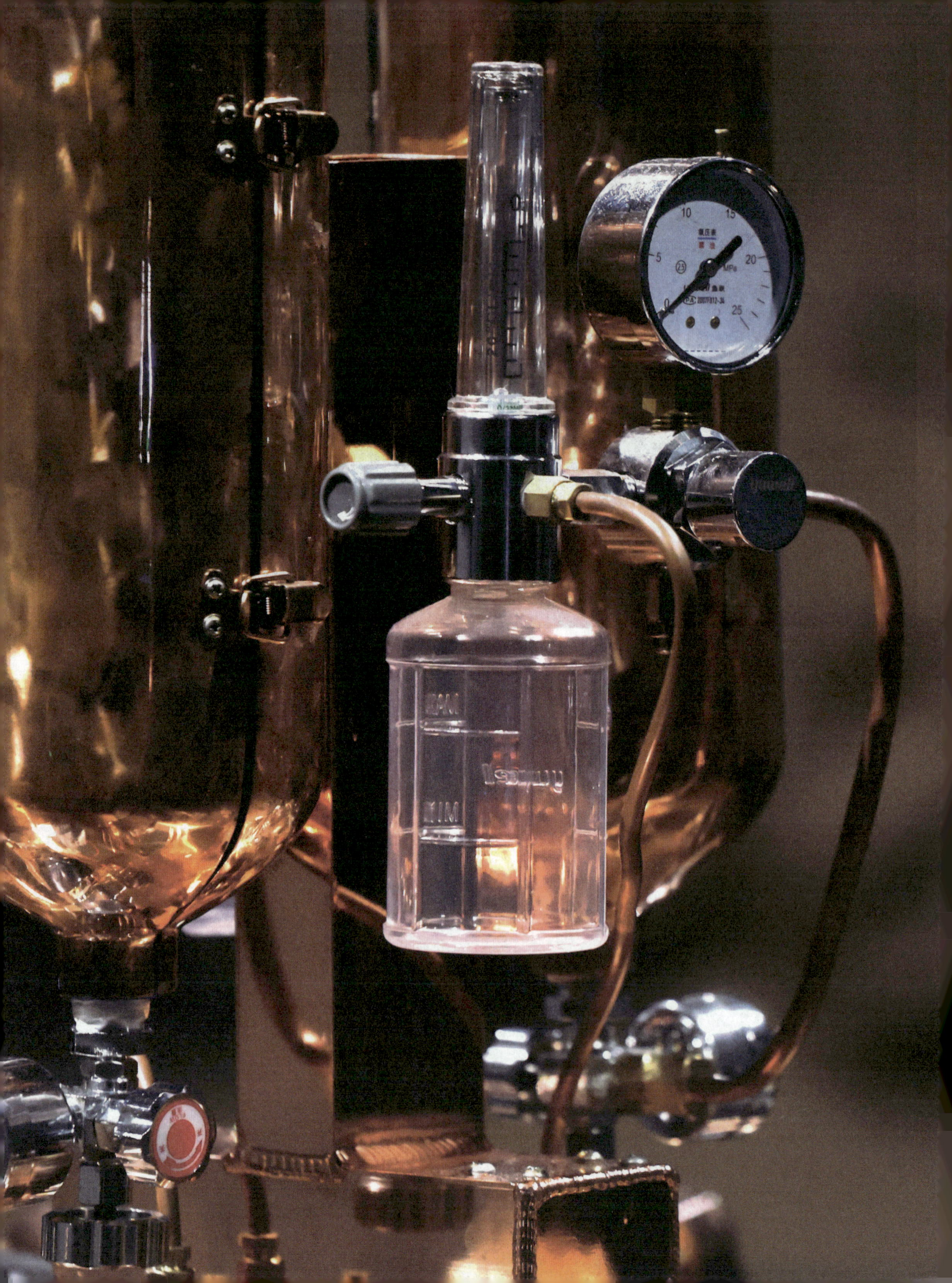

10
15
5
20
MPa
0
25

[80]

[81]

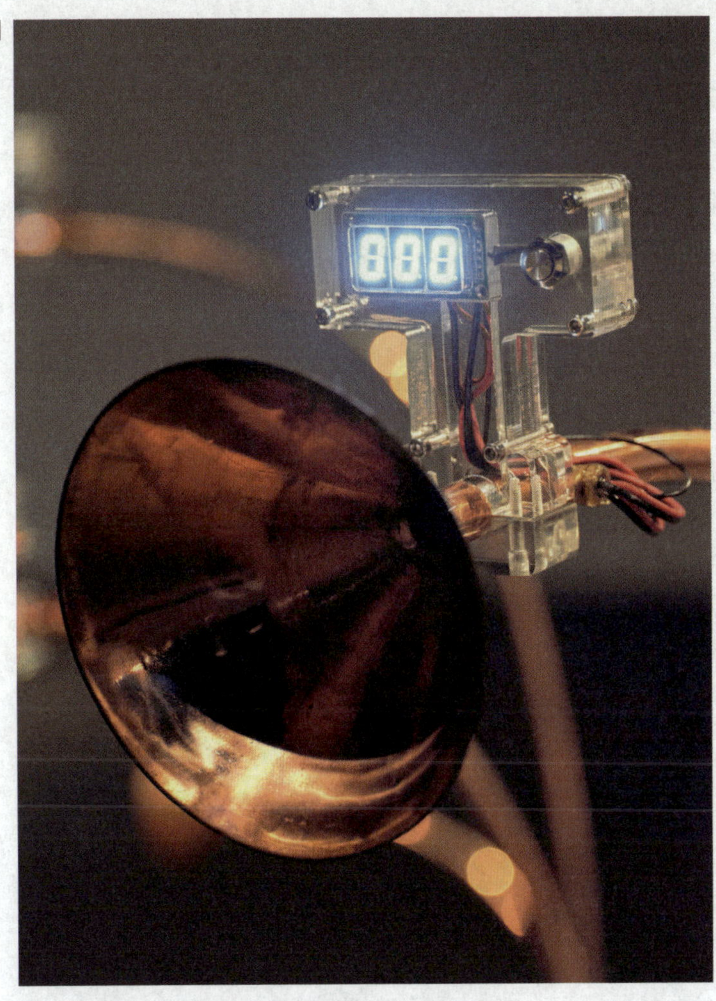

[80] [81] *Forgotten Memories*, 2024. Red copper, micro-computer, micro-motor, oxygen. 180 × 420 × 400 cm

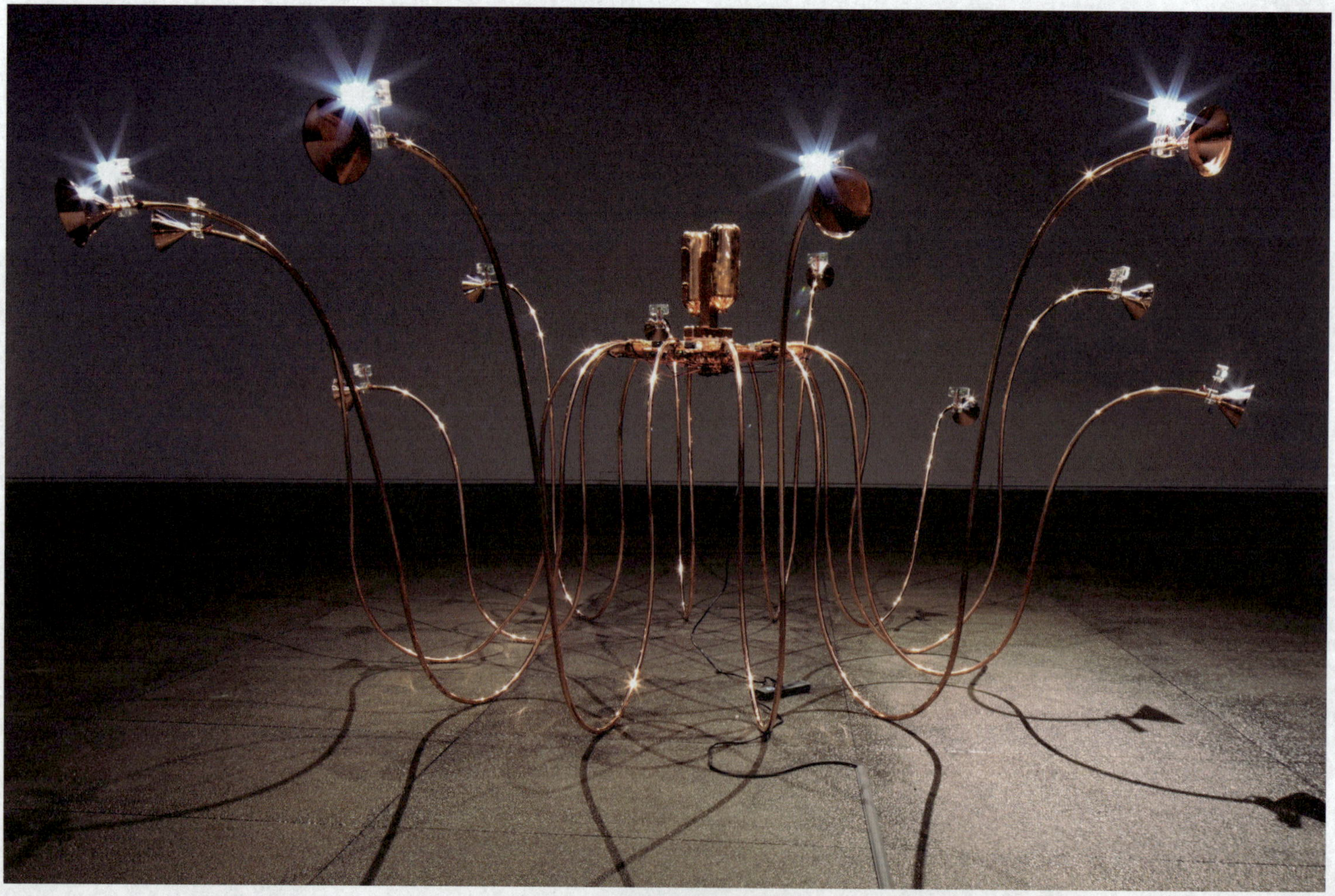

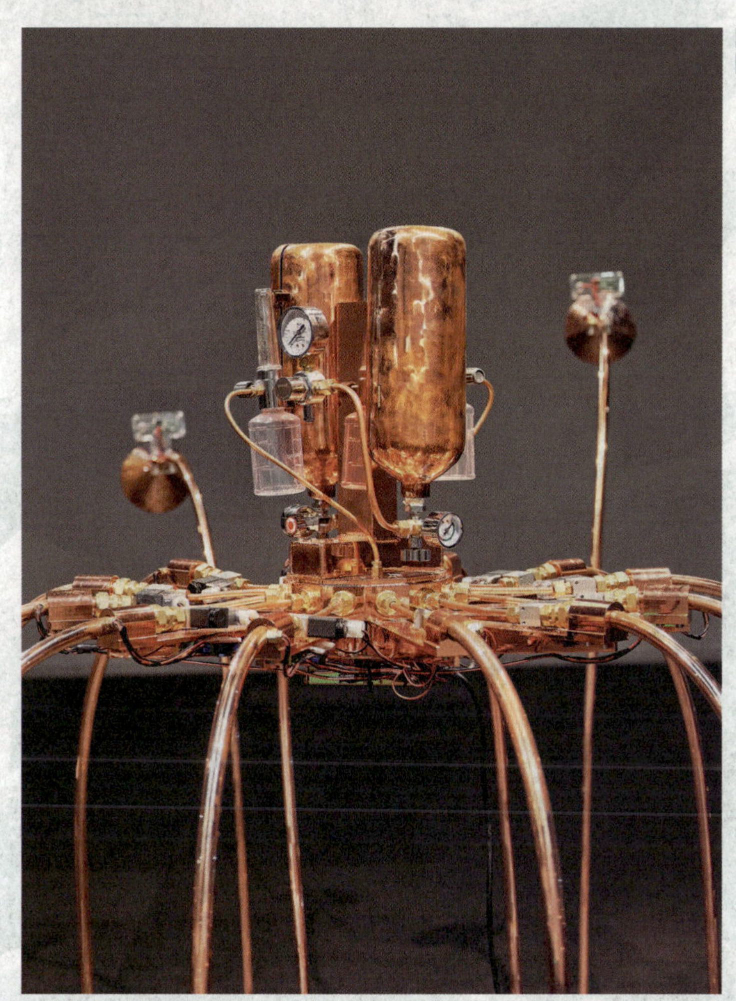

[83]
[84]

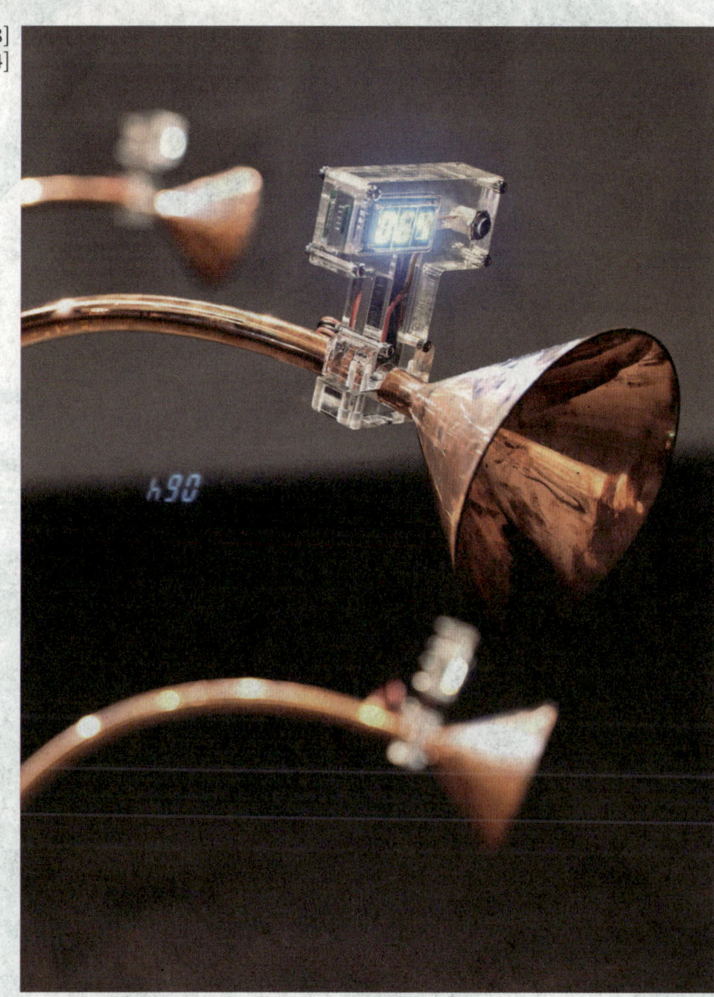

[82] [83, 84] *Forgotten Memories*, 2024. Red copper, micro-computer, micro-motor, oxygen. 180 × 420 × 400 cm

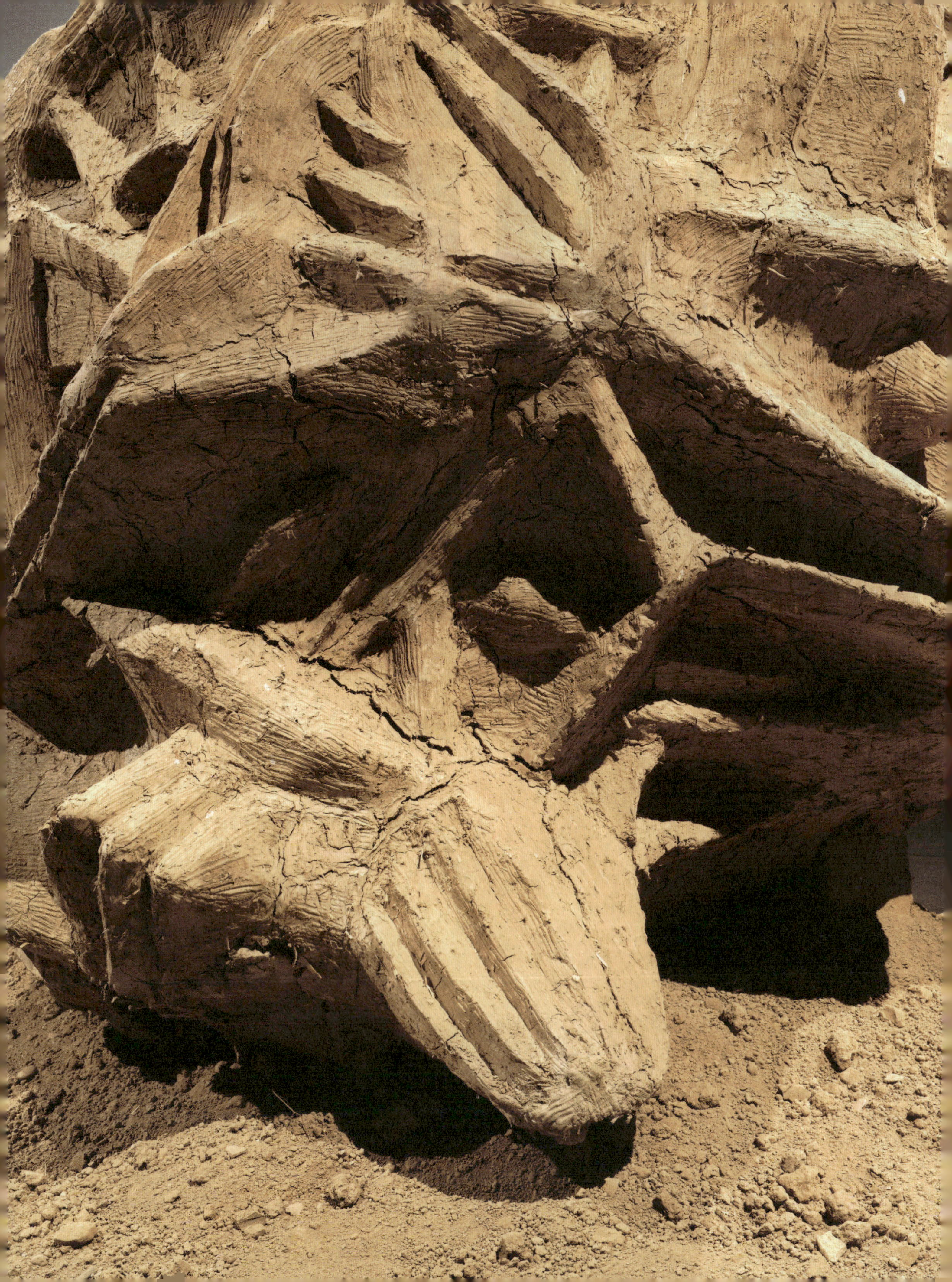

[85]

[85] [86]

Golem, 2022. Clay. 176 × 200 × 180 cm

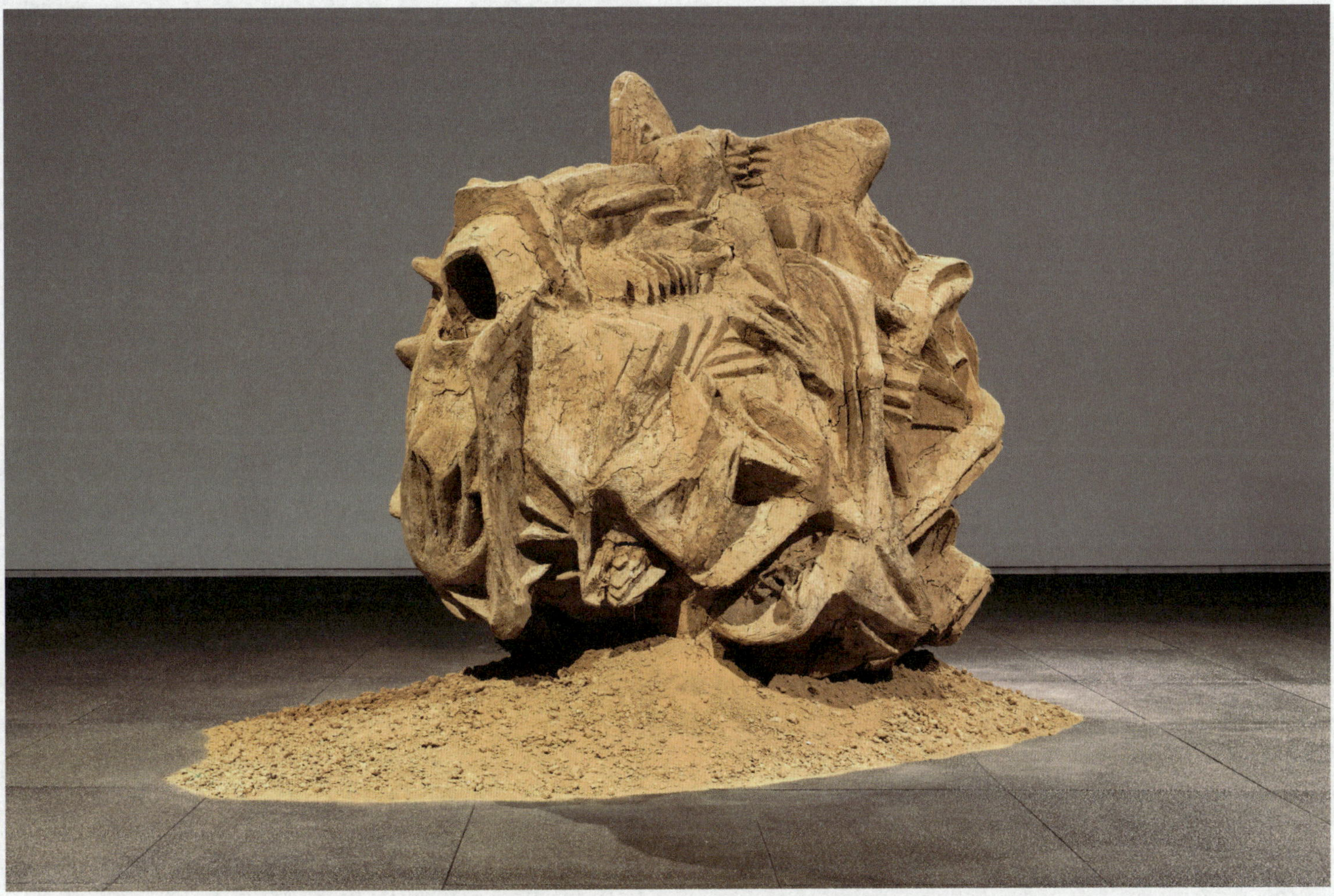

[87]

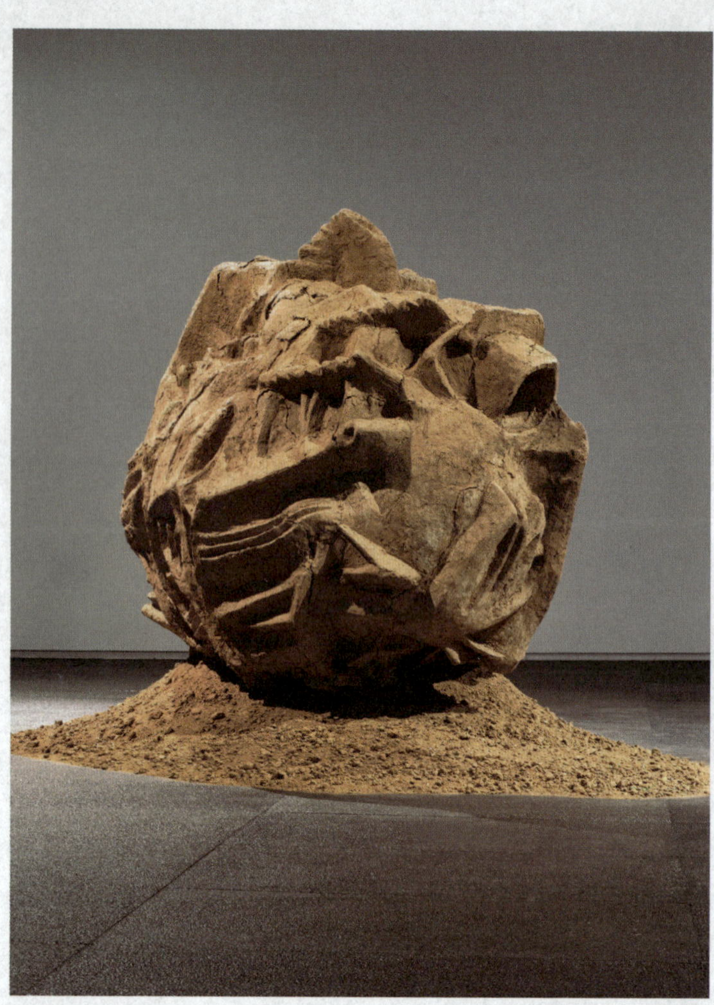

[87] [88] *Golem*, 2022. Clay. 176 × 200 × 180 cm

[88]

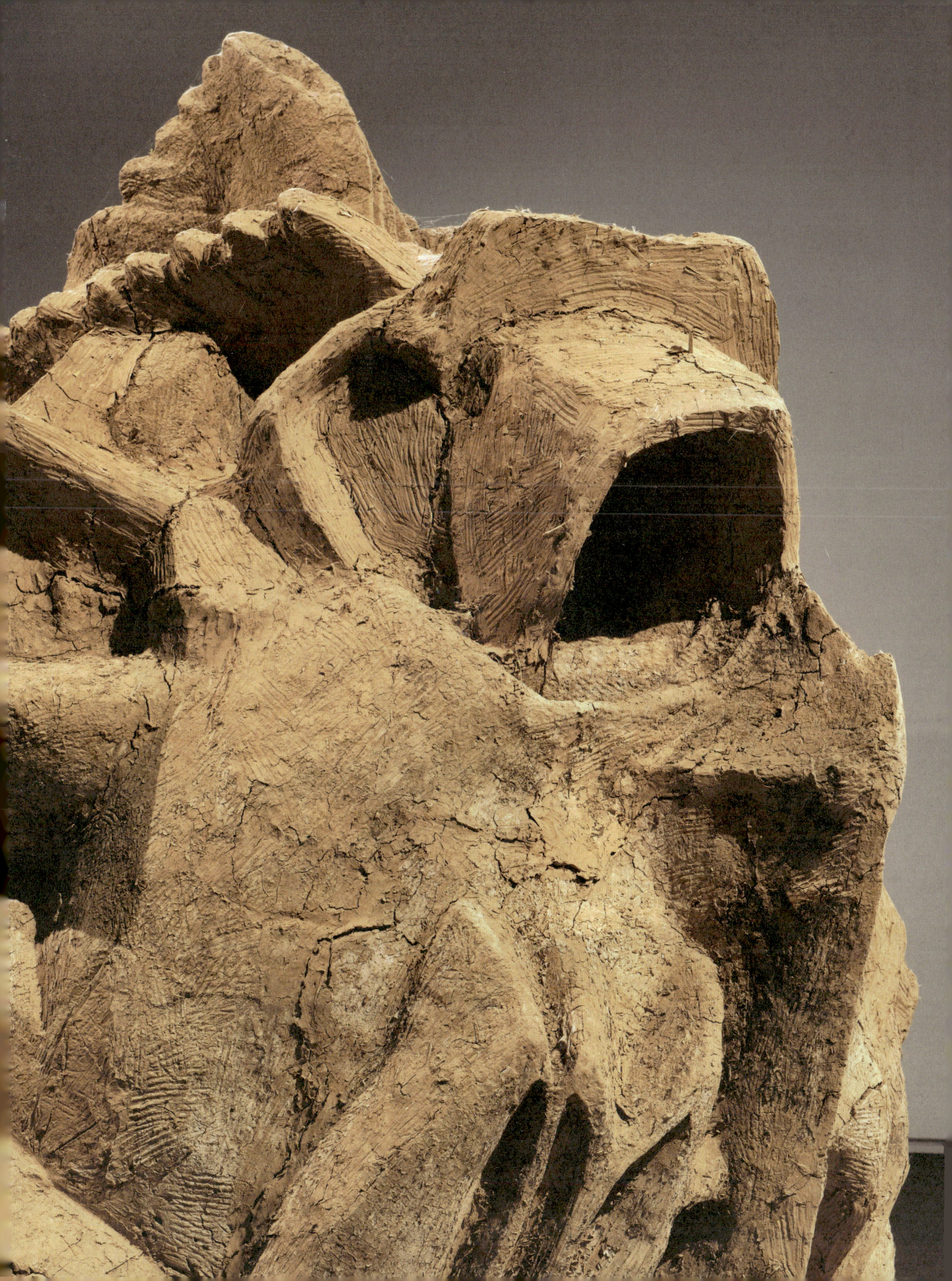

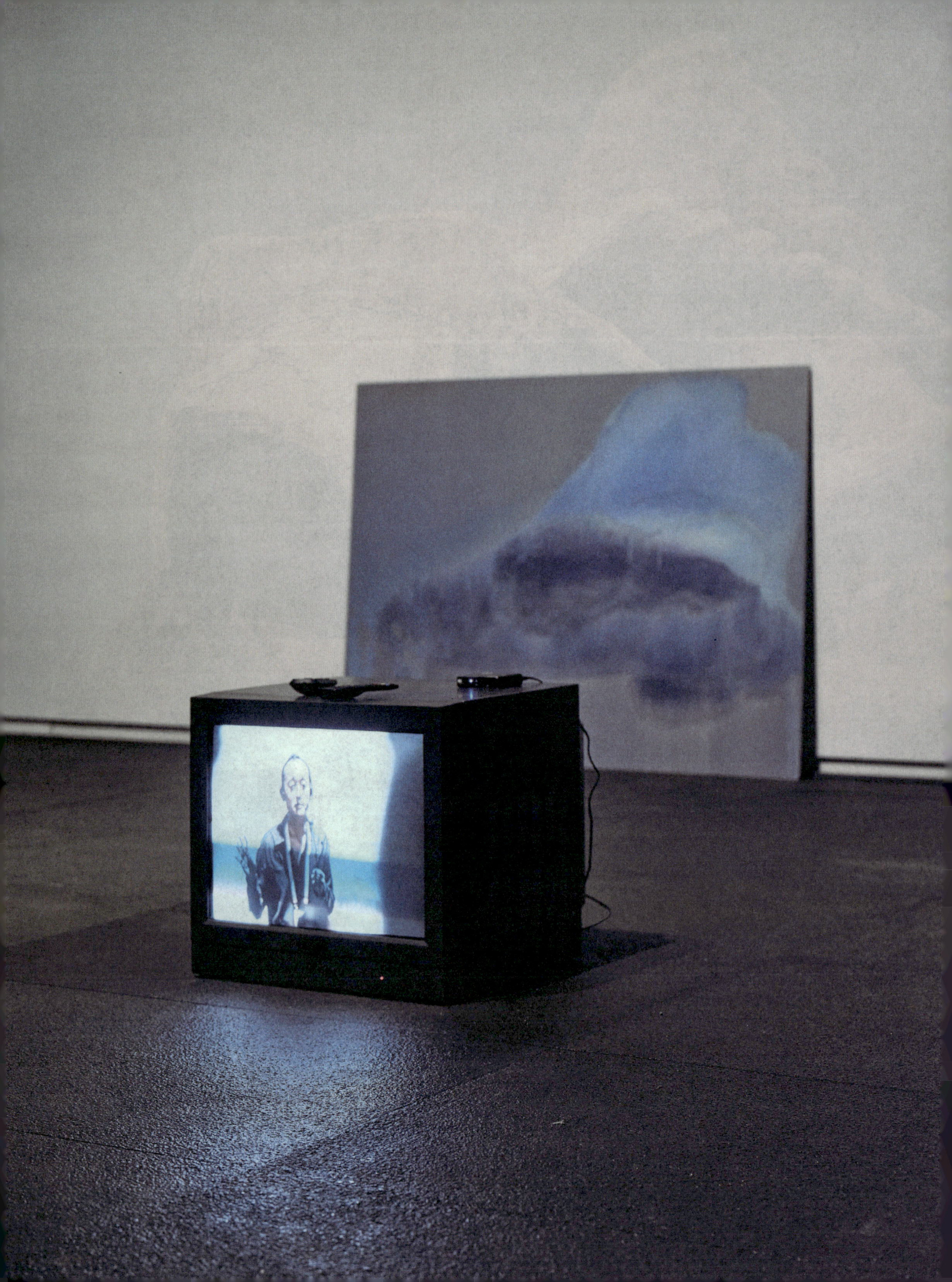

[89]

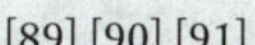

[89] [90] [91]

Release, 2024. Chair, monitor, aluminium plate. 150 × 270 × 250 cm

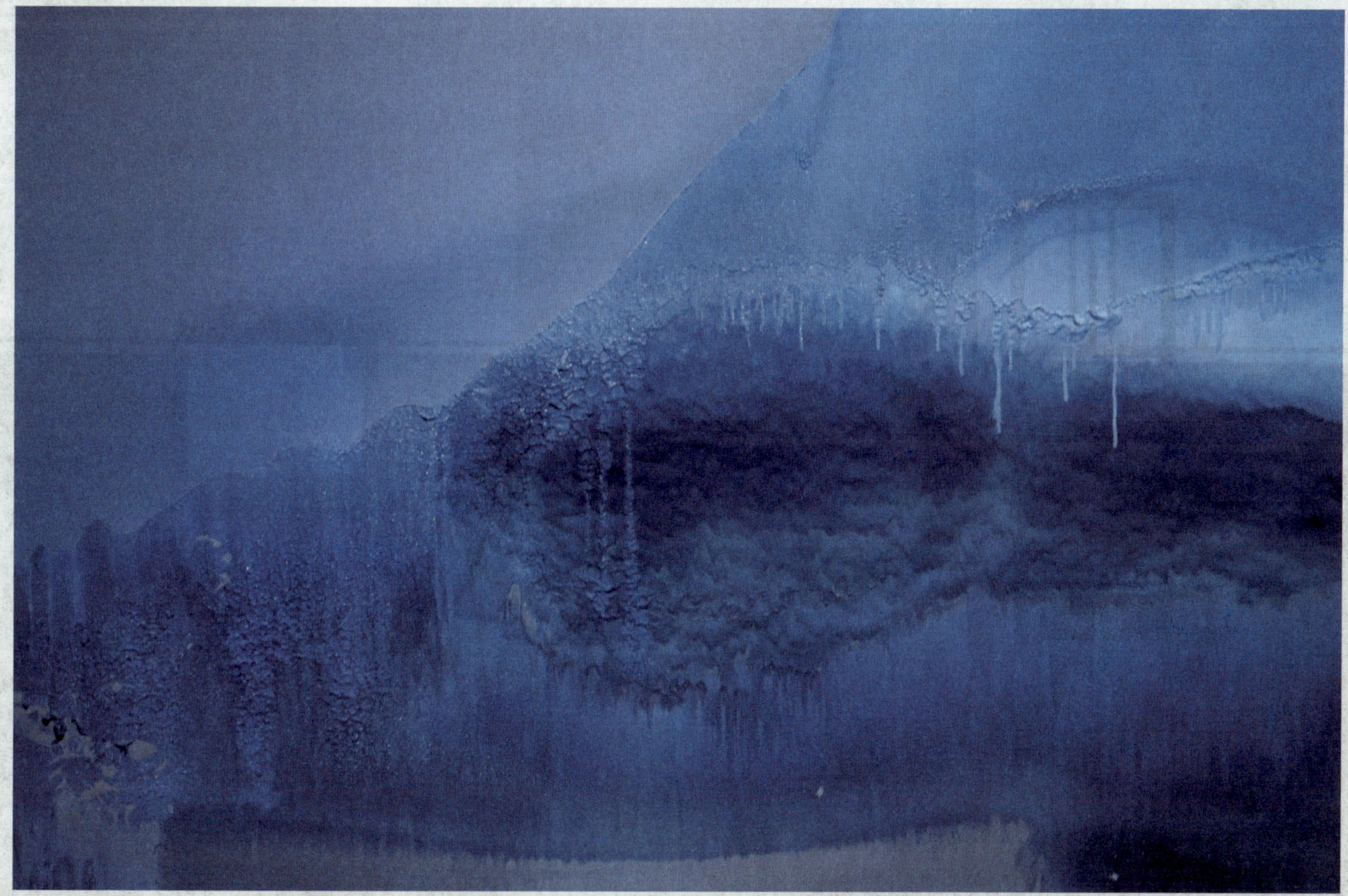

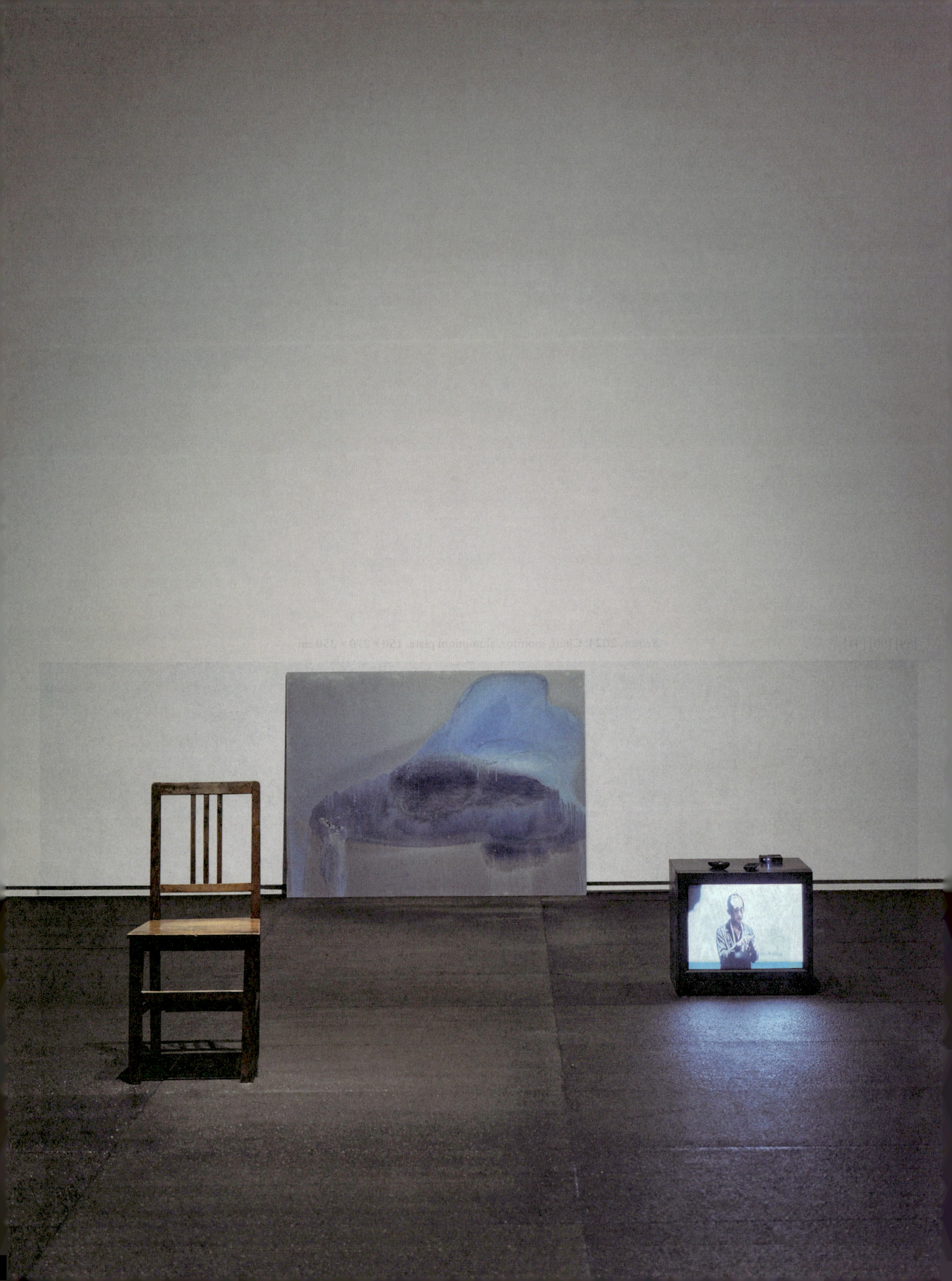

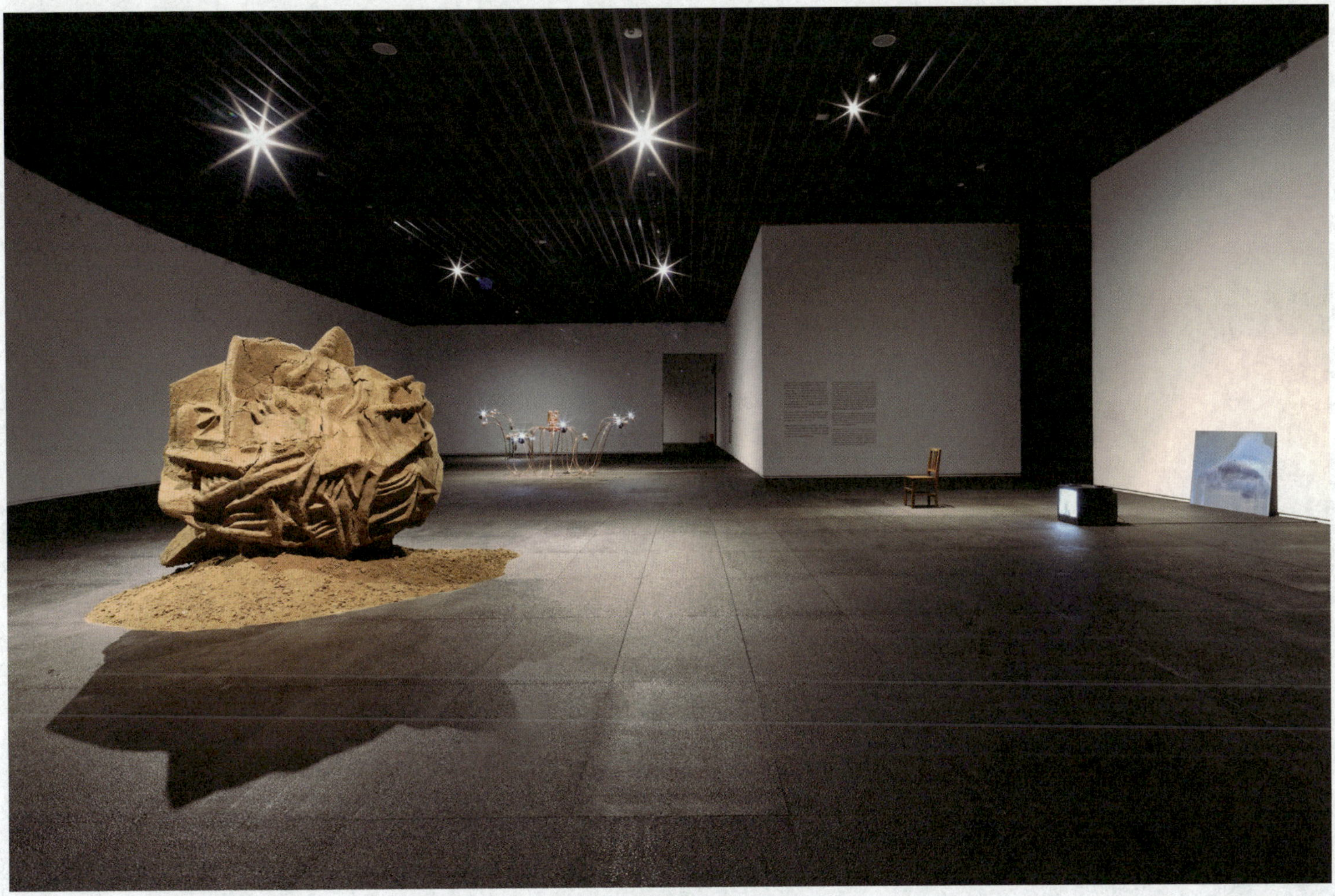

Wang Yuyang: Chaosmosis, Shenzhen Art Museum, China, 2024

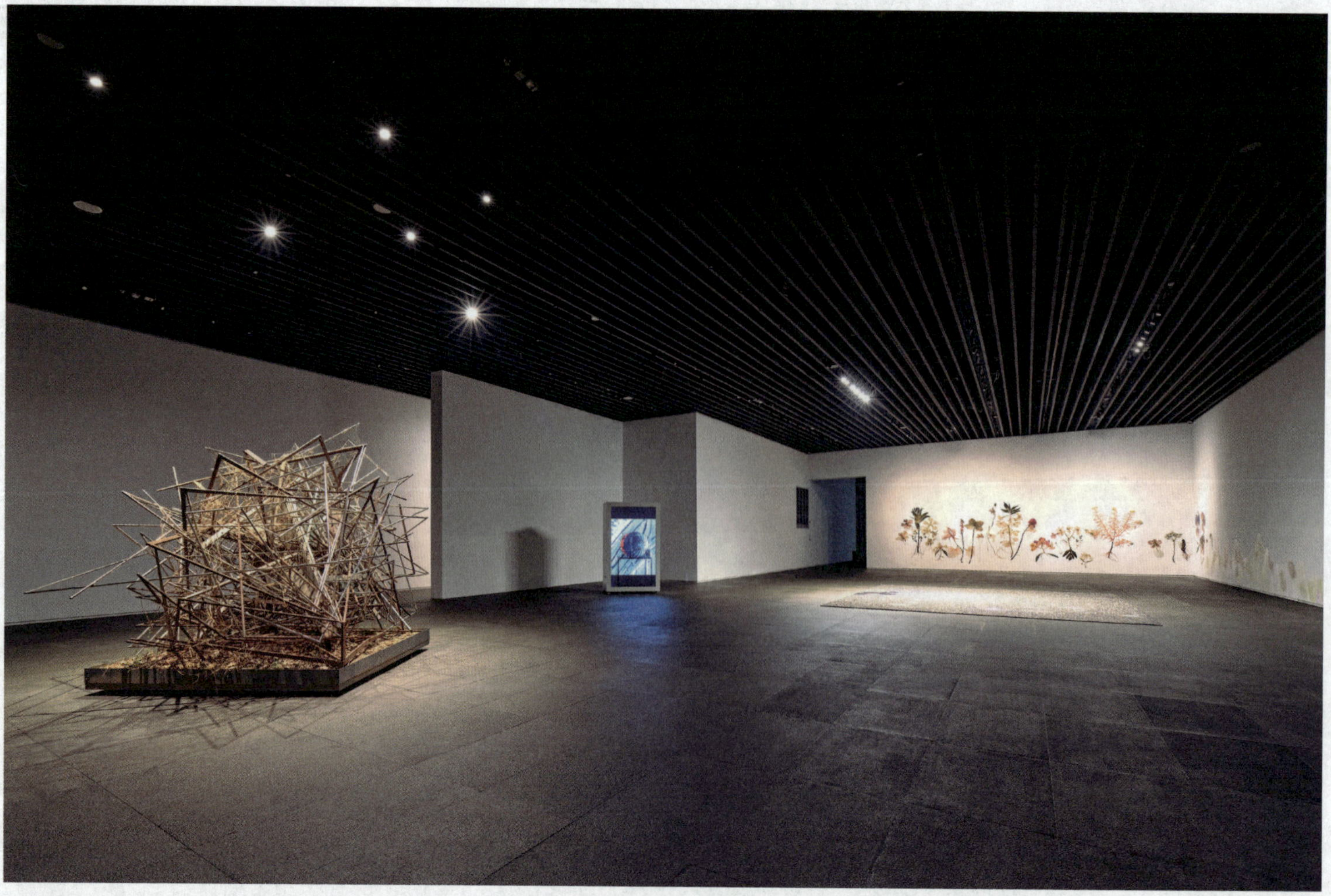

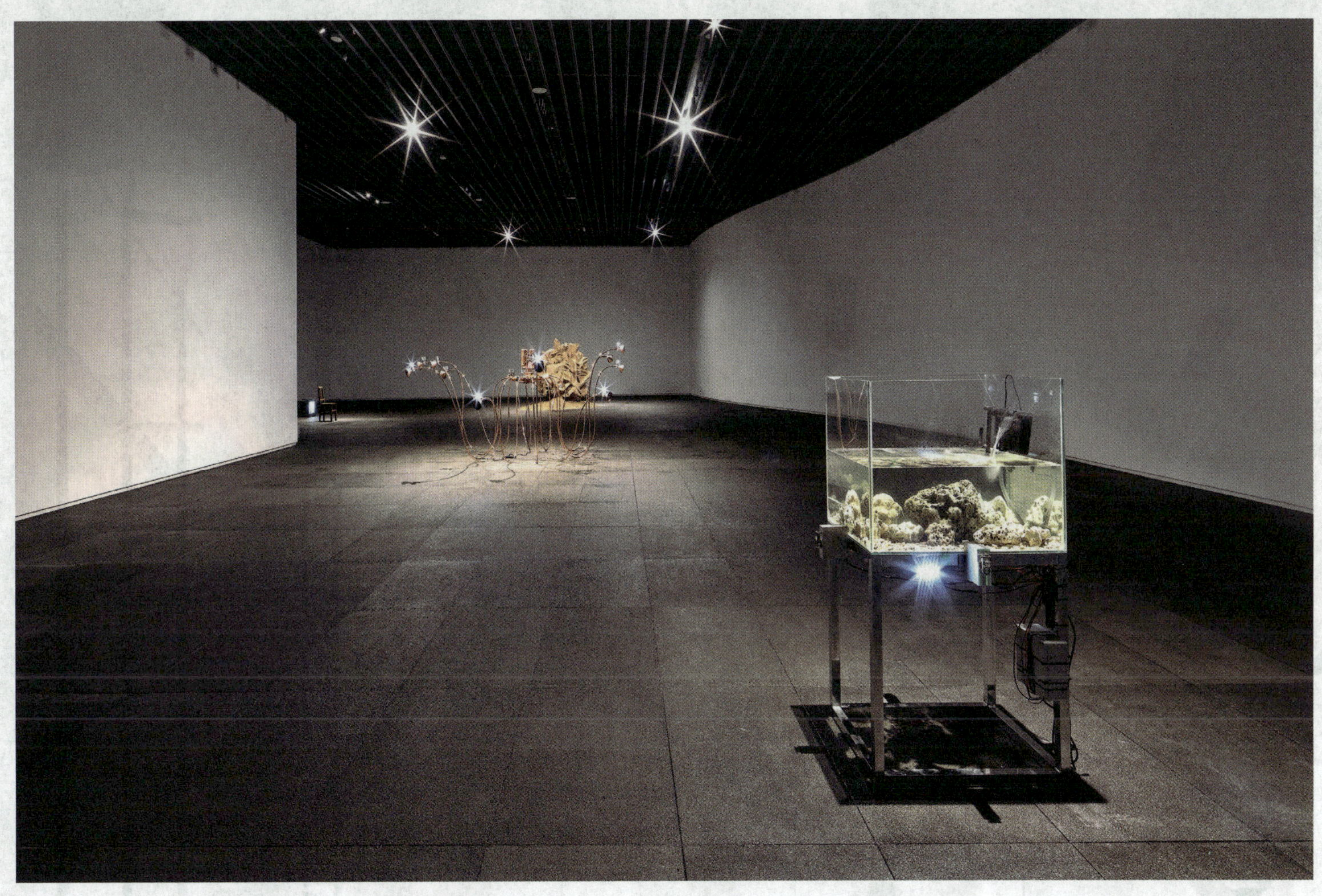

Wang Yuyang: Chaosmosis, Shenzhen Art Museum, China, 2024

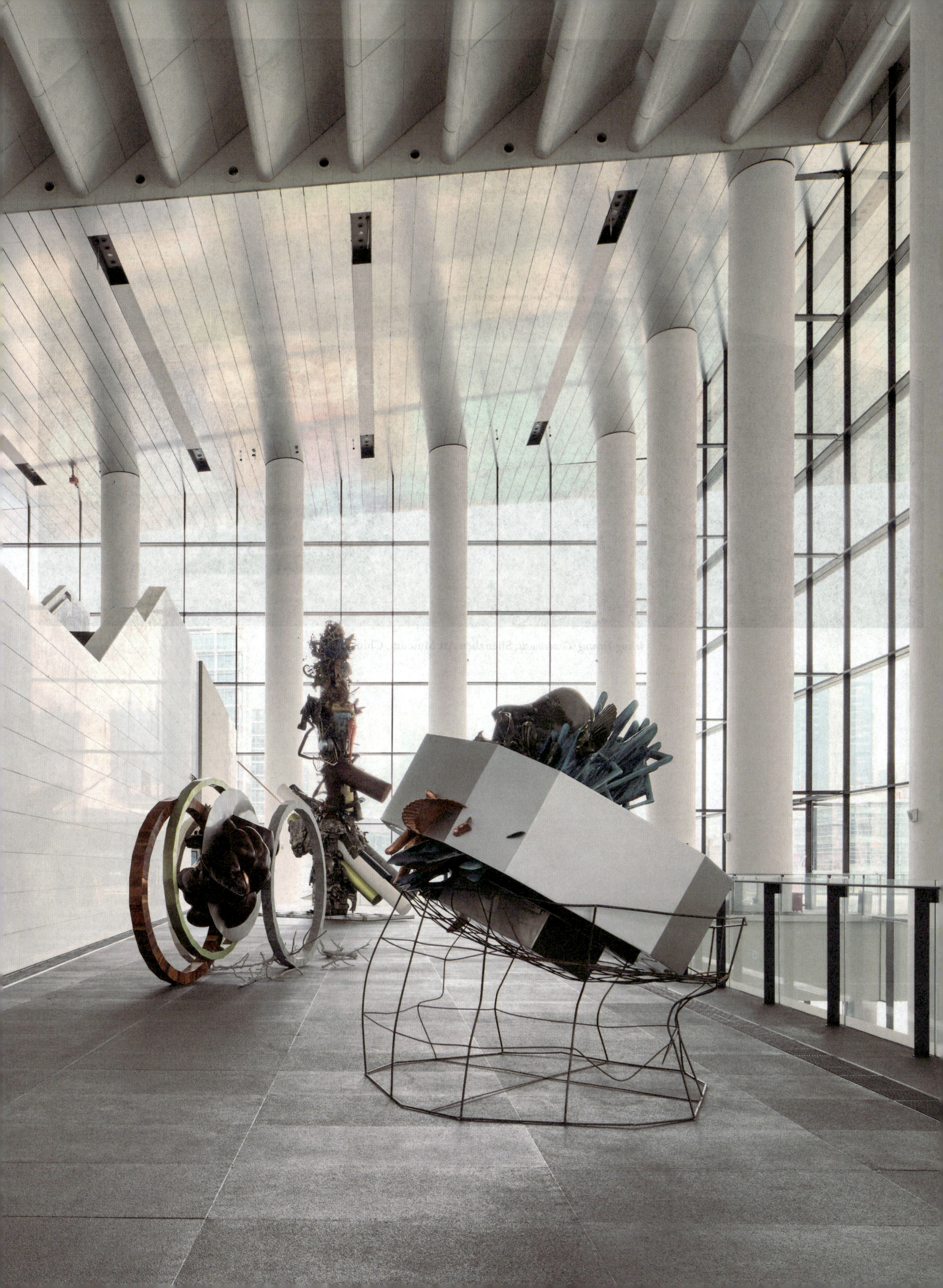

WANG YUYANG

(b. 1979) is a contemporary Chinese artist, and a professor at the China Central Academy of Fine Arts.

Focused on techno-art, his work explores the relationships between technology and art, nature and artificiality, material and immaterial, employing an interdisciplinary and multimedia approach. Wang's portfolio spans various fields such as artificial intelligence, genetic engineering, digital media, and mechanical devices. Utilizing computer programming, algorithmic generation, and data visualization, he creates dynamically changing and interactive art forms. Wang Yuyang's pieces not only reflect a critical examination of technological development but also brim with imaginative visions of the future, often presenting an unpredictable aesthetic challenging viewers' inherent perceptions. As an artist consistently innovating and pushing boundaries, Wang Yuyang has used technology to offer new possibilities to art, expanding the perspectives and expressions of techno-art with significant societal and cultural impact.

CHAOSMOSIS AND THE RETURN OF THE GRAND NARRATIVE

ZHANG GA

ZHANG GA
Professor of Curatorial Studies in Media Art, China Central Academy of Fine Arts

In Wang Yuyang's expansive 2015 exhibition *Tonight I Shall Meditate on That Which I Am* at the Long Museum in Shanghai, the artist unleashed a futurity conceived through the imbrication of the "that" in "I" and the "I" in "that." As I wrote then," That which I am conjugates the subject and the object, conflating the inanimate and the soulful and suggesting an emerging relationship between things and humans."[1] This meditative musing on the new paradigm of technicity and humanity characterized much of the artist's work at the time. Almost ten years later, with *Chaosmosis*, a mid-career survey show at the recently opened Shenzhen Art Museum extending his prolonged interest in investigating a plethora of subjectivities, Wang has ventured into an even more radicalized notion of nature and culture with a magnitude of geological immensity and minutiae of the microbial and everything in between. The artist's recent endeavors look out on a vista that beckons forth an "ecosophical" turn, which the late Félix Guattari proposed in *The Three Ecologies* (1989), and elicit a renewed grand narrative that transgresses human histories and invites reterritorialization.

1 Zhang Ga, foreword for the exhibition *Tonight I Shall Meditate on That Which I Am*, Long Museum, Shanghai, 2015.

WELCOME TO *CHAOSMOSIS*

If the series *WANG Yuyang#* (2015–ongoing), a hallmark of the artist's Long Museum exhibition, manifested a rupture away from an anthropomorphized object world and toward a reckoning with intelligences of another order, reversing the operational canon and delegating creative agency to the often subservient medium of tool being, *Symbiosis* (2023–ongoing), the first piece encountered in the Shenzhen Art Museum exhibition, indicates a second return of the human artist and the "utility of tool being." Here, the strange beauty of this monumental structure is a love child between Wang Yuyang (the artist in the flesh) and WANG Yuyang# (the artist in bytes)—a reconciliation of human fancy and machine vagary. The antagonism and intrigue that drive much of today's AI hype seem to find respite in a measured posture of transience and transcendence.

In *The Dubious of Entanglement by Plants* (2012–24), the derelict impregnates speculation about a sculpture that lives. Weeds grow thickly, and what was once an immaculate artifact is now an obscure object of desire in the imperceptible province of the biomolecular underworld where bacteria abound. In *I Don't Know* (2024), bacteria are particles crystallized in a plasma display of images derived from moss and liverworts. As structures and elements break down, fluctuate, and transpose, molecular bifurcation nurtures the birth of *Biological Klein Blue* (2022), a marvelous work of synthetic biology, while the floral arborescence sprawling along the wall propelled by the artificial mind yields abundance and fertility. Life, as in *Plant* (2024), flourishes in algorithmic prowess, too. In an age when semantics has acquired agential potency, to define is to code and to procreate, and it starts with the most rudimentary recipe of all life, DNA. All lives have a common ancestor; the evidence can be traced back to some 3.7 billion years ago, when signs of life first emerged in biogenic matter. But here the most rudimentary has become the most intricate and elaborate: a dictionary entry for the word "fungus" is translated into ATCG, the bases of DNA, and then injected into a eukaryotic organism. It is assumed that future generations of the fungus will therefore be hybrids of the original fungus's DNA and the human-language-reinterpreted DNA. Nature is bricolaged with the unnatural to become a third nature, a perfect symbiont that is much desired today. In *Define* (2022), the refurbished biomass sprawls between everything as if to make its indisputable claim that fungi and humans are of the same origin. All are unspeakable yet propagated and permeated by words, the code.

The meandering light tube in *Meandering* (2019–24) is alive and emanating, glowing, sometimes dragging its seemingly tired, slender torso; other times, at rest, it reclines into complacency. If we recall Wang's previous assemblages in which hundreds of them wiggled across the floor, twitching and carefully delineating their proximity to their neighbors, this solitary one seems more confident in its self-certainty and unambiguity as a being of consciousness.

Entropy and probability go hand in hand, according to Ludwig Boltzmann, and chaos precedes order, as announced by Nobel laureate Ilya Prigogine.[2] In *Indiscernible* (2024), white spots appear stochastically in a pool of black liquid, then suddenly converge into our narcissistic self-image, vanishing and re-forming as yet another portrait of a random human spectator, ad infinitum. This uncanny phenomenon invokes a working model of a dissipative structure, which has many implications regarding the self-organizing systems that have grown exponentially around us today.

Uncertainty and indeterminacy rule contemporary existence. But their genealogy runs all the way back to the Big Bang. Nobody knows the initial condition of the universe, since it escapes the laws of physics and remains unintelligible not only to humans but also to the infallible principles of mathematics, if that is considered a realm with or without human comprehension as the default intelligibility. The artist's amorphous physicality in the form of body odor, *I'm Not Sure About the Ones I Gave* (2024), reverberates with the syntactically sound but semantically absurd enunciations of artificial intelligence in *AI Quotes* (2024), infiltrating and osmosing, seeping through the roundabout of hallways in between the galleries.

As a hardware incarnation of the wetware series *WANG Yuyang#* (2015–ongoing), a telematic embrace infuses brain cells with iron and steel across time zones and coalescing consciousnesses both machine and human. Inside a sealed space with four glass walls, the industrial robotic hand of *Dream* (2016–24) moves agilely about, painting gracefully on the transparent panes—choosing colors, stroking a line, brushing a surface. It is the artist mechanically sleepwalking that makes the dream come true, albeit through the playfulness of an apparatus. Distance collapses and time diminishes, human becomes machine, and machine turns human. It is the sign of the times.

Collapsing is a thermodynamic norm. Everything collapses in the end—that is the irrefutable irreversibility of entropy. Destruction is the twin of construction, it's the primary law of conservation that everything is indebted to, including we humans. But then, entropy comes hand in hand with probability. We don't know when collapsing takes place, where the threshold is in which a phase shift comes to pass, in which the transition happens, chaos emerges, and things break down. The fish tank in *Collapse* (2024) is precariously equipped with a menacing metal probe that may strike it, shattering it at any moment, or perhaps not in our lifetime. Chance and aleatory events are out of human control. But today, even

2 See Ilya Prigogine and Isabelle Stengers, *Order Out of Chaos: Man's New Dialogue with Nature* (London: Verso, 2017).

chance can be programmed such that it becomes a controlled uncontrollability.

Enter eon, what the philosopher Quentin Meillassoux might call ancestrality, which is a world without thought: a "world without the givenness of the world, [but] a world capable of subsisting without being given," one registering geological timelessness and archaeological perpetuity.[3] This is a new grand narrative in which the history of human civilizations is deprived of any privilege. There is only the undead from which life may be resuscitated. In *Forgotten Memories* (2024), ice cores from glaciers hundreds of thousands of years old were harvested and turned into oxygen so that *Homo sapiens* of the twenty-first century may savor pristine air instead of the fumes and aerosols of our time, delivered from a Medusa-like structure with winding pipes and tubes that stored the ancient ice, then melted and oxygenated it. Life is breathed alive by the undead, and a world without the givenness of the world becomes the given world anew.

Life is godly (the air of the immaculate Ice Age is certainly divine), a breath blown into mud, so it goes. But here, life is also words or code turned living. *Golem* (2022) is invoked in the title of this monumental lump of mud and its unnamable growing form, and in that golem is an inanimate thing granted life by incantations and letters. The symbolism of a contemporary vision of code-engendered life is obvious. The form of the golem is a wretched portrait of artificial intelligence seeking to emulate the shape of the artist. It is fed by biometric data sets accrued from Wang—albeit deranged—becoming a crystalline form of the artist's consciousness. Climate, temperature, and environmental situations would sculpt and probably precipitate the eventual decay of the fragile clay (supposedly) humanoid figure back to dust at Shenzhen Art Museum in an archaeological future.

An empty chair—upon which Wang once sat—recounts the story of *Release* (2024), in which a robot dog, furnished with solar panels for life support, set off on uninhabited land in Lop Nur in northwestern China. The dog walked many miles, with satellite GPS following its whereabouts. Time went by, signals weakened, and eventually the dog disappeared. The finale is to vanish. To disappear is a victory over planned obsolescence. Nothing to be seen. Everything has already happened. Into oblivion marches technology, exhausted of power supply, like an organism that crumbles in breaking down its chemical bonds and rearranges its atoms to form new compounds. Dissolution and collapse may be the prelude to a new form of being. Out of chaos arises equilibrium

3
Quentin Meillassoux, *After Finitude: An Essay on the Necessity of Contingency*, trans. Ray Brassier (New York: Continuum, 2009), 28.

and order. That is again the physical law, against all human inventions and interventions.

Wang's world is an aggregation or conglomeration of discrete elements, a violation of continuum and consistence, where aleatory encounters agitate perturbation, in which precariousness is the norm and chaos persists. It is the atomic world of both the macro large and the micro small, convoluted in multiplicities of existence like the discombobulated finding of the double-slit experiment. Speaking of Lucretius, Michel Serres portrays chaos as the primordial atomic condition. But rather than endorsing a traditional atomist account of the chaos of fluxion, in which atoms move linearly, or fluctuation, by which particles fly in all directions, he elaborates on the laminar flow by the Lucretian image of "clinamen": that in the void, all directions are equal, neither ups nor downs are favored: "No point is privileged with respect to any other and none is univocally subordinate to any other."[4] All particles move uniformly and regularly, displaying no deviation in their homogeneous motion in the laminar flow, until a fortuitous atom unexpectedly changes direction, diverging from the given pathway. This swerve disrupts the invariable, degenerating into turbulence, much like a gentle sea breeze escalates into a storm: a butterfly effect. Serres therefore says that turbulence is order, and order turbulence—their perpetual reciprocity rules out a universal time and space. Out of these tumultuous disorders emerge new and singular temporalities and spatialities, each subsisting in its due course of continuance before disintegrating into chaos once again. In that cyclically eternal return, there is a multitude of times and spaces, enduring and dissipating each according to its own nature and rhythm.[5]

In his final book, Guattari coined the term "chaosmosis," unveiling the philosopher's vision of a fluid interplay between order and disorder, a world of metamorphosis and emergence, and the intricate exchanges and turbulent currents traversing many realms and scales of existence, encapsulating the gist of his ecological philosophy.[6] "Chaosophy" is "ecosophy," in which humans, societies with a technological turn, and the natural world intersect and transverse, giving rise to novel structures and new subjectivities that undermine the once-grand narrative of human history. It is an asignifying semiology empowered by agentic autopoiesis and outside the regime of the post-structuralist tool kit, an epiphany of the technic noumenon.[7] In the heyday of the deconstruction of the grand narrative, the vision of three ecologies resonated with a new type of grand narrative as Serres had advocated, that which "abides by two formats, both properly

4 Michel Serres, *Hermes I: Communication*, trans. Louise Burchill (Minneapolis: University of Minnesota Press, 2023), 5. See also Michel Serres, *The Birth of Physics*, trans. David Webb and William Ross (London: Rowman & Littlefield, 2018).

5 Christine Wertheim, "A Science of Exceptions: On Michel Serres's *The Birth of Physics*," *Los Angeles Review of Books*, August 14, 2018, https://lareviewofbooks.org/article/a-science-of-exceptions-on-michel-serress-the-birth-of-physics/.

6 Félix Guattari, *Chaosmosis: An Ethico-Aesthetic Paradigm*, trans. Paul Bains and Julian Pefanis (Sydney: Power Publications, 2006).

7 Mark B. Hansen, "Critique of Data," in *Critique and the Data*, ed. Erich Hörl, Nelly Y. Pinkrah, and Lotte Warnsholdt (Zurich: Diaphanes, 2021), 23–73.

universal: the laws of physics and the genetic code."[8] It is with this empathy and in resonance that we heed Wang Yuyang's grand narrative of chaosmosis, and this narrative, as Guattari had unequivocally enunciated, is their stories that unfold in an equally irreducible ethical-aesthetic paradigm.

8 Michel Serres, *Branches: A Philosophy of Time, Event and Advent*, trans. Randolph Burks (New York: Bloomsbury, 2020), 31.

ONE MUST HAVE CHAOS INSIDE TO GIVE BIRTH TO A DANCING STAR: SOME PASSAGES ON WANG YUYANG

SIEGFRIED ZIELINSKI

SIEGFRIED ZIELINSKI
Professor Emeritus of Media Theory, Berlin University of the Arts

In philosophical terms, trying to grasp the future is an absurdity.[1] Future is the mode of time that remains stubbornly closed to us; we cannot experience the future. However, what we as humans *are* capable of, in cooperation with machines and nature, is to creatively process the now and develop ideas and models of possible future presences by breaking with the realities we find. This is essentially what Wang Yuyang does, persistently and consistently. When we talk about such future realities, we are always referring to concepts, models, and designs, no matter how realistic they may seem. Wang plays with this particularly exciting relationship between past, present, and future, keeping us sensitive to this tension.

ΚΟΣΜΟΣ & ΧΑΟΣ

Kósmos and Cháos refer to the structure of the fabric that Édouard Glissant, the poet-philosopher from Martinique, called the Whole-World. It is what surrounds us and in which we are allowed to be guests. In ancient Greece and its complex mythologies, the two concepts were at strong antipodes. Kósmos designates a semantic field that is characterized by order, laws, constitutions, and political, legal, cultural, and mathematical rules. The cosmic also stands for equilibrium, for a beautiful appearance, for generated harmony and decoration. Kósmos clearly bears human hallmarks: it was invented by *Homo sapiens*. It is no wonder that at the beginning of the twenty-first century, when humans have developed into *Homo artefactus* and planet Earth is exposed to perhaps its

1
The title of this essay references Friedrich Nietzsche's preface to *The Birth of Tragedy* (1872).

2 See *NKA Journal of Contemporary African Art*, no. 46, special issue on "Rethinking Cosmopolitanism: Africa in Europe | Europe in Africa" (May 2020).

3 Athanasius Kircher, *Turris Babel* (Amsterdam: Jansson van Waesberge, 1679).

greatest test and can no longer be surpassed in terms of contradictions and conflict, the cosmic is booming: as cosmo-technics (Yuk Hui), as cosmo-media (Tang Hongfeng), as cosmos cinema (the 2023 Shanghai Biennale), once again as cosmopolitanism in different variations (including as Afro-politanism in the contemporary African art scene).[2] At the beginning of the twenty-first century, it is evidently not enough that late capitalism, under the verdict of the global—which has long since become a chimera and sunk into the depths of the exploited ocean—is trying, energetically and at the same time in vain, to drive conditions toward standardization and a high degree of compatibility among the various techno-economies. Many in the completely shattered human species are once again longing for strong forces of universalization and harmonization to which the subject can submit unconditionally. This promises a comfortable way of life, at least temporarily.

Cháos, on the other hand—depending on the worldview of the speaker—stands for raw, undivided, and consequently disorganized matter as the initial state of all existence. Cháos is the governor of the uncanny, the completely incommensurable. As such, in Robert Fludd's history of the micro- and macrocosm at the beginning of the seventeenth century, this state aesthetically took the form of the black square, three hundred years before Kazimir Malevich's iconic gesture for the radical new beginning in painting, and almost four hundred years before *One Square Centimetre* (2001), Wang's ironic play with miniature black squares on photographic paper—seven in number, one for each day of creation (including the day of rest). In the early modern period, Cháos also stood for an almost unbearable polyphony and Babylonian diversity (as in Athanasius Kircher's book on the Tower of Babel).[3] And Cháos must also stand for the absolute opposite, for the yawning void—the void to which the recently deceased London film and video artist David Larcher dedicated one of his most powerful electronic image works, *videøvoid* (1993).

In the deep time of our existence, Cháos is often ascribed the quality of the primordial. The Kósmos, on the other hand, is understood to be genealogically subordinate, as if it had developed from the chaotic state as a higher quality of being. Since the findings of quantum physics at the latest, this assumption has proven to be a mistake. In post-mechanical physics after Isaac Newton, the idea of a universal law for everything moving no longer works. The micro- and macro-physical realities are so complex that we can only understand them with the help of chaos theories. And Cháos is not simply a past state. Once harmony has been achieved,

4 Giuseppe Zigaina and Christa Steinle, eds., *P. P. PASOLINI organizzar il trasumanar / oder die Grenz uberscheitun* (Venice: Marsilio, 1995).

disharmony, hatred, and repulsion can develop again. Order, happiness, and harmony can plunge back into immeasurable Cháos at any time—into a reality characterized by fierce competition, war, terror, and tyranny. The origin is a trap, said Friedrich Nietzsche. Both states, each associated with archaic forms, can unfold in interaction as spaces of possibility, and historically can even be closely intertwined. The strong materiality of Cháos, however, forms a dialectical opposite to the concept of Kósmos, which tends toward the metaphysical. Practicing heterogenesis could be a solution in between—in thinking as well as in doing.

This brings us to the center of the universe into which Wang, as an artist subject, likes to emigrate, and in which he insists on his right as a guest. In his fundamental alienation from what people call their ordered reality, he needs the constant transgression of the set boundaries of the everyday as a self-evident free space. Like the resistant *enfant terrible* of Italian cinematic history, Pier Paolo Pasolini, Wang tries to organize his transgressions aesthetically, which is a strong paradox—*organizzar il trasumanar*.[4] For the means of transgressions, their media belong to the world of laws, structures, orders, techno-logics, regardless whether it is language, music, film, or computer. Wang's own world, on the other hand, is characterized by a fluctuating, constantly changing, and exciting interplay between order and disorder, censorship and fantasy systems, the calculable and the unpredictable. Only those who are able to reckon with the unknown are worthy of *máthēma* as a discipline, the application and formulation of the comprehensive knowledge we can acquire about the world. This is what each of Wang's artworks, created with and through thinking or even trivial machines, tells us.

As an artist, Wang himself is a chaosmotic subject. His works and actions repeatedly rise to the challenge of Félix Guattari's concept of "chaosmosis" by demolishing the confusing and disturbing manifold-ness and thus making it habitable, and even transforming it into a positive anti-place, a place of longing, a desirable porous state that is, however, stubbornly unattainable in reality. Such places were once called utopias. In post-human reality, they have largely given way to cacatopian sensations, the rules and construction principles, which Wang masters just as brilliantly. He staged the transition from one quality to the other already in 2007 with a reenactment, namely the first landing of US astronaut Neil Armstrong on the dream planet of humankind par excellence in 1969, in which the boundaries between the virtual and physically tangible or imaginable world become blurred. The vertical ladder that Armstrong used to step out of the

5
Understood as bringing forth, generating; in Heideggerian German, *Hervorbringung*. In view of the technical inventions produced by ancient societies, I still feel very modest today with my modern ego. For ancient Greece, see for example Kostas Kotsanas, *Ancient Greek Technology: The Inventions of the Ancient Greeks* (Pyrgos, Greece: Kostas Kotsanas, 2013).

6
See Francois Jullien's reading of Confucianism in chapter 3 of *From Living to Being: A Euro-Chinese Lexicon of Thought* (Thousand Oaks, CA: SAGE Publications, 2019), 13–20.

spaceship onto the surface of the moon seems to be the only constant in the vertical, the medium of swinging in and out with which people can both ascend to a higher place and experience a precipitous fall. In his brazen simulation of the iconic media event of the moon landing, Wang uses aesthetic means to make us curious about an existence in future techno-natures that is neither a unique poiesis (in the sense of the ancient Greek *techné*)[5] nor a dispositive frame. His art is in search of a third, which however is not located between the Heideggerian poles—the ideas of technology and technique that the German philosopher from the Black Forest essentially directed against artists, whom he denied the ability to transgress technical logics experimentally—but beyond them.

WE

Michel Serres was a mathematician and an outstanding philosopher of communication and the history of knowledge. Above all, I value him as a decidedly heretical thinker. His books *The Parasite* (1980) and *The Hermaphrodite* (1987) unfold their strength as provocations of established thought in masteries, systems, and skillfully constructed structuralisms. The new wisdom and the new morality that Serres called for do not come from this world with which we are familiar. Rather, they are brazen anticipations of possible future presences. The unconditional ego of European modernity is just as suspect to Serres as a figure of presumption as the cogito associated with it. Thought through Confucius the *cogito* means to become *disposable* for something or somebody. As soon as one holds on to a position, an ego coagulates. To put forward an idea, that is, to set light, already means to force others into the shadow. If you say *I*, you inevitably discriminate against the other. This is how Confucius paraphrases his plea for disponibility as a basic attitude towards the world.[6]

Serres's heroes are the figures of the in-between, of twilight, of ambiguity, of possible failure and fall: Hermes and Odysseus, the messenger, the angel, the parasite, the hermaphrodite. This heretical thinking reached a climax in his 1990 treatise *The Natural Contract*, a book from which Bruno Latour and many other thinkers learned a great deal. The treatise is a resolute plea for a radical paradigm shift, not only from an ecological point of view, but also from a media archaeological perspective. Serres calls for nature and its ecosystems—rivers, trees, animals, the Wadden Sea, mountains, oceans—to be recognized not just as objects to be used and exploited, but as subjects in the legal sense, as contractual subjects. What has become ethically and economically self-evident

7
Michel Serres, *The Natural Contract* (Ann Arbor, MI: University of Michigan Press, 1995), 38.
8
Serres, *The Natural Contract*, 80.

in Indigenous traditions of South America and Oceania, particularly in Ecuador, parts of Argentina, Colombia, and New Zealand, still must be fought for in the global West and in China.

My enthusiasm for Serres's treatise was awakened in the early 1990s, when I published my first explicitly media-archaeological projects, not only due to the demand for a recognition of the subject status of nature, which I also extended to technical existences, and for me that means the media apparatuses. In concluding the contract with nature, Serres argues that "our relationship to things would set aside mastery and possession in favor of admiring attention, reciprocity, contemplation, and respect."[7] It is striking that Serres here calls for attitudes that we are normally inclined to adopt toward works of art. In the arts, Wang is for me a post-romanticist, similar to Serres as a philosophical writer. Wang finds the unconditional nature of things in the richness of relationships that follow close listening and respectful observation. The virtual plants that his algorithms generated for the installation *Plant* (2024) are just as seductively beautiful as the biological reality on which they are based. At the same time, they act like bloodless shadows in the realm of Hades, from which there is no escape. The price of entry into Hades is the surrender of the body at its threshold.

Serres can only come to his unusual plea for a new, horizontally organized WE of nature, technology, and humanity because he succeeds in freeing knowledge and the sciences from the "epistemodicy" that generated the previous relationships "of science and law, reason and judgment."[8] This break with given reality is inherent in Wang's art. The symbiosis represented by his six-meter-high sculpture made of such heterogeneous materials as plaster, steel, sheet metal, copper, fiberglass, and sand can be understood as an invitation to reflect on the various individuations of the artist and his materials as well as their composition. The latter seems to follow a precise hallucination. The sculpture is a prosthetic god, an instrument of war, a pile of civilizational rubbish, and, in its utter uselessness, a bachelor machine par excellence. It does not want to produce or re-produce anything, and definitely not any kind of false harmony. From a media-archaeological perspective, I am tempted to interpret the tiered conglomerate as an invitation to abandon the cross of Western ideals. In verticality, the deep time of the manifold contexts of things finds expression. Individual condensations of objects and substances, on the other hand, seem to want to push into the horizontal of past constellations. The composition of both gestures gives rise to the necessity of a dynamic of departure. The dazzling and monstrous

9
Friederike Mayröcker, *Collected Poems 1939–2003*, ed. Marcel Beyer (Frankfurt: Suhrkamp, 2004), 631.

10
See Siegfried Zielinski, *[... After the Media] News from the Slow-Fading Twentieth Century* (Minneapolis: Minnesota University Press / Univocal, 2013).

sculpture *Symbiosis – Out* (2024) does not want to achieve anything beyond earthly existence at the upper tip, at its climax, nor does it want a transition to the metaphysical. I read the conglomerate of sprawling industrial waste, shiny scrap, and finely chiseled madness from top to bottom and not the other way around. The nearly twenty-six-foot-high sculpture challenges us not to accept the piled-up madness, but to use it as a scaffold for decadence. The monumental warrior thus becomes a vehicle for the departure from the cross. And when I look at the sculpture as a building, I associate it with a powerful poem by the Austrian writer Friederike Mayröcker, which is also a commentary on the artist's subjectivity:

what do you need? a tree a house
measure how big or small life as a human being is
how big how small when you look up to the crown
lose yourself in green, lush beauty [. . .]
you need a tree you need a house
none for you alone only a corner a roof
to sit to think to sleep to dream
to write to be silent to see the friend
the stars the grass the flower the sky.[9]

CHÁOS PILOT AND KAIROS POET

In the second half of the twentieth century, media art became an important stratagem in the global art scene. It had a rather short explicit lifespan of only about thirty years (which is almost nothing in art history). This strategy of art institutions and artists was less about a particular aesthetic or poetic sensibility than about access to machines, resources, and paid time in which to develop artistic works. The concept of artistic research only emerged when more complex technologies came into play in the arts. The digital became the last analogue of the alchemists' formula that promised the artificial production of gold. The magic world promised recognition if artists wore it like a label. By the turn of the last century, however, the media had become systemic. They were needed even more urgently for social, political, and economic infrastructures than in the arts.[10]

Now the media are no longer good for revolutions. This is a liberation for artists. They no longer have to work strategically but can concentrate on the noblest task of the arts: to make and keep us sensitive to the other, to what we stubbornly do not understand. This is where Wang's intervening activity begins. He is an artist of the twenty-first century. He needs not grapple with questions of the technical reproducibility of art, the simulability of things and processes, the technical conditionality of our existence, or similar ontologies. They had already been clarified to some extent, both theoretically and practically, when he began his experimental practice at the interfaces between humans and machines. With the arrival of learning machines in what Olympus reserved for the last refuges of the delirious *Homo artefactus*—making music, creating images, writing poetry, building spaces and sculptures, making films—the cards are being reshuffled. Just as artists are naturally integrated into this final stage of technological progress, machines and their inherent programs have become an essential part of that obscure world for which we have still not found a better name than art.

In 1959, the Belgian artist Henri Michaux, who is known for his mescaline-assisted transgressions in drawing and painting, among other things, formulated the subjectivity that also makes sense for Wang: "I paint as I write. To find, to find myself again, to find my own best, which I possessed without knowing it. For the sake of surprise and at the same time for the joy of having recognized it."[11] Wang's play with the famous quote from Henry Miller, "Tonight I shall meditate on that which I am,"[12] contains a comparable poetic enigma. Wang's objectification of his own self, however, is contrasted with his work on expanding the world of things toward its possible sanctity. In one of his estate fragments, Nietzsche uses the beautiful term "hyperborean."[13] By this, of course, he meant subjects like himself. The hyperborean lives with the world of facts, with everything that is the case, without submitting to the order of facts. This is great art, including Wang's.

I consider the generic sculpture *The Dubious of Entanglement by Plants* (2012–24) to be the masterpiece of such a hyperborean subject. The strictly geometrically ordered parts of the structure can hardly be surpassed in rigidity and hardness. At least in our macro-physical world of perception, they are dead. But wild flora, with their own laws of change and decay, unfold between the tangled, heavy metallic framework. This living plant world in turn attracts creatures such as spiders, which weave their webs between the dead and the living material. They have found their heterotopic place in this strange construct. Wang takes the endo-physics of a chaos theorist like Otto Rössler seriously and, as a participating inner observer, enters right into the center of the processes of the real, which is saturated and irritated by technology, in exchange with the processes of the imaginary and the symbolic. One of the most important faculties of future academies, which I have been working on for a good ten years, is a faculty for Cháos pilots. Wang is such a Cháos pilot, who also has the wonderful

11
Henri Michaux: Aquarelle, Temperabilder, Federzeichnungen, Mescalinezeichnungen (Frankfurt: Galerie Daniel Cordier, 1959), n.p.

12
This was the title of Wang's first major solo exhibition at the Long Museum Shanghai (2015) and the accompanying bilingual catalogue (2016).

13
I would like to thank Marcus Steinweg for pointing this out.

14
This is the title character of a fantastic book by Vilém Flusser and Louis Bec (Minneapolis: Minnesota University Press, 2012).

skills of the Kairos poet, a poet of the favorable moment, of the now, which has no extension, but which we must reckon with.

If it is the case that creativity is becoming a fundamental social competence in the face of limitlessly expanded possibilities of intervention at the interfaces of media-people and media-machines, and if the traditional model of the artist is being phased out in art itself, instead becoming a general guiding model of social action, then it is advisable to at least work on complementary identities. Wang convinces us of this with the means at his disposal as an artist. The competences that artists and intellectuals will increasingly need in the future can be grasped as tactical figures that cannot be translated into strategies: Cháos pilots and Kairos poets are basically uncensorable. They are artistic subjects who are able to not only deal with irreversibilities and complexities, but also organize them without administering them, and they are those who can seize the opportune moment (in the cinema, in the networks, on the stage, in the gallery, in the lecture theater, in the museum) and charge it with energy. Without an attitude toward the complex multiplicity of our reality, and without an attitude toward the time in which we are and which has us—both are inextricably intertwined in Wang's work—advanced thinking and advanced aesthetic practice will in the future no longer be conceivable. Just as we need artists who are able to intervene in those time structures that undermine our perception at the smallest level (such as the micro-intervals in high-frequency trading), we need thinkers and poets who can overflow space-time perceptions at the largest level (as in astrophysics). This faculty, which Wang possesses so excellently, is what I call "paleo-futurism." It is fantastically suited to exploring and developing the spaces of possibility of past and future presences and to generating those surprises in the relationships between media-people and media-machines that are vital for survival.

Forgotten Memories (2024) is also a frivolous thing, an animation with copper-red curved limbs and many glowing eyes that could have come from the depths of the seabed, a kind of *Vampyroteuthis infernalis*.[14] In order for the installation to allow the sensation-hungry museum visitor to experience past presences that date back hundreds of thousands of years, the artist has to consume extremely valuable natural material that has evolved over hundreds of thousands of years and is currently disappearing from our planet at an insane rate, namely glacial ice. The machine once again proves itself to be anti-nature grounded in nature. On the other hand, the delicate techno-structure with pistons, funnels, and an animalistic appearance actually makes paleo-ontological time tangible.

15
This is a term chosen by the biochemist Mahlon Hoagland in 1990 to characterize the epistemic value of experiments. I would like to thank Hans-Jörg Rheinberger for pointing this out.

Humanoids of the twenty-first century can breathe in the oxygen released by the ancient ice when the machine at the heart of the installation heats it up and turns it back into water. Humans can actively participate in the rapid disappearance of natural resources in the Anthropocene.

The clash of the two deep-time perspectives of past and future in this installation can also be understood as a balancing act between *facta* and *futura*, as a tension between the limited world of the given and the infinitely diverse spaces of possibility that we define as the future and that we want to preserve as open fields of action. The culturally coded sequence of geophysical and geopolitical facts would be replaced by a radical turn toward "dreaming ahead," as the philosopher Ernst Bloch emphasized the potential of utopia. He was aware that it would be possible to tip over into cacatopia at any time. The projection into the future must take the passage through the present and its agenda—its problems, challenges, aggregates of freedom and happiness—and link them with the utopian potential of the past. This is how "surprise generators" are created.[15] *Forgotten Memories* can also be interpreted as such a generator.

CULTURA EXPERIMENTALIS VS. TEST DEPARTMENT

With his minimalist installation *Linie* (2012), Wang experiments in a virtuoso manner with different forms of cognition at the interface between human and machine. Observation, reflection, imagination, and memory are thoroughly mixed up by the interposition of a computer in our consciousness. The calculation and simulation machine translates the handwritten line into visual code, which is rhythmically broken down and sent to the brain, processed by it as a medium, and projected outward again. In the extended interaction, the boundaries between the virtual and the real become blurred, as do those between the performances of consciousness and the machine in the process of perception.

In their strongest manifestations, museums of the future will be stimulating and exciting spaces for thought. As long as artists like Wang "play" them in the truest sense of the word, I can be sure that they will continue to delight us as generators of surprises. With his impressive aesthetic virtuosity, Wang also reminds us that artists should not primarily serve the decoration and ornamentalization of circumstances. Artists need not serve anyone but God, as Salvador Dalí never got tired of emphasizing. He did not mean a religious or even ecclesiastical God, but nothing less than the sovereign. Art has the potential to break with the current conventions of reality in order to enable a different view of the real. Wang closely observes the everyday and its particularities and makes them collide and explode in the art space. His magic creates something wildly divine that is difficult to describe discursively. I recently tried to formulate this phenomenon in the lyrics for a rock song. F. M. Einheit, the legendary rhythmic heart of the band Einstürzende Neubauten, translated the lyrics into music and sound. Finally, I would like to quote this text for Wang Yuyang:

art = resistance
there is no art without waste.
art works itself off on the material
so that it can appear or sound to others.
you have to break an egg to make an omelet.
As nature itself
material never is passive
the fabric is resisting
the processing by the artist.
matter is active.
active matter is
being in potentiality.

Potency potentials—
we open possibilities
natura naturans—
art is plastic and acoustic
exacerbated work
in the fiery matter

we don't just show,
what exists anyway.
artists are alchemists at the material.
the immense diversity of things
that do not and cannot exist
but that may be thought and believed
through the wild and wondrous world
of the power of imagination and experiment
before modern civilization finally commenced
its inexorable work of rationalization,
standardization and universalization.

potency potentials—
we open possibilities
natura naturans—
art is plastic and acoustic
exacerbated work
in the fiery matter

processing of the particular
the individual, the scattered
that nevertheless never
loses sight of the horizon of the whole.
alchemy is the dream
one is only just able to overhear,
one is able only to stammer.
when humans ceased
to be able to dream near their kilns
and to eavesdrop on matter itself,
the dream retreated back into the night.

potency potentials—
we open possibilities
natura naturans—
art is plastic and acoustic
exacerbated work
in the fiery matter

FEEDBACK FOR WANG YUYANG, OR, CYBERNETIC HISTORIES FOR CONTEMPORARY AESTHETICS

CAROLINE A. JONES

CAROLINE A. JONES
Allen Professor, Department of Architecture, MIT

"Feedback," in everyday English (and maybe also Chinese), is used colloquially to mean advice given from one human to another. But its origins are electronic. When the word first appeared in the English lexicon in 1920, "feed+back" meant pushing (feeding) part of an output signal back into a machine circuit, as input.[1] Such electronic loops changed conceptions of technology in the twentieth century, layering onto earlier ideas such as eighteenth-century "systems" (emulating clockwork) and "dampening" (from the time of steam).[2] A scant decade after "feedback" was coined, electronics were continuing to offer new notions for cultural uptake, such as the "push-pull" concepts that moved from mechanical engineering to describe the excitation and dampening of neurons, as in British scientist Charles S. Sherrington's book *The Brain and Its Mechanism* (1933). Those "push-pull" electrical impulses flickering across the brain in Sherrington's theories came to inform artists such as Hans Hofmann, who was pushing intensely colored pigment onto canvas "Push-pull" ideas also colored cultural uptakes of computation in the 1931 "differential analyzer" by Vannevar Bush, its calculations running on the push of gears and the pull of pistons. By the time Bush wrote about his computers for the popular press, he could describe them as an "enlarged intimate supplement" to human memory.[3] Their contribution to feedback theories was immediate, becoming our own cognitive prosthetic.[4]

Feedback was implicitly part of how these "push-pull" theories became useful to Hofmann, describing how visual phenomena

1
"Feedback," Online Etymology Dictionary: "1920, in the electronics sense, 'the return of a fraction of an output signal to the input of an earlier stage,' from verbal phrase, from feed (v.) + back (adv.). By 1955 'feedback' was in use in broader parlance, as 'information about the results of a process.'" https://www.etymonline.com/word/feedback.

2
Étienne Bonnot de Condillac's *Traité des sistêmes, où l'on en démêle les incovéniens & les avantages* (La Haye: chez Jean Néaulme, 1749) reflected the clockwork universe, whereas James Watt's patent of the governor mechanism (1788) ushered in a relationship to the steam-powered universe.

3
Vannevar Bush received US patent no. 2,032,253 for the differential analyzer he completed in 1931 while working at MIT. The quotation comes from his now-prophetic essay, "As We May Think," *The Atlantic*, July 1945, written when he was director of the US Office of Scientific Research and Development.

4
David Mindell, *Between Human and Machine: Feedback, Control, and Computing before Cybernetics* (Baltimore: Johns Hopkins University Press, 2004).

5
For the impact of Sherrington on neuroscience, and other mechanical engineering concepts from science-impacting engineer-turned-artist Hans Hofmann's "push-pull" aesthetic theories, see Caroline A. Jones, *Eyesight Alone: Clement Greenberg's Modernism and the Bureaucratization of the Senses* (Chicago: University of Chicago Press, 2006), 180 and 466 no. 83.

exerted forces on the perceptual system of trichromatic humans. Decades later and on a different continent, Wang Yuyang made notions of feedback exceedingly strange by foiling artistic choice and intuition regarding painterly hue in a 2019 series on the moon. For Hofmann, saturated hues in the "hot" range appeared to push to the foreground of a pictorial surface, while "cool" blues and greens receded demurely into the background [FIG. 1].[5] Wang had no idea about these "inputs," since he blocked color from his eyes by wearing various kinds of color-removing goggles while he painted.

Feedback is intuitively present in all aesthetic relations that involve making something and then evaluating it. Eye-hand coordination, at minimum, is the artist's most basic form of bodily feedback when generating handmade images, manipulating clay, carving wood, *or tweaking algorithms*. A touch is made, delivering a pigment or trace or bit of code; it has an effect. That gets eyeballed as a change in the visual field, and adjusted with the next touch. Painterly prostheses extend the intuition to the end of a pencil, the tip of a loaded brush, or the click of a mouse as feedback migrates from paper or pigment to screen-based design choices in endless iterations. Wang, insisting on introducing color to the actually monochrome surface of the lunar satellite, nonetheless allowed the algorithms filtering color from his vision to rule. Although sensitive to the tonal range of what was on the end of his brush, he essentially applied pigment while blind to its chromatic hue. The paintings are beautiful *by chance* [FIG. 2].

What do such analog feedback protocols have to do with our rampantly technological moment? (Hofmann left engineering after war, turning to art to get away from mechanical feedback, initially by teaching German veterans art as therapy in the 1920s; Wang was specifically commenting on the black-and-white unknowing of 1960s videos of the moonshot, aiming at a retro imaginary.) Clearly, as we operate in 2024 under the reign of GenAI (generative machine learning programs described as "artificial

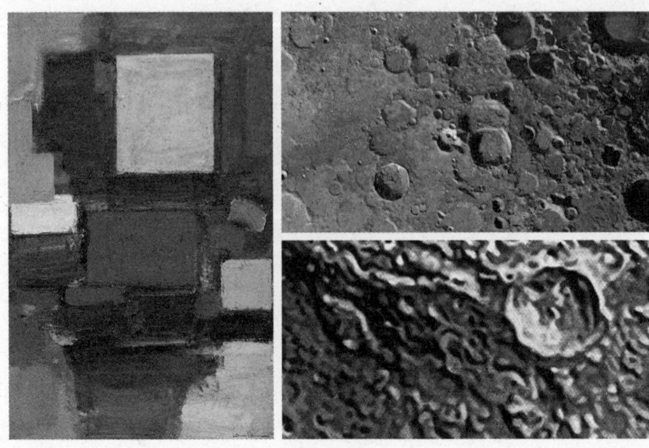
[1]

[FIG. 1]
Left: Push-pull aesthetics of feedback in Hans Hofmann, *The Gate*, 1959–60 (oil on canvas, 190.5 × 123.2 cm), Guggenheim Museum, New York. Right: Foiling intuition, feedback in Wang Yuyang, *Moon*, 2019, involves a monochrome headset that confounds color choices. Shown with detail from a different canvas in the series. Images courtesy of MASSIMODECARLO (https://massimodecarlo.com/channels/the-moon-landing-project)

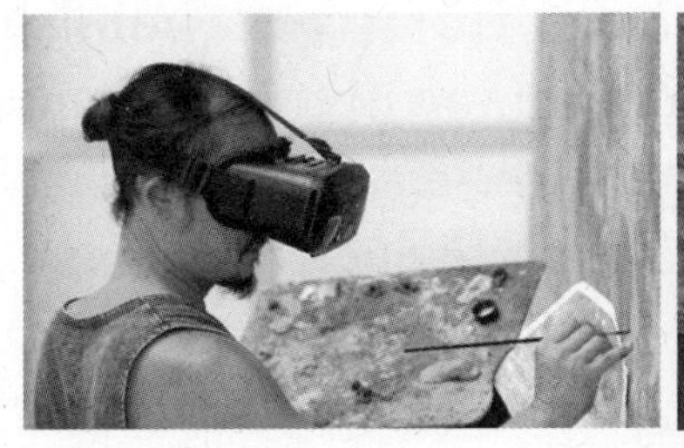
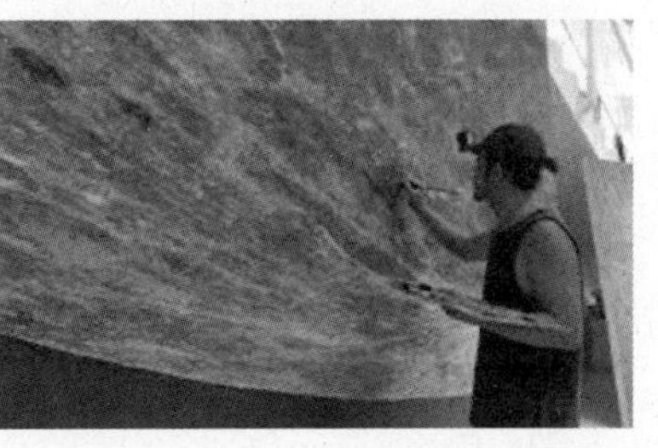

[2]

[FIG. 2]
Wang using goggles that remove color from the painterly feedback loop. The artist may know where hues are placed on his palette, yet removes himself from knowing the effect they have when placed adjacent to other colors on the canvas. Images courtesy of the Artist, as found on https://news.cgtn.com/news/2022-11-16/Chinese-artist-explores-art-boundaries-with-a-restless-soul-1f0nh8VsUMg/index.html

intelligence"), we must attend to patterns of feedback from artists, following how they resist technological "solutions" for human problems, yet use contemporary technological models to inform radical pictorial procedures in their time. Wang critiques the chromatic control of a compositional author, while Hofmann pushed the power of abstraction to detach chroma from the real, as cybernetics first burst into named existence in the mid-twentieth century. Historically, the radical move away from figuration into abstraction (with Hofmann's push-pull feedback) already resonated with the utterly abstract, feedback-obsessed cybernetic art of the century's second half. This essay will argue, from an art historical perspective, that the cybernetic art of the 1960s can be instructively compared to Wang's combinatorial arts of the 2020s, revealing just how deeply we are now inside technologies that were once seen as outside us, and imagined to be under human control.

In our own epoch of generative algorithmic thinking and stochastic collaborations, cybernetic concepts offer useful "feedback," and Wang's work proves good to think with. As cybernetics emerged to theorize feedback, we left the mechanical metaphors of push and pull. Instead, mathematical ideas about "signals" and "receivers" contributed to new sciences of information as well as biological theories of homeostasis and semiosis in organismic life. Wang correspondingly shifts from the way the US moonshot looked on black-and-white film in the late 1960s to the way signals are conveyed today: massively parallel computational programs that sift images as bits of binary code over the information superhighway of the World Wide Web, possibly even assembling these bits only at the interface where human eyes make sense of them. Each of these concepts—feedback, information, bits, and signals, as they are recognizable and available to artists now—were refined in the immediate postwar period. Cybernetics aimed to rule them all.

Coined as a word and a science by mathematician Norbert Wiener in a 1948 book by that name, cybernetics soon became a juggernaut. But not everyone was ready to jump on the bandwagon. Indeed, the very phrase "artificial intelligence" was coined in 1955 to hold off cybernetics and Wiener's functional machine talk in favor of more speculative symbolic language models.

Following on the Turing test (published in 1950), mathematician John McCarthy came up with the idea of an "artificial intelligence" to ask whether machines could be "made to *simulate* . . . aspects of learning."[6] Such a *simulation* only aspired to be *artificially* intelligent. Why did McCarthy and those who gathered with him, such as polymath W. Ross Ashby, want the word "intelligence"? They were well aware of the difference between our chemically sensitive wetware and the engineered mechanics of, say, a thermostat. As Ashby put it in 1956, "A simple machine appears to be extraordinary when viewed psychologically." He continued, "When part of a mechanism is concealed from observation, the behavior of the machine seems remarkable."[7] As with the shock of the man-on-the-moon videos from the US *Apollo* mission in 1969[8] or the existential wanderings of Wang's solitary light bulb in Shenzhen in 2024 (*Meandering* [2019–24]), purely machinic protocols can generate profound meditations on what it means to be human.

Art is accomplished at such tasks of enchantment, yielding luminous meaning rather than dry functionality. For the nascent science of computing machines, the apparent magic concealed by engineering's "black box" allowed computer scientists to exaggerate their power and emulate this kind of enchantment, breathlessly cautioning that machine learning may make humans extinct.[9] This aura of magic around AI is defiantly questioned by Wang, whose studio instead dwells on AI's senseless "meanderings" as algorithms search for answers to a human or mechanical prompt. Strategically, McCarthy's phrase "artificial intelligence" was suggested as a new, agnostic and neutral term that would avoid the mess of "automata theory" and hold off "cybernetics."[10] By contrast, automata and cybernetics are exactly what I want to engage in interrogating Wang's art. If today the notion of "simulation" is disavowed, with iterative machine learning routines (based on outputs fed back as inputs, or feedback) ideologically constructed as actual cognitive processes with "neural nets," we humans need to question that anthropomorphic fetish.

Wang's art destabilizes the current fad for AI algorithms as autonomous cognitive or creative agents. Instead, Wang seems to embrace the almost Dadaist absence of forethought that these machinic collaborators offer. His use of algorithmic processes is more consistent with contemporary mediatic sociality (sampling, riffing, weighting with human-coded preference) than "intelligence" per se. I apply the term "cybernetics" to Wang's works to secure a history for his experiments, particularly in China and in dialogue (for me) with the Chinese diasporic engineer-

6
My emphasis. John McCarthy et al., "A Proposal for the Dartmouth Summer Research Project on Artificial Intelligence," submitted to the Rockefeller Foundation in 1955, with the meeting held in 1956. Online at http://jmc.stanford.edu/articles/dartmouth/dartmouth.pdf. For Turing test see Alan Turing, "Computing Machinery and Intelligence," *Mind* 59, no. 236 (October 1950): 433–60.

7
Notes from Ashby's talk taken by Trenchard More are reprinted in Grace Solomonoff, "Ray Solomonoff and the Dartmouth Summer Research Project in Artificial Intelligence, 1956," n.d., available at https://raysolomonoff.com/dartmouth/dartray.pdf, p. 11.

8
These restored videos were utilized by Wang in his *Moon* series (2017–ongoing). See NASA posting of the July 1969 footage, restored in 2009, at https://www.youtube.com/watch?v=S9HdPi9Ikhk.

9
Note the 2023 warning by "godfather of AI" Geoffrey Hinton, saying that AI will eventually outperform humans and take over the world, feeding this headline (on CNN): "Experts are warning AI could lead to human extinction," May 30, 2023. https://www.cnn.com/2023/05/30/media/artificial-intelligence-warning-reliable-sources/index.html.

10
". . . as well as him potentially having to accept the assertive Norbert Wiener as guru or having to argue with him." Solomonoff PDF, p. 6.

turned-cybernetic-artist Wen-Ying Tsai.[11] Finding two artists born in China to put in historical conversation around cybernetics is not an essentializing move. It is to recognize that important theorizing by some contemporary Chinese philosophers (for example Yuk Hui) opens the possibility of a separate epistemological path for Chinese cultural thinking about chance, technology, and feedback.[12] I am an outsider to that effort, but I assert that cybernetic thinking is certainly embedded in the feedback technologies we all inherit and inhabit.

Wang's fondness for alien agents and devices as collaborators (which is to say, sources of feedback), regardless of whether they operate as machines, algorithms, or organisms, is notable. As with ancient modes of the "combinatorial arts" that invited chance and aleatory procedures into the process of art making, Wang's art confounds notions of "art" or "intelligence" as premeditated. Patterns may be found in the work as we look at it, but the processes that generated the art are positioned as "ignorant" of aesthetic outcomes (as in the color choices in the *Moon* series). This absence of aesthetic intention is intentional: the intentional act of the artist is to confound intention by collaborating with aleatory and stochastic agents, yielding results that cannot be predicted. The choice to share agency was earlier pegged as WANG Yuyang#—"the artist in bytes"—yet whatever that digital avatar was, whatever it produced, was then paradoxically annealed to "the artist in flesh," since singular authorship will always be secured by an art world organized around author names.[13] The artist-as-producer here promotes a discourse about giving up authorship (and perhaps even *artistry*) to agents that might be described as more than human, whether these be organic life forms, flows of machine vision in a headset, or the algorithms crafted to mimic such lively feedback loops.[14]

Consider the digital-biological sculpture *I Don't Know* (2024, [FIG. 3]), consisting of fermenters, microorganisms, transparent digital screens, computers, and cameras. The artist acquires state-of-the-art technological objects such as the stunningly transparent digital screens, which reveal machinery inside the box whenever they are not flashing images across their plasma surfaces, and a toggle then illuminates the interior. As we look, we see intermittently the churning bioreactor device inside, and then are dazzled by stars, swooshes, and fragmentary photographs illuminating the screen "skin." There is a deep cybernetic relationship between the interior and the exterior of this sculpture. The intermittently visible "guts" of the assembly are there to introduce chance, by way of the burbles and churn of a standard bioreactor

11
I am grateful for research assistance by, and inspiring conversation with, Lun-Yi London Tsai of the Tsai Foundation.

12
I am neither linguistically nor philosophically competent to question Yuk Hui's somewhat exceptionalist description of China's technological path, but I welcome his efforts to bring five thousand years of this history into global techno-philosophical conversations. See Yuk Hui, *The Question Concerning Technology in China: An Essay in Cosmotechnics* (Falmouth, MA: Urbanomic, 2017); Yuk Hui, *Recursivity and Contingency* (Lanham, MD: Rowman & Littlefield, 2019). For a useful dialogue exploring Hui's positions see Geert Lovink, "Cybernetics for the Twenty-First Century: An Interview with Philosopher Yuk Hui," *e-flux*, no. 102 (September 2019): https://www.e-flux.com/journal/102/282271/cybernetics-for-the-twenty-first-century-an-interview-with-philosopher-yuk-hui/.

13
Eponyms are by Zhang Ga, "Chaosmosis and the Return of the Grand Narrative," written to accompany Wang's 2015 exhibition at the Long Museum, Shanghai. On the dominance of the author name in the art world see Caroline A. Jones, "The 'Artist Function' and Posthumous Art History," *Art Journal* 76 (Spring 2017): 1.

14
"Artist-as-producer" intentionally echoes Walter Benjamin, "The Author as Producer," an address delivered at the Institute for the Study of Fascism, Paris, April 27, 1934, trans. Edmund Jephcott, reprinted in Walter Benjamin, *Reflections: Essays, Aphorisms, Autobiographical Writings* (New York: Harcourt Brace, 1978).

15
Explanation provided to the author by Wang and his studio via email, May 13, 2024: "The images on the monitor are generated by open-source AI for images on the web, controlled by text and words corresponding to binary codes converted by the data of bioreactor."

16
Caroline A. Jones, Huma Gupta, and Matthew Ritchie, "Visual Artists, Technological Shock, and Generative AI," August 2024, available at https://mit-genai.pubpub.org/pub/l62ipwcb/release/1.

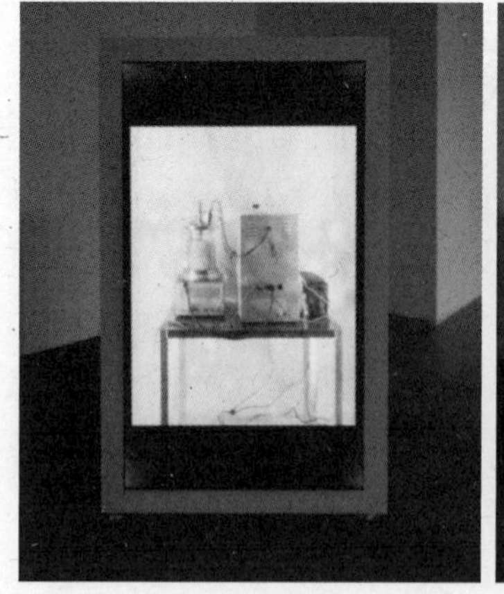
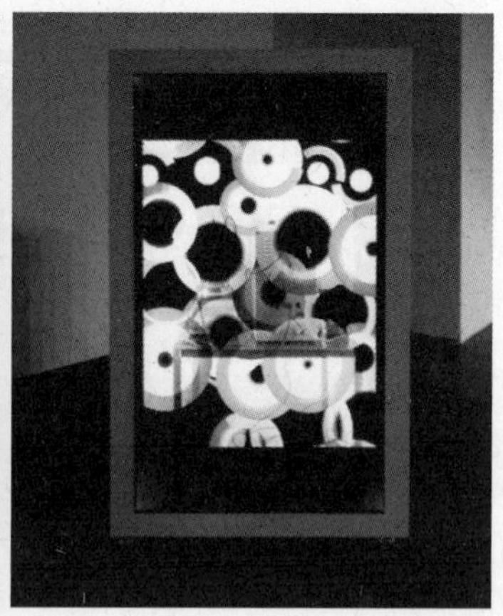

[3]

[FIG. 3]
Wang Yuyang, *I Don't Know*, 2024. Shown in two of a theoretically infinite number of phases. Image from https://www.cafa.com.cn/en/news/details/8332452

or fermenting device that we can see within the box. The churning liquid contents are filmed by a camera (also in the box), which generates data that then gets fed back into the computer to filter open-source imagery to generate the "broadcast." Put simply, inside the fermenter there is liquid food to feed a fungal workhorse, brewer's yeast (*Saccharomyces cerevisiae*), the friendly microbe domesticated by humans since bread and beer were first produced in ancient Egypt. Also living happily on our skins and inner mucosa, yeast varieties need little more than some organic material to eat, plus oxygen, warmth, and water, to multiply happily.

With Wang's camera trained on their churn, machine learning can extract data such as "fermentation temperature, dissolved oxygen concentration, pH, feeding quantity, stirring speed," which is then treated as binary code to filter images flowing from the web.[15] Able to run on consumer-grade computers, the programs used are primarily diffusion models (such as stable diffusion) used for generating still or video imagery. This type of machine learning takes up random fields of pixels that are then de-noised in a progressive process guided by comparisons with existing images, discerning latent images within the pixelated flow. *I Don't Know* reflects a state of unknowing in both the artist and the algorithm. The pleasure of stable diffusion (and some other AI tools) is not having a clue what details will show up from any given prompt, since we are in machine-vision-AI early days. The glitchy results of diffusion models (and, for that matter, all the generative programs in use at this time) are closest to the century-old art movement of Surrealism, whose accidental mimicry in AI is often misnamed "hallucination."[16]

I Don't Know's pulsations are dazzling. Bombarding viewers with an image flow that just as quickly stills to darkness (which allows us to see the stirring fermenter within) is a virtuoso performance of feedback. Yet while we see that there is a system in action, its feedback mechanisms remain mysterious. Its operations are internalized, even "self-absorbed" (granting the composite entity,

17 The French physicist André-Marie Ampère used the word *cybernétique* in 1834, plumping for a science of government. This earlier usage of the concept emerged in English only after Wiener made it famous. Wiener's own account is that the concept came out of his collaborations with leading Mexican physiologist Arturo Rosenblueth in the summer of 1947. See Andrew Pickering, "The Birth of Cybernetics," in *Foundational Papers in Complexity Science*, ed. David Krakauer (Santa Fe: Santa Fe Institute, 2024), 115–27.

with its inside and outside, could be figured as a "self"). It has no awareness of its viewers, and its feedback loops are only in dialogue with yeast, temperature, image flow, and algorithms. Both inside and outside of the box are noisy in terms of information, yet each is configured to submit its noise to cleaning up—by more-than-human mechanical and microbial processes that some call intelligent. Cybernetics embraces such a paradoxical relationship to agency. A program is given to a machine, which iterates routines based on its own outputs reconfigured as inputs. By the rules of cybernetics, Wang's *I Don't Know* is utilizing concepts of first-order machine learning; it stays within the machinic circuit and does not take account of an observer (second order) that might alter the routine.

Why does cybernetics remain a useful concept for thinking about Wang's art? Claims of "immersion" that have become frequent in art world discourse are analytically available to cybernetic questioning: What systems are we immersed in? Can we alter the response of the system? Are we part of the system? These are tools of critical thinking made available by second-order cybernetics, alive and well in philosophies of aesthetics today.

Entering culture with a promise to tackle feedback in animals, machines, and "men" (human beings), cybernetics' post–World War II mythography began with its name, which Wiener coined from the Greek word for "steersman"—*Κυβερνήτης* or *kubernétés*—a masculine figure channeling power, knowledge, and instinct at the helm of a ship. Predicting the arrogance of the emerging computational science, this mythography built on a metaphor in which others (galley slaves, or maybe fungus) provide the labor, allowing the steersman to program where the boat will go with a light touch on the rudder. As taken up by Wiener[17] and applied to machine feedback systems, "cybernetics" already smuggled in this idea of a man in charge, somewhere within the system and presumably the prime mover setting everything in motion. "Cyber" was already linked to modern English through the Latin that had converted Greek *kuber* to *guber*—the root of "gubernatorial" and "governor," the name chosen by British inventor James Watt in 1788 to describe his feedback device for dampening a runaway steam engine [FIG. 4].

This first order of cybernetics was electromagnetic (circuits were soldered onto breadboards), but its programs yielded the dance we recognize today between hardware and software. Such dancing runs on feedback loops in which repeating routines contribute new inputs, subtly changing the next output. With machine learning in play, as the output becomes input it triggers a change in

18 Heinz von Foerster, ed., *Cybernetics of Cybernetics: Or, the Control of Control and the Communication of Communication* (Minneapolis: Future Systems, 1995).

the preset program, yielding potentially unanticipated results. The machine evolves with environmental shifts as it learns to write new code to adapt to changing inputs. Emulating human cognition by naming layered subroutines "neural nets," computer science structures programs to learn by producing their own algorithms. Yet these can only respond to a training set taken from the past. In machine vision, this means old material, now equipped with weighted priors that sift noise to find signal.

The idea of a second-order cybernetics emerged in the 1960s as cyberneticians began to understand that the observer of any system has impacts on that system, provoking the need for a "cybernetics of cybernetics," as Margaret Mead put it. In the words of crucial cybernetician Heinz von Foerster, second-order cybernetics could also be described as "the cybernetics of observing systems" in which any observer is herself being observed by the system, becoming a part of the feedback that alters the system going forward.[18] Wang makes contemporary art that is rich in reference to these feedback complexities. *I Don't Know* will presumably never be the same twice. The extended agency of the artist includes the installation crew and preparators at the museum, who must feed the yeast and ensure that there is enough oxygen in the tank and electricity to run the bioreactor effectively. In that sense, humans tending the yeast are no longer mere outside observers but causal agents of what is being observed. Yet the setup does not perform this potentially second-order complexity by including us observers in its data gathering; it appears to be only talking to itself.

The crucial distinction between first- and second-order cybernetics is muddied by the term "neural nets," used by programmers to designate machine learning layers that (cybernetically) take outputs as inputs to guide further outputs. Polemically: the electromagnetic switching inside computer processing is not remotely like neurons, which function in some (not all) animal bodies through chemical *and* electrical processes, deeply engaged

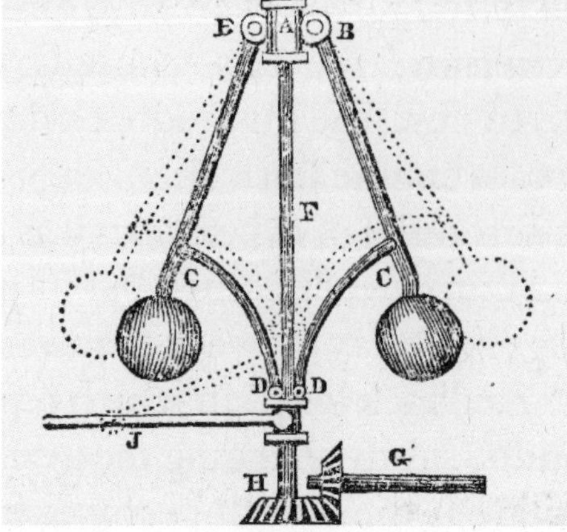

[4]

[FIG. 4]
James Watt, governor for a steam engine, 1788. As steam increases, it drives the shaft that spins the weighted balls. Gravity then pulls the balls back down and dampens the steam—a feedback system that "automatically" adjusts the machine and minimizes effort on the part of the human engineer

with a planetary environment in which nervous systems evolved in bodies—continuing to inform cognition, in concert with their symbionts.[19] The "gut brain" is linked deeply to cognition and mood; gut symbionts produce brain chemistry for animal neurons every day—a completely alien concept to computer science.[20] "AI" and "neural net" mislead us about how intelligence works. They each pretend that computers are human brains, and suggest falsely that the cranium is the only site of cognition. Wang deploys both a gut brain (the fermenter) and machine circuitry (computer, camera, stirrers, and more) in *I Don't Know*. The very title confesses that the "I" of the artist is not in charge. *But neither is the computer.* Silicon, yeast, internet, electricity—all are agents in making the art into a lively object for our gaze.

Wang's work allows us to put aside fetishes of the neuron to consider broader systems such as bacterial "quorum sensing," microbial responses to changes in the environment (a fundament of cognition per se) that are robust and entangled. Yeast can't tell the plasma screen what to flash at us unless these creatures' water and nutrients (usually some kind of glucose) are allowing its reproduction and thriving. Thus, even the "closed" system of such a cybernetic artwork needs dosing and feeding from a much wider world. Out in the wild, fungal entities related to yeast are terraforming the planet. Invisible to humans, the spores partner with algae to create lichens, taking down mountains and digesting wood lignin all over the world. Fungal hyphae of numerous species link trees in old-growth forests through feedback systems that nurture the health of the forest as a whole, rather than favoring a specific tree or even a specific species. Think of it—during leaf season in the Pacific Northwest of the North American landmass, certain kinds of deciduous smaller trees (aspen, alder) will yield nutrients through the mycorrhizal (fungal) network to feed the evergreens (fir, pine) in a hydrostatic relationship that reverses once leaves have fallen, at which point nutrients flow to the leafless ones from the trees that never drop their small photosynthesizing needles.[21] All of these separate species are linked in ecologies of thriving, functioning as a symbiotic holobiont—an entity of interlinked species that maximizes chances of survival for all, with the metagenome (fungus, trees, and other soil makers) evolving together.

Wang's *The Dubious of Entanglement by Plants* (2012–24, [FIG. 5]) cuts a planar section out of such symbioses in the wild state, to produce a quasi–still life of these ongoing processes for our aesthetic and analytic contemplation. It is unclear what the "suspicion" of the title might mean (the word is sometimes translated as "dubious"). Multiple Chinese words engage this concept,

19
For a variant on this polemic see Caroline A. Jones, "Symbiontics: a Polemic for our Times," in Jones, Natalie Bell, and Selby Nimrod, *Symbionts: Contemporary Artists and the Biosphere* (Cambridge, MA: MIT List Visual Arts Center and MIT Press, 2022): 13–49.

20
For example, a cow's rumen and its neurons will not develop until bacteria found on grass is ingested by the weaning baby calf. These new bacteria "cue" a process in the gut that folds animal tissue inward to form a rumen to house the bacteria in the developing stomach. It is the bacteria that digest grass and release its nutrients, further cuing neurons and blood vessels to arrive to supply the microbial rumen's needs. Without such symbionts, cows couldn't eat grass.

21
Per the research of forestry scientist Suzanne Simard, replicated by thousands of studies of deep forest symbiosis.

22
Ideograms from https://dictionary.cambridge.org/dictionary/english-chinese-simplified/suspicion.

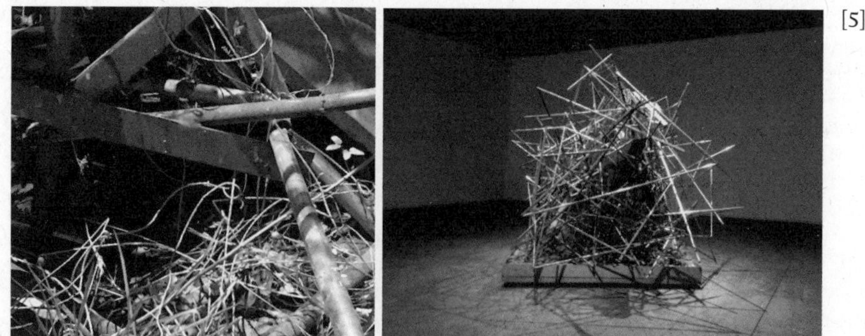

[5]

[FIG. 5]
Symbiosis and mineral metabolism in Wang Yuyang, *The Dubious of Entanglement by Plants*, 2012–24

ranging from a belief that something could be either true or false (a state of dubiety), to a feeling that someone or something has committed a crime (怀疑; 嫌疑).[22]

Perhaps the crime is the artist's wanton neglect of the original sculpture! For *The Dubious of Entanglement by Plants* to happen, the sculpture first has to be forgotten, left unloved and abandoned, somewhere on the ruderal edge of Beijing. Then the wilding begins, as vines, grass, fungus, sprouting tree seeds, and insects begin to utilize the metal (itself oxidizing in a mineral "metabolism"). The originally artistic structure becomes mere support for organic processes of growth: twining to reach the sun, collecting dew dripping from condensation on metal surfaces, metabolizing rust to extract food value, catching smaller insects in webs stretched between structural members. In the Shenzhen Art Museum, this assembly was constrained by a metal container, positioned under dramatic lighting in a darkened space. Surely most of these life processes were on their way to dormancy if not death, isolated from the circadian rhythms of their ecosystem. Yet even after transport and installation, the sprouts and tendrils and spiders were attempting to continue their metabolic interactions, evincing the tenacity of life. Genetic sequencing of the artwork would yield a holobiont of the no doubt symbiotic entanglement.

Wang's *Golem* (2022, [FIG. 6]) would also yield a metagenome of its holobiont were we to sequence the crustal materials falling off its dusty surface. But that would only acknowledge the organic dreams buried in this anthropomorph, its title alluding to the legendary system of magical animation via "code"—although in medieval telling, it was the divine code of all the different names of a monotheistic G*d that provided the animating force to a man made of clay. If the original golem strode out of Jewish folklore, supposedly stomping through Prague as a protector brought to life by divine alphanumeric powers, Wang's *Golem* performs itself as utterly dead. Once again, algorithms that sift the artist's biometric data are revealed as spectacularly inept in understanding the relation of those alphanumeric bits to the human body. The software yields a 3D file for sculpting a surprisingly primordial lump

[FIG. 6]
Challenges to divine animation in Wang Yuyang, *Golem*, 2022 (detail)

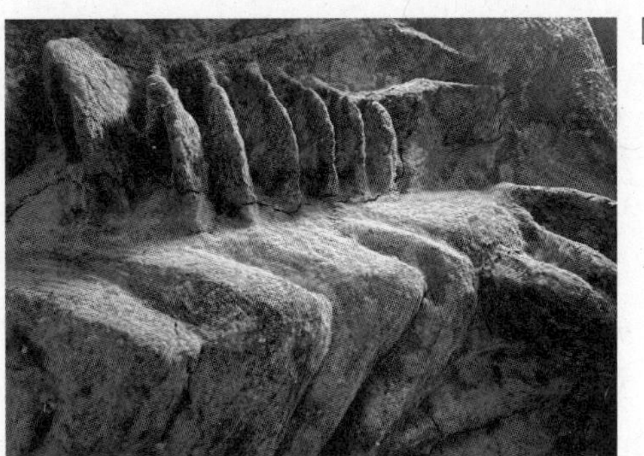
[6]

of matter, looking more like the proud assemblage of a dung beetle (*Coleoptera: Scarabaeinae*) than the noble animal placed at the pinnacle of evolution's Great Chain of Being. *Golem* presents the inadequacy of machinic notions of creation—the result of what the artist thinks of as a "dismal" processing of his own biometric data through design software that inevitably, stochastically, fails to animate anything that even resembles a muddy humanoid form. What look like ribs or gill-like structures in the surface poke out of a large dusty sphere, as if all the metallic shine we associate with a robot has oxidized into dung. Cybernetically speaking, it is the opposite of what Weiner warned us about in his 1964 *God & Golem, Inc.*, where "the machine which learns" and the "machine that reproduces itself" prompted that theorizer of cybernetics to warn about matters metaphysical and religious.

Wang's broad interests in these kinds of questions motivate artworks that are sometimes animated and sometimes not. The studio enters a wide variety of collaborations, experimenting with plants (*The Dubious of Entanglement by Plants*), with algorithms and yeast (*I Don't Know*), and, still to be discussed, with robots (*Dream*) and syn-bio-generated fungal pigment makers (*Biological Klein Blue* [2022]). What is newly evident from an art historical perspective, assessed during this first quarter century of a new millennium, is how every one of these complex orders (computational, vegetal, microbial) can be artistic, offering new chance operations and sources of random variation that are tenuously programmable for art. This distinguishes Wang's moment from that of earlier artists, whose cybernetic moment was exclusively focused on electronics and machines—a contrast that becomes vivid when comparing Wang's work to that of previous generations.

Those earlier generations matured in an optimistic, technophilic postwar moment, three decades before Wang was born. Certainly, China was undergoing great turmoil and political change, even as the United States witnessed an intense marrying of art and technology. In the 1960s, wartime surplus flowed into the hands of peacetime artists and gave rise to some who claimed systems and cybernetics as guides for their art, some of whom were

East Asian, others European, all finding a haven in New York. Part of what the technology made possible was to plunge viewers into the midst of cybernetic systems of feedback, exemplified by German American artist Hans Haacke's photo-electric immersion set up in a New York gallery in 1968, and Wen-Ying Tsai's responsive cybernetic environments triggered by visitors that very same year [FIG. 7].

Haacke himself assiduously distanced his meditations on feedback from the term "cybernetics," insisting on the name "systems art" for what he was doing (partially influenced by his friend and interlocutor Jack Burnham, who published "A Systems Esthetics" in *Artforum* that same portentous year, 1968).[23] Yet if Haacke would stick with systems, at the very same moment (and in the same New York gallery), the Chinese-born artist Tsai would proclaim his work to be "cybernetic sculptures," later even dubbing his entire oeuvre "Tsaibernetics." Soon, Tsai would show with others in ICA London's blockbuster *Cybernetic Serendipity* (1968). Artists in this rapidly expanding art-technology circle were embracing responsive, mechanical-sensing technology in search of new capacities to plunge humans into the experience of a fully techno-social, electronic-infrastructural surround. As observed by the curator and distinguished professor Zhang Ga in his assessment of Tsai from our own time:

> Today we are in a completely technological era, in a social environment of technological time and space. Technology is everywhere and permeates our lives all the time. Many of our thoughts and lifestyles are constructed by technology, which is constructing our behavior patterns and ways of thinking. How do we face such a historical moment? How do artists respond in such a situation?[24]

Wang's work inherits this "situation," but much further along the technologizing path, where machine learning, cybernetics,

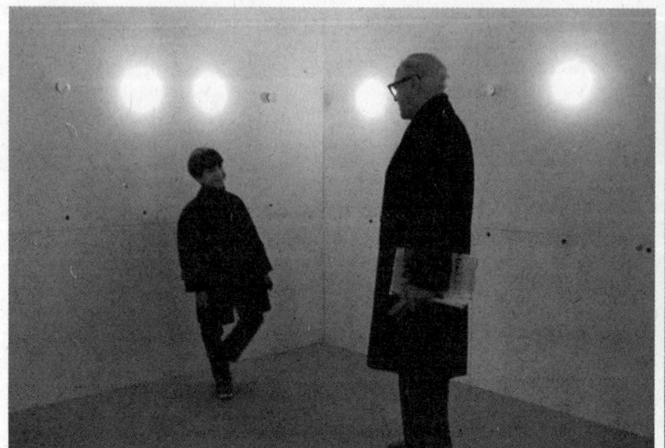
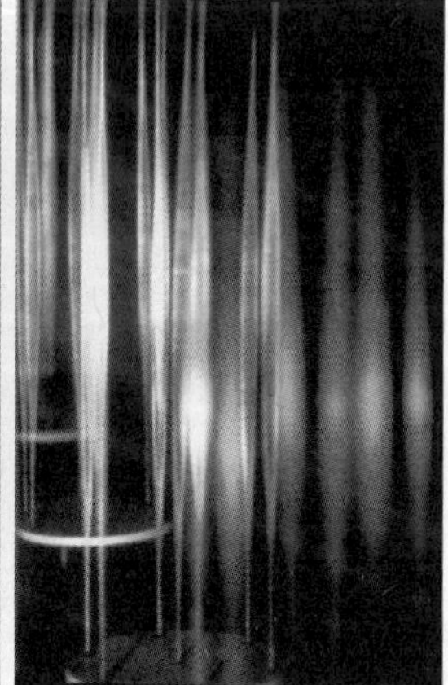

[7]

23
See Caroline A. Jones, *Hans Haacke 1967* (Cambridge, MA: MIT List Visual Arts Center, 2011).

24
Zhang Ga, "The Imprint of Art History in the Age of Technology," in *Tsai*, ed. Lun-Yi London Tsai (New York: Tsai Art and Science Foundation, 2018): 168.

[FIG. 7]
Left: inside the feedback loop in Hans Haacke, *Photo-Electric Viewer-Controlled Coordinate System*, 1968; right: detail of Tsai Wen-Ying's vibratory, responsive *Cybernetic Sculpture System #1*, 1968

25
Yuk Hui usefully historicizes this organicist trend in philosophy, for which see *Recursivity and Contingency*.

and non-cranial cognition by fungal, bacterial, and plant forms of "intelligence" are now all part of the system.

It is historically interesting that prior to notions of feedback in the early 1920s, the idea of machine intelligence might have taken the form of automata—wind-up or water-driven animated machines with fixed programs that merely repeated themselves. This was definitively replaced by cybernetic systems thinking, which launched itself from the centuries of cultural history behind automata (found throughout all technologically tinkering cultures, including China, Japan, the Islamic Middle East, and early modern Europe). Those linear machines had been configured as producers and actors: writing, shitting, playing chess, making music, serving food and drink. But significantly, sensing was not a priority in these mostly eighteenth-century machines, a limitation surpassed in the twentieth century with cybernetic "organicism."[25] Wiener, for example, learned from animal physiologist Arturo Rosenblueth about how creaturely homeostasis works, crucially based on sensing and adjusting to a wider environment. Thus cybernetics began to shift engineering to sensing devices such as photoelectric cells, pressure pads on the floor, audio-triggered servomechanisms, and of course the lowly temperature-sensing thermostat. All such feedback sensitivities began informing the new field of cybernetics, distinguishing it from the old, early modern amusements of repetitive performing machines.

Wang's painting robot *Dream* (2016–24) brings in both automata theory and its cybernetic critique. On the one hand, the industrial robot inside the transparent box is preprogrammed like an automaton: its limbs can only move in certain directions defined at the industrial plant that built it. On the other, within the constraints of the arm's movements, the machine can be programmed in real time. Wang links himself like a cyborg (cybernetic organism) to the robot's servomechanism, recording his dream state in medical EEGs (electroencephalograms) and streaming that data to shape the robot's mesmerizing mechanical dance between brush, paint can, wall, and ceiling. The painting robot then "feeds back" images to Wang and us visitors in the form of colorful, brushy abstractions floating on the transparent walls and ceiling of the robot's confined space, which certainly do not convey anything of the actual imagery of Wang's dreams.

Tsai, six decades earlier, had also been interested in translating between organic body data and machine movements, also in real time, but his interface was necessarily strictly analog. Sounds made by a visitor would set undulating rods in motion, triggering the movements of quivering machinic fronds, described as "vegetal"

[FIG. 8]
Tsai, Paik, Wang: Control or not? The inheritance from automata. Left: Tsai Wen-Ying, *Cybernetic Sculpture Environment*, 1970, Galerie Denise René, Paris. Middle: Nam June Paik, *Robot K-456*, ca. 1968. Right: Wang Yuyang, *Dream*, 2016–24. Photo by the author, Shenzhen Art Museum, March 2024

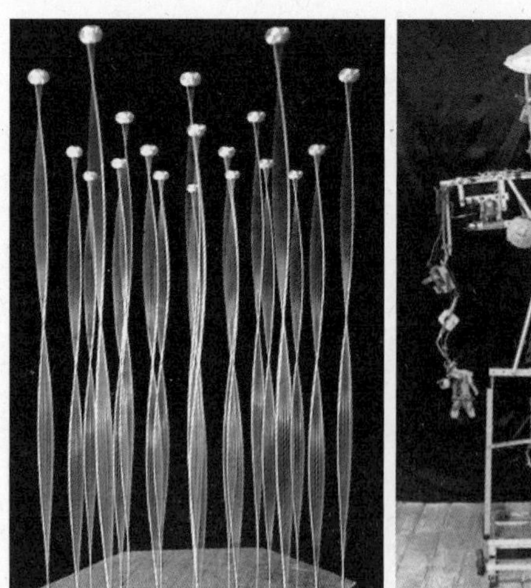
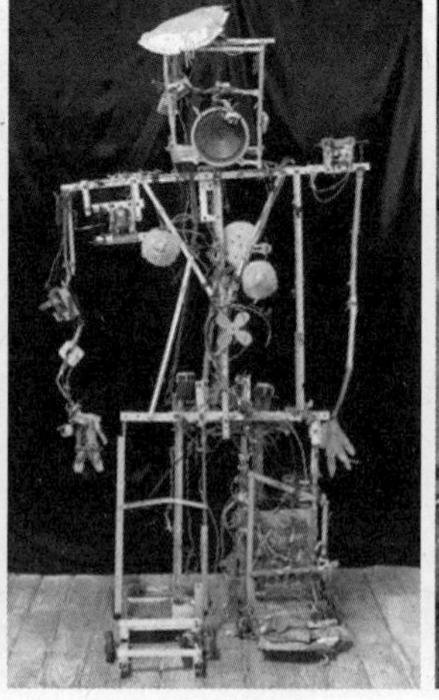
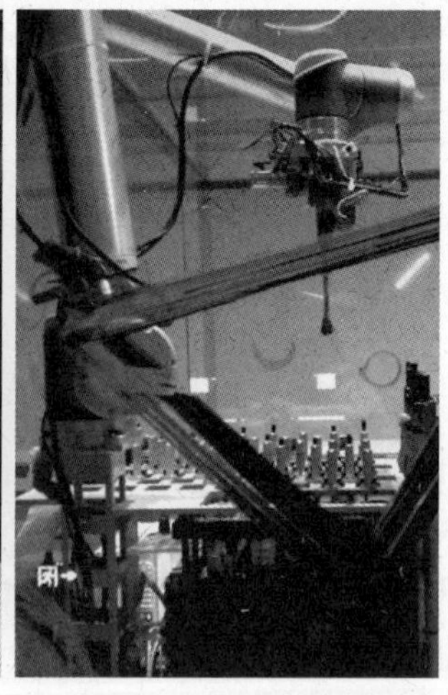

[8]

or "aquatic" by observers at the time. At that same moment, Korean-born Nam June Paik wanted feedback to come from radio-control joysticks operated by a human, leaving his robot in the gendered tradition of automata, commanded by the man in charge [FIG. 8]. In contrast, both Tsai and Wang explore, through technology, our symbiotic relations with the planet and with our prostheses (biology and technology being functionally different in what we fantasize that we can control).

Paik wanted a cybernetic art based on analog movements that had more to do with instinctive drives and postwar sexual politics than chance or dreaming. Paik and Shuya Abe's robot, for example, was given a penis in Japan and fitted out with breasts in London—a malleable entity modeling relations with what the French philosophers Gilles Deleuze and Félix Guattari have called the "machinic phylum." Wang's wandering fluorescent bulb and the dreaming/painting robot might be distant cousins of Paik's outrageously gender-fluid robot. But Wang reminds us that we have now passed into the fully immersive space in which technology is not confined to a single machine, but is a nature-culture interweaving that crisscrosses the planet.

Meandering, unlike *Dream*, is informed by data internal to the system [FIG. 9]. The program generates an uncanny stuttering across the floor, the slender, luminous fluorescent tube performing in a cavernous, dark gallery (at Shenzhen Art Museum, the space was vast). Humans entering the gallery are irrelevant to the wan light's distracted dragging. Suspended by a wire just long enough to allow it some slack as it is pulled along the ground, the tube's peregrinations are governed by a magnetic carriage motor that holds the wire and traverses the two axes of movement with mechanical deliberateness (while presumably also "feeding" the fluorescent tube with the stable electricity needed to fuel its glowing phosphors). The speed and angle of movement are generated by algorithms that are never explained, but nonetheless generate affect (as the artist Dan Flavin first experienced in the 1960s when experimenting with his diagonal installations of fluorescent light, describing the first as a "diagonal of personal ecstasy").[26]

Each of Wang's works can be grasped as first-order cybernetics, meaning that there is no accounting for the observer in the system (although the observer of the art certainly reacts). There is no autonomous learning by machines from environmental sensory cues, whatever they might be. Yet in the constant provision of feedback from biological systems (whether the artist's dreaming, his body biometrics, or yeast's unpredictable reproduction cycles), there is a strong link to the organicism that Yuk Hui discerns in cybernetic thinking, a neo-vitalism current to our present moment.[27]

In the rapidly developing art-technology interface in which cybernetics had its first explicit impact on art, Polish-born émigré Jasia Reichardt's aforementioned 1968 extravaganza in London, *Cybernetic Serendipity*, stood out. In addition to Tsai's work, this amazing show included Paik's robot, a suspended dance of "male" and "female" mobiles that signaled each other, crafted by theater designer Yolanda Sonnabend and cybernetician Gordon Pask, and many other hybrid creatures. These art world assemblies put "sensor organs" (electronic eyes, motion sensors, microphones) together with "effector organs" (electronic breadboards, switches, lights, hydraulics, pneumatics). No sort of "electronic brain" or "thinking machine" was present in the art I've mentioned, but immersive, responsive technological entities were everywhere.[28]

Tsai's sculptures, like Wang's *Wandering*, evoked behaviors indicative of life. In his flocks of responsive frond-like entities, emergent behaviors were often likened to life forms by observers. Not surprisingly, theorizer of the vampire squid Vilem Flusser was very keen on these works and their gentle, unpredictable behaviors. Flusser explicitly called out their sense of "play" and identified the sculptures as "botanical."[29] As György Kepes would muse: "To see [Tsai's] work in an 'exhibition,' one discovers

26
Artist Dan Flavin described one of his first diagonal placements of simple fluorescent fixtures, the *Diagonal of May 25, 1963* (1963), as a "diagonal of personal ecstasy," describing its "forty-five degrees above horizontal" angle as being in "dynamic equilibrium." See Dan Flavin, "'...in daylight or cool white.' an autobiographical sketch," *Artforum* 4 (December 1965): 20–24.

27
Hui, *Recursivity and Contingency*.

28
Jasia Reichardt: "*Cybernetic Serendipity* [deals] broadly with the demonstration of how man can use the computer and new technology to extend his creativity and inventiveness." The three categories she set out in her curatorial vision of the exhibition were: computer-generated graphics, films, music, poems, and texts; cybernetic devices as works of art, "cybernetic environments, remote-control robots and painting machines"; and machines "demonstrating the uses of computers and an environment dealing with the history of cybernetics." I am not discussing the computer artworks, which could not be immersive (apart from the sounds generated by computerized music compositions). Jasia Reichardt, ed., *Cybernetic Serendipity: The Computer and the Arts* (New York: Praeger, 1969; reprint of a 1968 *Studio International* special issue that served as the catalogue for the exhibition).

29
Vilem Flusser, "Aspects and Prospects of Tsai's Work," *Art International* 18, no. 3 (March 1974): 55–57.

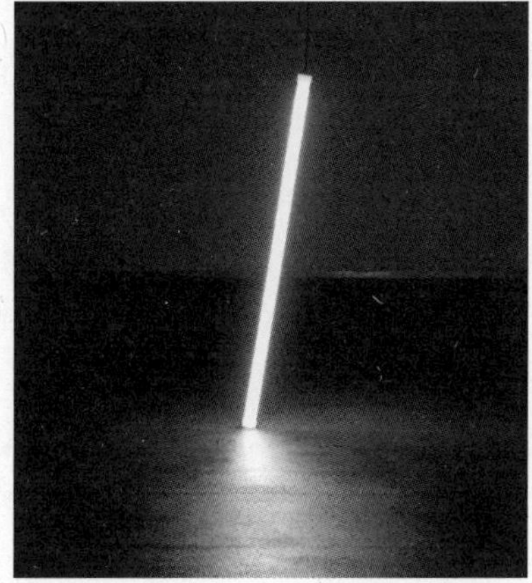
[9]

[FIG. 9]
Wang Yuyang, *Meandering*, 2019–24

soon enough that the term 'exhibition' does not fit anymore. [They] transform the space and make you a part of it."[30] Tsai's sculptures are on pedestals that hide their motors. They are self-contained and do not surround us. But period descriptions should be taken seriously: the works put the human inside an environment saturated by the techno-responsive, affective behaviors of machines. As another early commentator on Tsai put it, "The ecology of these 'organisms' demands not only electric power but also the presence in their environment of a different species—the human participant."[31]

Ambitious for both humans and machines to become intra-active agents, Tsai worked for almost a year to produce the Hong Kong public art project *Living Fountain* (1980–88), in which the structure of the flow would alter in response to ambient sound in the public plaza.[32] Such cybernetic interfaces imperceptibly inaugurated what philosopher Gilbert Simondon terms *technophany.* Echoing "theophany," the ecstatic becoming-visible of the deity, this neologism describes the fulgent manifestation of the technological-human relation (in implicitly positive, even beatific form).[33] Notably, there is nothing computational in this interface, and nothing needs to be "thinking." Technophany acknowledges distributed, collective forms of cognition that are more like the planet than the bot. For Tsai, these planetary interactions were strictly limited to humans and simulated organic movements. For Wang, the palette of possible materials includes living organisms at the microbial scale.

This leaps forward to what distributed creaturely cognition looks like in 2024. Although its responsiveness to humans might initially seem obscure, works such as Wang's *Biological Klein Blue* [FIG. 10] are indeed living entities in a feedback loop that takes up the more-than-human spores of bacteria entering the gallery, some of which drift off our bodies with every movement we make. (This is, then, a "response" to human presence, slowly growing though it may be.) What we see in the gallery is a horizontal mat of deeply saturated indigo, the result of a synthetic biological process in which *E. coli* bacteria have been given extraneous genetic material through the CRISPR-Cas9 technology that has revolutionized biology.[34] Bioengineers in this case introduced genes that produce "outputs" of botanical indigo-type chemicals, in this case indigoidine. Traditional botanical indigo is found in several plants through many precursors; the usual precursor of "indican" needs to ferment with a strong base or alkali to form the prized blue color that Isaac Newton put between blue and violet (although "indirubin" is a *red* isomer of the molecule that is the major active

30 György Kepes, "Introduction," in *Tsai: Cybernetic Sculpture Environment* (New York: Galerie Denise René, 1972), n.p.

31 Jonathan Benthall, "Cybernetic Sculpture of Tsai" (1979), reprinted in *Tsai*, ed. Lun-Yi London Tsai (New York: Tsai Art and Science Foundation, 2018): 74.

32 See *Living Fountain*, https://www.wikiart.org/en/wen-ying-tsai/living-fountain-1988. See also Lin Qi, "Chinese-Born Tsai's Works on Display at Tate Modern in 2016," *China Daily*, 2015, https://www.chinadaily.com.cn/culture/art/2015-04/07/content_20012718_3.htm.

33 For a useful introduction to Simondon's cybernetic philosophies see Pascal Chabot, *The Philosophy of Simondon: Between Technology and Individuation*, trans. Aliza Krefetz and Graeme Kirkpatrick (London: Bloomsbury, 2003). On technophany specifically, see pp. 66–68.

34 The CRISPR technology was derived from a palindromic genomic sequence found in archaeobacteria that helped them defend themselves from viruses. Used in synthetic biology as a precision "knife" to excise desired genes from one bacterium to insert into another, the original function of these codons was immunitary; they produced a protein for the bacterium that cut DNA found in a viral phage, to destroy it. For a glossary of other technical tools in synthetic biology see Jones et al., *Symbionts*.

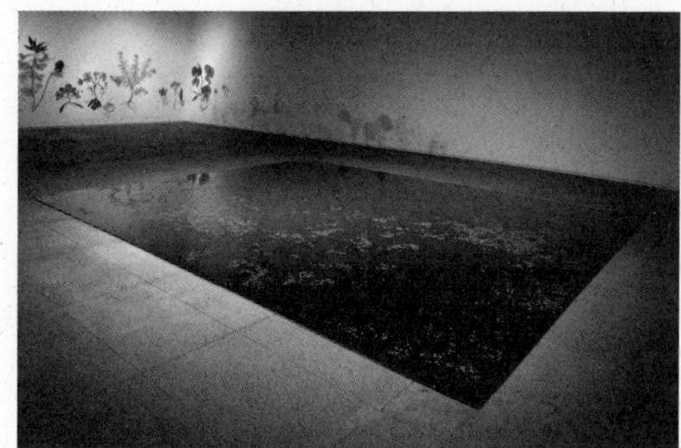

[10]

ingredient).[35] Synthetic indigo is a prized industrial target, motivated for some by the deep colonial shame of the Euro-American indigo trade, which relied on enslaved laborers to do the smelly work of fermenting the indigo plants in animal urine. Further drivers are to replace toxic chemical processes based on fossil fuels (aniline synthetics) by using rapidly proliferating bacteria (almost always *E. coli*) to generate this beloved hue.[36]

Wang's "Klein" blue is not an exact substitute for the color of French artist Yves Klein, since the latter possessed a specific ultramarine hue (from pigment he purchased in bulk and blended with a synthetic resin binder). Klein claimed to have patented this hue, but what he innovated was a binder that yielded his specific aesthetic: the deep matte surface of a velvety, seemingly infinite ultramarine.[37] Differently, Wang's saturated blue is indeed a kind of indigo—inherently associated with dyes and transparency rather than absorptive depth. In keeping with twenty-first-century methods, Wang experiments not with paint chemicals but with the Shanghai-based firm Abiochem. These "bio-intelligent" manufacturers use "rational protein design and directed evolution methods" to grow the syn-bio indigo in a broth that the *E. coli* wants to eat; as it multiplies, the altered strain of bacteria produces the chemical precursor (indigoidine), which is then fermented to produce the indigo itself, over time [FIG. 11].[38]

Following fermentation, the bio-synth blue dye is then separated from the bacteria and added (for the artistic installation) to a massive expanse of agar (an algae "soup" common in all biology labs) that is poured into a shallow tray on the gallery floor. But now, in the supposedly antiseptic environs of the art world (the "white cube"), we are far from the industrial syn-bio clean room. In the living biotope of the museum, the vividly blue agar *gets going*, hosting and feeding "various microorganisms in the environment in a living and dynamic process, ultimately forming the artwork," in the artist's description.[39] Not only do our own bodies "vent" microbiotic entities that might become patches of fuzzy growth on the artwork's surface, but the spores that the artist has applied in washes of color to the nearby gallery walls

35
Per "Indigoidine Introduction," a document supplied to the author by the artist on May 13, 2024, authored by Abiochem (a firm collaborating with Wang). Abiochem aimed to synthesize indigoidine, which is chemically analogous to other precursor chemicals such as indican, indoxyl, indigotin, isatin, and indirubin, but has a different pathway to producing the blue pigment. Intriguingly, indirubin is connected to a traditional Chinese medicine named *danggui longhui wan*, perhaps an unintended allusion embedded in Wang's *Biological Klein Blue*.

36
Huifang Yin et al., "Efficient Bioproduction of Indigo and Indirubin by Optimizing a Novel Terpenoid Cyclase XiaI in *Escherichia coli*," *ACS Omega* 6, no. 31 (2021): 20569–76, available at https://pubs.acs.org/doi/10.1021/acsomega.1c02679.

37
Klein worked with the chemical manufacturer Rhône-Poulenc to produce a colorless polyvinyl acetate resin called Rhodopas M60A. He mixed this with alcohol and commercially available synthetic ultramarine pigment to produce the painterly surface he dubbed IKB (International Klein Blue), patent no. 63471, registered in Paris on May 19, 1960.

38
Abiochem, "Indigoidine Introduction." The glucoside indican, with the formula C14H17NO6, is the commonly found botanical precursor to indigo chemistry. Yin (2021) used tryptophan and hydroxyindole to feed their genetically altered *E. coli* to make indican and indirubin.

39
Wang Yuyang, email communication, May 13, 2024.

[FIG. 10]
In the foreground, Wang Yuyang, *Biological Klein Blue*, 2022. Visible in the background, Wang Yuyang, *Plant*, 2024

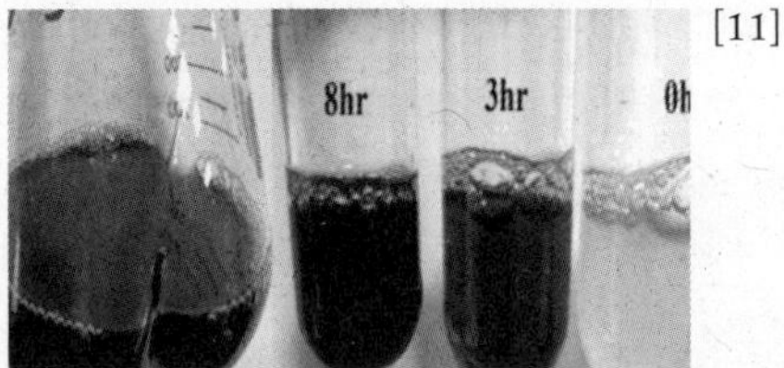

[11]

must surely play a part, wreaking havoc on the white cube and the horizontal field of blue as they grow.

Wang's work has been good to think with, allowing us to trace more than a century of feedback notions into the technophanies of today. As feedback blossomed from electronics to cybernetics, it stretched to include biological homeostasis and sensing as ways of calibrating life within environments. These organicist complexities, increasingly performed by Wang's art, are needed to confront today's breathless claims for AI. Even as the artworks can be contrasted with the shy machines and brassy robots of an earlier cybernetic age, Wang embraces more-than-human collaborators and releases artistic agency to other forces, acknowledging our planetary condition of entanglement and symbiontic codependent arising.[40] Sporulating fungus, nutritious algae, bacterial quorum sensing, and emergent machinic behaviors—these offer evidence of the feedback loops entangled with Wang's machinic and organic phyla. In appreciating this art, let us look not to "artificial" intelligence but to our own, in symbiosis with the planet, producing as it does critically engaging art, technoscience, prosthetics, and nature-culture with all the Anthropogenic urgency we can muster.

40
For an exploration of symbiontics in the context of Buddhism in the work of Japanese mycologist Minakata Kumagusu see Caroline A. Jones, "The Labour of Symbiosis," in *The Edinburgh University Press Companion to Curatorial Futures*, ed. Bassam El Baroni and Matthew Poole (forthcoming spring 2025). I am indebted to the work of scholar Eiko Honda and artist Jenna Sutela in coming to an understanding of Minakata's extraordinary, cosmic biological research.

[FIG. 11]
The chemical production of synthetic indigo from indigoidine by the Shanghai firm Abiochem, 2024

THE AESTHETICS OF THE SUPERJECT, OR WHY WANG YUYANG IS AN ACCIDENTAL MEDIA ARTIST

MARK B. N. HANSEN

MARK B. N. HANSEN
James B. Duke Distinguished Professor of Literature, Duke University

For the artist . . . the fact [is] that these cyborgs breathe the same air as their human audiences.
—Robin Peckham[1]

Is Wang Yuyang a media artist? This frequently asked question returns interesting though often rather oblique less-than-equivocal answers. Most commentators readily acknowledge that Wang's artwork engages media in a consequential manner, but once that point is made, qualifications begin. For curators Kang Li and Wu Mo, Wang is "good at creating artistic works with new media," but unlike most media artists, his interest is less technology itself than the "artistic qualities brought by the 'outdated' technologies, the 'destructive' aesthetics and the material waste."[2] Similarly, for curator Sun Dongdong, Wang, although "long known for making new media art," seeks less to interrogate "modernization on a technological level" than to step directly "into the situation of media and human beings."[3] Art historian Pamela Lee concurs, suggesting that Wang's work turns away from media as object to "probe the . . . existential . . . quandaries . . . media raise about objects, subjects, and the human agents formerly imagined to broker th[eir] relationship."[4] Finally, and perhaps most bluntly, for critic Robin Peckham, Wang's interest in "media new and otherwise . . . very rarely reflects the techniques and aesthetics that characterize the . . . category" of new media art.[5]

1
Robin Peckham, "Wang Yuyang: Things That Should Not Be," in *2002–2013 WANG YUYANG* (Hong Kong: Blue Kingfisher, 2013), 142.

2
Kang Li and Wu Mo, "Preface to Wang Yuyang's Solo Exhibition *A Painting*, CAFA Art Museum," in *2002–2013 WANG YUYANG*, 268.

3
Sun Dongdong, "The 8th Exhibition of Art Changsha: Foundation," in *The Marvelous Clouds* (Changsha, China: Hunan Tan Guobin Contemporary Art Museum, 2022), 29.

4
Pamela M. Lee, "How We Became Posthumanist," in Wang Yuyang, *Tonight I Shall Meditate on That Which I Am* (Milan: Flash Art Books, 2016), 46.

5
Robin Peckham, "51 m² #16: Wang Yuyang," in *2002–2013 WANG YUYANG*, 236.

The common thread running through such observations is echoed and expanded in the artist's own statements. When, for example, Wang suggests that media can be both content and agent, both "materialized" and "materializing," he envisions media themselves as forces working at cross-purposes to and in excess of their "characteristic of functionality," and he sees his role as artist to be that of letting "different mediums . . . make use of each other" and also "work against each other."[6] That media are "materializing" forces in their own right helps explain Wang's claim to be an "accidental media artist."[7] Media have "materialized" him as media artist, and in a quite literal sense. Entering into co-creative relations with objects and the world, Wang has variously sought to share—and in some instances to relinquish—his own agency. Neither topic nor object, media is Wang's *medium*: from his earliest student projects to the works in the *Chaosmosis*, his 2024 show at the Shenzhen Art Museum, Wang has invested in media as catalyst and operator of worldly or "cosmic" mediation, and he has incrementally—often by recycling and rejuvenating his own past work—developed a powerful and wide-ranging "superjectal" aesthetic of mediation as process.

PROCESS

"Process" philosophy's most important proponent was the great British mathematician-cum-speculative-philosopher Alfred North Whitehead.[8] Whitehead developed a generic metaphysics that is neutral in relation to the plurality of ontologies it supports. Its fundamental tenet is that process, rather than substance, is primary. Rather than viewing the world (or the cosmos[9]) from the standpoint of one of its privileged products—the human subject—a focus on process enjoins us to view it in terms of its "own" elementary processes. From the process standpoint, all of the entities we normally take for granted, subjects and objects alike, appear instead to be derivative compositions of atomic elements of process, and if we are to garner a proper understanding of them, we must view them through, and indeed *as*, the processes composing them.

Process occurs through the incessant repetition of a twofold operation: the genesis of "actual occasions," and their "objectification" and addition to the world in the form of "superjects." Whitehead terms these two phases "concrescence" and "transition," respectively. In the phase of concrescence, emerging actualities "feel" (or, in Whitehead's technical term, "prehend") the entirety of the world they inherit (the superjectal world) and are composed as a unique mixture of positive feelings (direct engagements

6
Wang Yuyang, "Let Things Tell: Interview with Yang Juan," in *2002–2013 WANG YUYANG*, 154.

7
Robin Peckham recounts that Wang referred to himself in this way when they first met in 2008. Robin Peckham, "Algorithm, Rendering, Object: Art for Systems," in *Tonight I Shall Meditate on That Which I Am*, 60.

8
Prior to emerging as a speculative philosopher in the 1920s, Whitehead coauthored the multivolume *Principia Mathematica* with his former student Bertrand Russell.

9
Whitehead subtitled *Process and Reality* (his most systemic presentation of process philosophy) *An Essay in Cosmology*.

with the world) and negative feelings (non-engagements, which are nonetheless still relations). Once this phase is completed, actualities become "objectified" and added to the world, where they carry on as "superjects"—objects with lingering potentiality for future process.

Process philosophy is thus a proposal for understanding the incessant oscillation that is at the heart of reality: new actualities are continually produced from the potentiality of past realities and then become part of past potentiality for the subsequent production of new actualities, which in turn are added to the world, and so on—until, as Whitehead put it, the "crack of doom."[10]

WORLD AS MEDIUM

Distilled down to its essence, process philosophy aims to grasp the world from the standpoint of its actual concrete happening, which is to say, from the perspective *of the world itself*. To do that, process thinking seeks to view the products of process—enduring entities at all scales, from the atom to the solar system—in terms of the concrete acts through which they are created. Process thinking thus treats each act of process as an internal perspective *of* the universe itself, not an external perspective *on* the universe as object.[11] At the core of process philosophy, we thus discover a radical claim about media: the world is its own medium.[12] As "a medium for the transmission of influences," the world is at every instant rife with superjectal potentiality for the future—the potentiality of what could have been but wasn't—and indeed, "each actual world" is itself "a medium," the medium of its own concrete genesis.[13]

This understanding of the world as medium allows us to grasp the world from the perspective of its actual concrete becoming. This does not mean, however, that we can *know* the world from this standpoint. Indeed, process occurs prior to any possible experience of it: the "transmission of influences" hosted by the world occurs through the *real togetherness* of processual units (actual occasions) in which disparate superjectal elements compose together into "complex unity." Such unity is originary and preanalytical, "prior" to separability. An insuperable gap exists between the concrete happening of process and any effort to know or otherwise engage it. Simply put, the very happening of process—of process that creates experience—exceeds any possible experiential perspective on it.[14]

ABSTRACTION

As experiential beings, we can only know or engage process through what Whitehead calls "abstractions," experiential perspectives on

10
Alfred North Whitehead, *Process and Reality: An Essay on Cosmology* (New York: Free Press, 1978), 228.

11
I borrow this helpful distinction from Belgian philosopher Didier Debaise. See Didier Debaise, *Nature as Event: The Lure of the Possible*, trans. Michael Halewood (Durham, NC: Duke University Press, 2017).

12
See Andrew Murphie, "The World as Medium: A Whiteheadian Media Philosophy," in *Immediation I*, ed. Erin Manning et al. (London: Open Humanities Press, 2019), 16–46. I develop an account of Whitehead as a media theorist in Mark B. N. Hansen, *Feed-Forward: On the Future of Twenty-First-Century Media* (Chicago: University of Chicago Press, 2015).

13
Whitehead, *Process and Reality*, 286, 284.

14
This is why Whitehead calls his philosophy speculative: ungraspable in its happening, process can only be gestured at through a speculative construction of what must have happened for experience to be what it is. Whitehead makes this apparent from the very first page of *Process and Reality*: "Speculative Philosophy is the endeavor to frame a coherent, logical, necessary system of general ideas in terms of which every element of our experience can be interpreted" (3).

process that necessarily select from integral process and thus emphasize certain features and entirely overlook others. There is, simply put, always more in the process informing any particular experience than that experience is capable of knowing. That is why Whitehead defines philosophy as the "taking care of our abstractions," and it is why abstractions can be "good" or "bad," depending on whether or not they recognize their irreducible partiality—that is, their status as abstractions. When they don't, they commit what Whitehead calls the "fallacy of misplaced concreteness"—taking an abstraction for what is concrete, for process itself in its integral operation.

As a selective delimitation of process, every abstraction provides a double perspective on the process that produces it: in addition to the delimited, experiential perspective it affords *on* process—the perspective from which it knows itself and the world—it also instantiates—indeed simply *is*—a partial perspective *of* process itself, and for this reason, includes more than it can be aware of or know. Every abstraction, in short, is informed by the entirety of the "causal efficacy" of the process from which it abstracts even though it cannot grasp it in its entirety. For this reason, abstractions differ categorically from Immanuel Kant's "representations" (*Vorstellungen*). They are not different in kind from the object of their knowledge, the so-called "thing-in-itself." Rather, as partial perspectives on process itself, abstractions are both vehicles to know some part of a process that categorically exceeds them *and* themselves products, not representations, of that act of process in its unknowable entirety.

Because of their duality, abstractions can be vehicles for extending the scope of perception and knowledge in ways that expand their grasp of the causal efficacy informing them. The techniques of modern science provide a perfect example: as expansions of human perception, they let us grasp "more" of the reality whose product they are. Abstractions are thus vehicles for knowing the excess of process from the standpoint of experience, and for this reason, they can also be technologies for expanding the experiential grasp of process.

MEDIA AS AGENT OF ABSTRACTION

With his double aim to let process happen and to subordinate his own agency to that happening, Wang effectively creates artworks that are abstractions in precisely this sense. They stage interventions into process with the express aim of putting experience into relation with the processual excess from which it abstracts, and in that way letting that excess, or some portion of it, become active in the forging of new experience.

To stage such interventions into process, Wang deploys diverse media as agents of abstraction. In this vocation, media "relate," and what they relate are not (just) things in the world but *the superjectal force* of those things, the potentiality they harbor for generating new process. Wang thus deploys media as means to catalyze *the mediation that is process itself*, following Whitehead's proposal that each actual world is the medium for its successor. If Wang is indeed a media artist, his medium is worldly mediation itself, the cosmic process that unceasingly generates new worldly sensibility.

Consider *I Don't Know* (2024). Encountering this work, the viewer sees a large, transparent, rectangular case containing a blocky desktop computer connected by tubes and wires to a glass vessel filled with a soup of microorganisms. Expressly constructed to simulate some sort of scientific experiment, the work is composed of the incessant generation of images that are the product of the "becoming-together" of computational and biological operations. If this work is meant to be received as an experiment, however, what it experiments with is precisely the operation of process as worldly mediation. The images it produces—images generated by computation itself as it processes the "activity data" of the microbiotic soup—are products of a mediation that precedes them and that is "preanalytical" in Whitehead's sense. Indeed, if these images are random and unpredictable, it is precisely because they are the product of a mediation of the indeterminate—a mediation that cannot be known in advance precisely because it does not preexist its own happening. *I Don't Know* is in this respect an expressly didactic work, one meant to instruct us, Wang's viewers, about what his art, and what his use of media in his art, can do. In it, we see process and product at the same time: we literally watch the soup of microorganisms growing and changing while simultaneously viewing the images in whose genesis they participate.

I Don't Know is a key work for another reason as well. It marks a culmination of sorts of Wang's career-defining gesture of displacing himself from the position of authority that the modern artist canonically enjoys. Most prominent in Wang's series *WANG Yuyang#* (2015–ongoing) this gesture involves strategies for sharing agency with other elements of process—most notably, computational operations—in differing configurations. In the *WANG Yuyang#* series, this gesture yields works that are produced through a collaborative process but that are in the final instance products of computational randomness operating independently of the artist's oversight. *Chaosmosis* marks a new stage in this strategy of divestment for two reasons. First, as the sculptures in Wang's *Symbiosis* series (2023–ongoing) attest, his gesture has become more complex: no longer aiming to displace himself entirely from the process of production, Wang now conceives of his agency as one element among others in co-creative process.[15] And second, Wang's use of biological processes in particular—a distinguishing feature of the work collected in *Chaosmosis*—allows him to add another element, a non-computational *and* nonhuman element, whose "living" agency introduces a further source of indetermination to the mix.

To grasp the significance of this double complexification, let us contrast *I Don't Know* with an earlier, similarly didactic work, *Speak* (2010). *Speak* stages the encounter of an audiotape with its own genesis. To produce it, Wang used an audiotape to record the sounds of the material process involved in recording an audiotape. He then plays the recording in an installation setting, affording listeners the opportunity to hear the tape "tell" the story of its own genesis as medium. Like *I Don't Know*, *Speak* thus stages a situation in which media product is made to confront the process of its own production—the mediation through which it comes into being. Reminiscent of certain strands of Postminimalism,[16] the work however affords a meditation on the status of the "object" that exceeds the Postminimalist strategy of undermining its autonomy. Here, the subjectivity that compromises its autonomy is not added onto the object as a phenomenological supplement but is intrinsic: it is the subjectivity of process itself—the "other-determination" of superjectal potentiality. *Speak* can thus be understood as a personification of process. By letting the tape tell its own story—by letting it play the recording of the process of its own recording—the work allegorizes the oscillation constitutive of process. As one critic astutely puts it: *Speak* shows "how an object exercises the rights of subject and objectivizes itself again."[17]

Speak thus proposes that the object is itself a process. It is a process in which superjects—that is, objectified actualities—become together in order to produce new actuality, new superjects. Wang's introduction of the biological, and of biological indeterminacy,[18] complicates this picture of process-qua-object yet further. Specifically, it introduces a source of *living* indeterminacy alongside the *physical* indeterminacy of computation. As a surrogate for the indeterminacy of the artist's whim, this living indeterminacy allows Wang to exit the scene but without removing the operation of living contingency, without subordinating it to physical contingency—and also, it is important to note, without fully divesting his own authority. That is why *I Don't Know* marks the culmination of Wang's effort to "let process speak": the double perspective it "objectifies," that makes it an object-qua-process, does not require the

15
One commentator refers to the new phase in Wang's trajectory as the *Co-Create* series. See Sun Dongdong, "Wang Yuyang: The Marvelous Clouds," in *The Marvelous Clouds*, 40–43.

16
Robin Peckham observes that *Speak* "enters into a remarkable conversation with the fabled Robert Morris piece *Box with the Sound of Its Own Making* (1961), mimicking the same strategies of overdetermination in cognitive reception but inserting very explicitly (indeed, so explicit it becomes almost boring) the question of media as genre into this equation." Peckham, "51 m² #16," 236.

17
Su Wenxiang and Tan Xin, "Preface to Wang Yuyang's Solo Exhibition 51 m² #16, Taikong Space, Beijing," in *2002–2013 WANG YUYANG*, 220.

18
Polymath mathematician Giuseppe Longo draws a categorical divide between physical randomness and biological randomness, the gist of which is that biological randomness cannot be predicted in advance, even in ideal conditions, since the processes in which it inheres do not preexist their own becoming and are constantly—or in Whitehead's terms, incrementally—changing. Giuseppe Longo, "Letter to Turing," *Theory, Culture and Society* 36, no. 6 (November 2019): 73–94.

19 Wang Yuyang, "I Want 'Things' to Talk," interview with Sun Dongdong, in *2002–2013 WANG YUYANG*, 328.

20 Longo, "Letter to Turing," 73–94.

human viewer-listener to lend it "life"—following one key formative strategy of Wang's earlier work that finds exemplary expression in his breakthrough *Breathe* series (2006–13). Instead, as itself living, *I Don't Know* "objectifies" the double perspective of the object-process, and the oscillation it frames is one that it also catalyzes. What in the earlier work could only take form as allegory here becomes literal. The work operates through its own continual objectification, producing its object anew in each iteration, in each image it generates.

AESTHETICS OF FAILURE

"Life," or living indetermination, is the crucial element informing the shift in Wang's practice. Long a theme in his work, living indetermination becomes the superjectal agent of his most recent work. *Chaosmosis* thus represents a culmination, but also a rejuvenation, of earlier experiments with the fundamental difference between physical and living indetermination. Exemplary here is *Electricity*, an oft-commented-upon work from 2007, that takes form as an installation featuring a battery lying on a chair alongside a case containing a brainwave device with an accompanying video depicting the process of the work's creation. The installation and video provide a document of Wang's attempt to capture, convert, and store the energy of his own thinking in the form of a battery. But this was not the artist's original intention; Wang initially envisioned a different installation altogether, one in which the battery storing his mental energy would be connected to a lightbulb. Illuminated at the beginning of the exhibition, this bulb would gradually dim and go out entirely, thereby "delivering a kind of sorrow and sentiment." With its aim to "change the power of thinking into functioning energy," Wang's original plan was thus to produce an equivalency between a living brain and an inert battery, between two forms of energy, living and physical. His effort failed because the "brain power" stored in the battery was "too weak . . . to light up a bulb."[19] Yet from this failure came success, in the form of the work Wang did manage to realize, concretized through the blunt juxtaposition of brainwave apparatus and battery. Confronted with the results of this failure —the impossibility of functional equivalence—the viewer is encouraged to reflect on the "myth of the digital" currently driving our accelerationist techno-culture.[20]

The failure of Wang's original intention and the recuperation of *Electricity* as a testament to this failure led Wang, or so I want to speculate, to a crucial insight: that physical and living processes are not inter-convertible without loss. From this came a realization that any collaboration with physico-technical processes would need to take form as an imbrication of functionally distinct operations, initially those of artist and computer and, now in the works collected in *Chaosmosis*, of biological and physical processes more generally. In this new dispensation, the physical and the living relate to each other not on the basis of functional or material equivalence (or its failure), but rather through the sheer fact of their co-becoming in and as real togetherness of process.

Consider *Dream* (2016–24), the work in the current cycle most reminiscent of *Electricity*. Like the earlier work, *Dream* involves the interface between brain and computer. Specifically, the work features a painting machine—a robotic hand attached to a large, mobile computer inside a glass-enclosed room—that processes input from EEG signals and eye movement data produced by the artist's brain and recorded while he is sleeping. Fed with this input, the machine moves around the space painting swatches of different colors on the glass walls. Like *Electricity*, the work features a correlation between living energy (the psychic energy of the artist dreaming) and mechanical energy, but here what becomes most insistent is the absolutely enigmatic nature of this correlation. We simply cannot know exactly how the data determines the pattern of painting, and that is precisely the point: physical and living indetermination come together in a form that evades the grasp of any abstraction whatsoever. Like *Electricity*, *Dream* stages its own failure to realize a concrete inter-convertibility between living and mechanical processes. Yet the very fact that it works attests to its success: it captures how living and machinic elements compose together through preanalytical togetherness in an age when the artificial and the natural freely interpenetrate at scales ranging from the microscopic to the cosmological.

This same pattern takes different form in other works in *Chaosmosis*. Like *Dream*, both *Golem* (2022) and *Release* (2024) succeed on the basis of their failure. *Golem* exposes the contemporary fantasy of a "data self" in a stark, almost brutal manner. A gigantic hunk of sand, clay, and weeds modeled by an AI system processing biometric data from the artist and images of his artworks, *Golem* bluntly proposes that our current technophilic fantasy of simulation is mere illusion. The blob does not resemble Wang—at least not in any way we can fathom—and even if we take it to be his simulation, as we are invited to do, its material fragility and eventual decay over time say more about the artist as a living being than anything we can divine concerning its genesis. While data can give no more than a snapshot of a life, the sculpture's material disintegration captures something of the contingencies informing life as process.

21 For example M. Beatrice Fazi, "Beyond Human: Deep Learning, Explainability and Representation," *Theory, Culture and Society* 38, nos. 7–8 (2021): 55–77.

Similarly, *Release* allegorizes the hubris of our techno-culture by staging the failure of its animating dream of producing life mechanically. This complex work centers on a robot dog that Wang released in a desolate area of Lop Nur in northwestern China. Equipped with a source of energy (or "life") in the form of solar panels and connected to satellite GPS, the dog made its way farther and farther into the wilderness until it lost connectivity, disappeared, and at some point presumably "died." In the gallery, the work takes form as an installation that explicitly reproduces the format and layout of *Electricity*. It features an empty chair positioned next to a monitor behind which stands an abstract painting of a blue blob leaning against a wall. The monitor displays a video documenting the artist, seated in the chair adjacent to it, holding a cell phone containing the data of the dog's adventure, as he explains the project and its results. In contrast to *Electricity*, however, here the failure of the project is a foregone conclusion, and the work's interest lies instead in the becoming-myth of the dog's adventure, as Wang recounts it for us and for the future beyond. With the dream of equivalence sidelined from the get-go, it is the pathos with which we imagine the dog's adventure that takes center stage.

BECOMING "DISTINCTLY TOGETHER"

As experiments variously staging the failure of the equivalence driving digital culture today, these works—*Dream*, *Golem*, and *Release*—are all in some sense transitional projects that pave the way for the "superjectal aesthetic" informing the most ambitious and thought-provoking works in *Chaosmosis*. *I Don't Know*, as we have seen, captures the consequential shift informing this aesthetic: Wang's gesture of giving the living, and the specific indeterminacy informing the living, autonomy, and, with it, independence from the human. In the wake of this shift, what was figured in early works like the *Breath* series as a "simulation" of the living has now become the failure of simulation, the revelation that our contemporary logic of simulation is rooted in the reductive modeling of computation on the image of the human and the prototype of human intelligence. Wang's various stagings of the failure of equivalence thus make experientially salient what a certain strain of contemporary media theory has insistently proclaimed: that we can dream of equivalence only because we constrain computation to the human frame we impose on it.[21]

Through their patent difference, a pair of works from *Chaosmosis*, *Plant* (2024) and *Define* (2022), suggest an alternate path forward, one that explores precisely what becomes possible on the far side

22 Caroline A. Jones, Natalie Bell, and Selby Nimrod, eds., *Symbionts: Contemporary Artists and the Biosphere* (Cambridge, MA: MIT List Visual Arts Center and MIT Press, 2022).

of the fantasy of equivalence. *Plant* consists of a series of objects depicting exquisite, colorful plants and flowers wallpapered onto the gallery's walls. These objects are results of algorithmic processes generated through machine learning of images of plants and controlled by random numbers. Literally the products of the physical indeterminacy informing computation, these images offer a lure of simulation that is immediately undermined by the simple fact that their processual genesis remains beyond the grasp of any abstraction. Simply put, we have no way of fathoming how they were made or what exactly they signify. Mounted on the walls immediately adjacent to *Plant*, *Define* presents a series of colorful blobs that on initial glance seem to mimic the plant objects beside them. In fact, however, these blobs are the products of living microorganisms that have been injected with DNA manufactured by translating a dictionary definition of "fungus" into the base pairs (A, C, G, T) of genetic code. Far from being simulations of life, these blobs are "symbionts"[22]—products of superjectal other-determination—that interweave natural and synthetic elements into an inscrutable real togetherness.

Perhaps envisioned by the artist as a joint unpacking of the two elements informing *The Dubious of Entanglement by Plants* (2012–24), these two works signify as a pair, one presenting the creativity of computation freed from the imposition of a human model, and the other, the creativity of life as preanalytical process. The convolution of all three works suggests that these two distinct sources of creativity—computation and life—themselves operate most powerfully when they co-operate "distinctly together," through superjectal composition, as elements of complex processual unities. Through this speculative connection to *Plant* and *Define*, *The Dubious of Entanglement by Plants* may indeed signify more as a generic promise of future entanglement than as a monument to entropy. Literally the product of Wang's abandonment to the elements of an earlier computationally generated sculptural work, *The Dubious of Entanglement by Plants* results from a contingent composition of superjects. Not unlike Wang's own experience of becoming a media artist, it becomes an artwork by accident.

DISSOLVING INTO AIR

Like the accident that derailed *Electricity*, this accident paved the way for recent works that stage the agency of living and physical indetermination as distinct but entangled forces in our synthetic world. Outsourcing living indetermination to living processes themselves also transforms Wang's agency as artist: no longer the giver of life to things, he has become a "channel" linking disparate worldly operations.[23] As a channel for cosmic mediation, Wang becomes superject, swapping bodily self-reference for the free play of worldly other-determination well beyond the terminus of the human body.

Forgotten Memories (2024) is certainly Wang's most radical work in this respect. A tentacular metal sculpture composed of winding pipes and tubes, it offers a portal from an ancient world, a world that is "alien" because anterior to the appearance of the behaviorally modern human, which is to say: *anterior to us*. The network of pipes and tubes connects to two glass vessels containing oxygenated air obtained from ice cores that have been extracted from ancient icebergs hundreds of thousands of years old. Exhibition visitors are able to breathe this ancient air through masklike protuberances at the ends of the tubes. With its emphasis on the superjectal revivification of ancient air through the act of breathing today, the work makes salient the power of Wang's superjectal aesthetics to forge heteronomous relationalities without limit. Far from marking a radical disjunction between our world and the world before the human, *Forgotten Memories* celebrates the power of mediation itself, and the power of air as the most capacious medium of them all. Able to connect anything with anything, air is the quintessential superjectal host, the most cosmic form of "between-ness" there is.[24]

In the most provocative works in the *Chaosmosis* exhibition, Wang dissolves himself into a channel for the anomic play of superjectal other-determination that connects across vast divides and disparate scales. This play allows us to inherit the ancestral past as present potentiality. The mediations it can forge, however, are not limited to those at the cosmic scale—nor to those at the microscopic scale, as in *Biological Klein Blue* (2022). Yet another work from *Chaosmosis*, *I'm Not Sure About the Ones I Gave* (2024), brings the mediating power of air back to the primal scene of Wang's practice: his own body. The work features six transparent containers, each with a small door at the top powered by a small motor attached to it by wires, and inside each container is a tissue that has absorbed sweat from the artist's body at moments when he was experiencing distinct emotions. The doors of the containers open periodically in response to instructions produced by random numbers, allowing scents from the artist's body to escape into the atmosphere of the gallery. By dematerializing and rematerializing his body into odors imbued with emotion, the work releases Wang himself to the play of superjectal other-determination: as the odors intermingle with the surrounding air, Wang literally becomes air

23
"I didn't want to delete or reduce anything in order to make only a 'single' clue. Thus comes the concept of 'wormhole,' which is just like the connection between two time-spaces, channeling between a black hole and a white hole, with openings on both ends, one to our understanding of technology, the universe and the world, and another one to our body and daily life. The two holes are linked up by a channel, which is probably me." Wang, "I Want 'Things' to Talk," 326.

24
In this sense, *Forgotten Memories* exemplifies and brings to its final fruition the aim of engaging the spaces between things that Edward Sanderson astutely recognizes to be Wang's guiding principle from the very start: "One feature in Wang's work that may be seen as the closest thing to a principle for them, seems to be an approach to looking at the world through gaps between things—but not 'through' gaps: maybe a better word is 'with'—'with' the gaps between." Edward Sanderson, "Wang Yuyang," in *2002–2013 WANG YUYANG*, 136.

and, as air, becomes available to be inhaled by, and thus to enter into some form of togetherness with, visitors to the exhibition and any other "cyborgs" that "breathe the same air."[25]

The significance of this dispersion becomes particularly salient via its contrast with the work located across from it. *Questions for Us* (2024) is a wall installation of manifold LED screens of various sizes that pose questions generated by an AI trained on disparate data sources. These questions are addressed to us by the machine, and the fact that they are syntactically correct but nonsensical makes us immediately, and in a way viscerally, aware that what we here confront is an "intelligence" fundamentally different from our own. As the standardized shapes of the LED screens suggest, this intelligence is imprisoned in language and lacks all capacity to test its statements referentially, in relation to a world exterior to it.[26] The stark contrast of this work with *I'm Not Sure About the Ones I Gave* once again lays bare the fundamental difference between physical and living contingency at the heart of Wang's recent work. Where the AI spells out questions that only make sense to it (if at all)—"What voltage is a license plate?" or "Swimming would be blooming if you eat an insect"[27]—in the process further underscoring its terminal imprisonment in language, the transfiguration of Wang's body into odor releases it to an outside world of endless "osmotic" relationality, one that connects, through the cosmic "between-ness" of air as medium, to the oxygen released from the prehistory of the Earth by *Forgotten Memories*. Through this connection, we encounter a powerful expression of the "neutrality" of process which ranges across all scales of cosmic mediation. Yet we also get a sense for its inclusion of specifically human process as one mediation among many, a mediation whose privilege—one we enjoy, for example, through our ability to appreciate Wang Yuyang's artwork—is itself processual, and not ontological, substantial, or essential. Breathing the same air as the works themselves, we become together with the ever-changing superjectal force informing Wang Yuyang's *Chaosmosis*.

25
This phrase is taken from my epigraph citing Robin Peckham.

26
Media theorists commenting on ChatGPT have described this well. For example N. Katherine Hayles refers to the "fragility of reference" of these systems in "Inside the Mind of an AI: Materiality and the Crisis of Representation," *New Literary History* 53, no. 4 and 54, no. 1 (Autumn 2022/Winter 2023): 635–66.

27
On-the-fly translations by the exhibition's curator, Zhang Ga.

WANG YUYANG'S DREAM OF COLOR

RUDOLF FRIELING

RUDOLF FRIELING
Curator and Head of Media Arts,
San Francisco Museum of Modern Art

Viewers in a museum like to contemplate and admire finished compositions. That has not changed over the last sixty years, even as artists have disrupted and even transcended the binaries that govern the traditional notions of art (artist versus public, studio versus museum, contemplation versus participation, et cetera). Challenged by this pursuit, the public has also gradually accepted and even embraced time-based, processual, open-ended, and participatory situations. The questions raised today are thus not that things change and evolve, but how they do this, under what conditions, and with what effects or results. The public still loves to look at a pond of lilies in a painting, and yet it is even more mesmerized when it can sense the depth, the flow, a kaleidoscope of particles, differences in temperature or color, evocative sounds, and last but not least living agents within this open field. A live animal as art in the gallery is a fascinating sight to behold, and live performers or performative processes visibly change the atmosphere in any given art space. But what if change happens at a non-visible level, and over such an extended period of time that viewers can only speculate and contemplate what might happen in the future?

In this essay, I will look at some specific installations in the oeuvre of Wang Yuyang that dream of slow change and other dimensions of sensing art, and argue that the artist embraces the notion of "nature" or live biological agents as well as the sensorial experience of color as key operative agents within his artistic pursuits. Wang works within situations that not only generate change, but do so by gradually letting go of artistic control—essential notions not only in the works that operate with live matter and aspire to a symbiosis between technology and biology, as I will argue here, but in his oeuvre in general and perhaps in the post-technological state of media art today, in which "media constitute components of material systems rather than structuring purely cultural or symbolic circuits."[1]

BLUE

The color blue is a key agent not only in Wang's work, but in the history of art and technology. Let me start by evoking three specific historical references in this regard to set the stage for my argument. To collage two electronic images seamlessly in a recording, the color blue is often used as a placeholder for a second image feed. It signals to the camera a blank to be filled with other content in a live mix or in postproduction. The invention of this so-called blue screen by a production team at RKO Radio Pictures first made its way into film with the special effect of a genie flying out of a bottle in 1940's *The Thief of Bagdad* as an evolution of the traveling matte technique. The blue screen entered the realm of the electronic image under the term of "chroma keying," which theoretically can be done with any color that is uniform and distinct, but it all started with blue backgrounds, as they differ most distinctly in hue from any human skin color.[2]

A second reference addresses the use of pigments in painting. "Historically," notes Lee Down, "blue dyes were difficult to come by and expensive to manufacture. The most popular blue dye was derived from the murex shellfish, which was harvested from the Mediterranean Sea."[3] The dye could only be used in small batches and was labor intensive. Ultramarine, a different blue pigment made from lapis lazuli, was hard to acquire until the nineteenth century, remaining a rare and expensive pigment often reserved for the use of royalty. The blue pigment thus not only symbolically signaled the extraordinary status of a painted figure, but also visibly demonstrated the resources of the painter who had to acquire it (the Dutch painter Johannes Vermeer being an example). Blue, as it was later discovered, also offered a particular sensitivity to light, which eventually led to the use of "blueprints" in architecture.[4] In addition, blue is typically associated with emotions of peace, calmness, and a sense of infinite space, as in vast, unlimited expanses of sea and sky.

These are clichés, but they nevertheless provided the French artist Yves Klein enough motivation in the 1950s to test his first monochromatic paintings and the audience's emotional response to his palette of blue, orange, and pink. Eventually, Klein officially

1
Robin Peckham referencing media theorists Jussi Parikka and McKenzie Wark in "Algorithm, Rendering, Object: Art for Systems," in *Wang Yuyang: Tonight I Shall Meditate upon That Which I Am*, ed. Zhang Ga (Milan: Flash Art Books, 2015), 61.

2
It is a little-known fact that the more commonly used green screen today was a consequence of mostly male newscasters wearing blue jackets and shirts, compromising their appearance on television, an effect artists like Peter Campus used to explore the specificity of video in the 1970s.

3
Lee Down, "History of the Colour Blue in Art," *Arts Artists Artwork*, 2022, https://artsartistsartwork.com/history-of-the-colour-blue-in-art.

4
"As a result of a chance mixing of potassium and iron sulfides in 1709, Johann Jacob Diesbach created a potent blue. In German it was known as *Berliner Blau* or in England as Prussian blue. . . . The discovery by Sir John Herschel that the hue holds a unique sensitivity to light and could be put to use as a medium for producing copies, proved invaluable to architects who could create multiple versions of their maps, plans, and drawings of buildings for the first time." Ksenija Pantelić, "The Long and Fantastic Story of Blue Art Pigments," *Widewalls*, December 6, 2016, https://www.widewalls.ch/magazine/blue-art-pigments.

registered a particular blue as IKB, or International Klein Blue, putting his name on a version of ultramarine he had ordered from the workshop of Edouard Adam, a Parisian art paint supplier. IKB uses a synthetic resin binder that allows the pigment to maintain as much of its original intensity as possible. Klein stressed again and again how the pigment itself worked most profoundly when not compromised by mediating matter such as binders, water, et cetera. His blue was a matte, deep ultramarine with no reflection of the environment. Picture a monochromatic blue in the center of a room—it immediately commands attention (very much like a moving image). Klein spaced paintings generously when exhibiting his monochromatic works to allow for the "pure" perception of their color.

The third historic reference about time-based practices is a very personal one. I recall experiencing strong emotions when attending the premiere of Derek Jarman's 1993 film *Blue* at the Venice Film Festival. The feature-length film consists of a single continuous shot of International Klein Blue on celluloid (according to Wikipedia, with these detailed chromatic coordinates: RGB 0, 47, 167, CMYK 100, 72, 0, 35). This hue fills the screen as the sole visual, accompanied by a soundtrack where the narration describes Jarman's life and the effects of AIDS on his deteriorating vision. The term "resonance" best fits the description of an encounter that took me initially from the impatience of waiting for the first "image" to the disbelief that a filmmaker was refusing to deliver the primary task of providing a visual experience. With a mix of irritation, resignation, enthusiasm, and ultimately a simple calmness in accepting what Pauline Oliveros would call "deep listening," I realized that a monochrome field of blue affects the viewer differently than the black of nothingness, of the absence of light, because it is, after all, the result of projected light. As the visual equivalent of a space where any form might appear at any moment, here blue is not only affectively potent, but also generative.

These historic references set the stage to address Wang Yuyang's contemporary practice and experiments with color and generative processes of change. In my focus on works that operate with the symbiosis of technology and biology, the case of Wang's *Biological Klein Blue* (2022) is particularly central, as its titular blue, at the conclusion of Wang's 2024 exhibition at the Shenzhen Art Museum, had completely vanished, just like the blue screen in television that appears only by accident, revealing the composite nature of the video recording or broadcasting apparatus. Blue thus can be the most singular, attractive color in a room

—imagine one of Klein's monochromatic blue paintings or sculptures—but it can also operate as a mediating presence and absence behind the scenes. Blue is potent, affecting the symbolic but also the physical realm of the imagination.[5]

COLOR

How do these references prepare or relate to any reading of Wang's "dream in color," as the title of this essay states? Prompted by the experience of his *Biological Klein Blue*, I began to look for works where the use of color took center stage in a career mostly dedicated to redefining notions of sculpture and authorship. In fact, Wang's innovative use of algorithms was on full display at the grandiose presentation of his large-scale, precisely titled *Symbiosis* sculptures at the entrance to the exhibition in Shenzhen, foregrounding shape, texture, and scale. Color in these works is a side effect of materials in works like these, and its presence never seemed to have played the role of the main character in his entire practice until about ten years ago, with the creation of two significant works: the paintings of the *Moon* series (2017–ongoing) and the robotic installation *Dream* (2016–24). *Moon* was not the first endeavor to "land" on the moon in Wang's own personal quest. In the early works *Artificial Moon* (2007), *Dust Is Dust* (2008), and the *Moon Landing Program 4* (2009), the optics of how to approach an object so charged with symbolic significance were staged either through a microscopic lens on actual matter or via the juxtaposition of historic record and remake on two parallel screens. The new *Moon* paintings, however, took a leap from examining the materiality and constitution of a found image toward the imagination of a completely new reality. Compared to his innovative use of algorithms and new technologies, this was at first sight a step back to the traditional medium of paint, entirely dependent on the artist's hand to simply color black-and-white photographic representations of the moon's surface. The artist's statement, however, repositions our gaze: "Since black and white photographs were invented and NASA or space agencies share images, our perception of the moon has been that it is colorless. I believe that perhaps the moon, beyond what we think, could actually be colored. To make these paintings I wear digital glasses that convert all colors to different tones of black and white. What I see, including the paint on the palette, is black and white. Following and referencing an image of the moon, I paint what emerges to become a multicolored moon, once I have removed the glasses. This different image of the moon is like a representation of the moon *in another dimension*."[6]

5
I once witnessed a visitor to a private collection who, detecting a Klein blue sponge sculpture casually exhibited in a corridor, dared to touch its delicate surface in a moment of solitude, following the irresistible urge to physically sense the deep blue matte surface.

6
Wang Yuyang, email to the author, July 25, 2024, my emphasis.

What Wang calls glasses looks more like a VR headset, goggles of the most advanced kind that completely shut out any glimpse of the outside world. We could thus claim that his main concern here is not the specific or subjective coloring or texture of the various paintings, but the translation process of a mediated prompt by simply using a different lens.[7] Operating inside an optical space of discoloration, his handcrafted reproduction of the moon is translated back into the artistic realm in such a way as to render our perception of it completely fresh beyond any known—and considered truthful—historical representation. Imagine landing on such a colored moon, a feast for biologists and chemists exploring the apparent sheer diversity of lifelike traces on the barren, remote landscape. These colors would speak to the vision of a vibrant life of bacteria and plants—"another dimension," as the artist states.

My argument here, however, pertains to the desire to see life emerge and at the same time—a main feature of Wang's practice—to effectively circumvent conscious choices and open his process to randomized algorithmic interventions and mediated production methods. Here, an optical device automatically renders a historical artifact as a "nature" of a colorful life, even if remote and inhospitable, for all we know. In other words, Wang's use of the traditional paintbrush was prompted by a desire to expose the limitations of perception, re-mediating a machine vision into something tangible and dismantling our trust in the truth of historical memories so ingrained in the black and white of documents. This counters dramatically the very contemporary use of AI in the reconstruction of color in black-and-white film records. Wang's kind of "Technicolor" trusts the truthfulness of his dreamlike filter. It occupies and embodies "another dimension," something we have never seen before. Now, if we can dream the moon, we should be able to dream the Earth at the same time.

ANOTHER DIMENSION

Let's take once more a step back in our historical framework. The imaginary realm opened up by astronauts traveling to the moon at the end of the 1960s resulted in another important milestone, and that was the photograph of a blue Earth, a pictorial event that allowed us humans to perceive the globe with its billions of microscopic worlds as one holistic environment. This event was rightfully celebrated not just nationally by the US federal agency NASA or by the global media, but also on a local level, particularly by the Californian community that had imagined this holistic perspective as an alternative vision for the existing modernist and

7
On a related trajectory, in 2020 he created *Artificial Moon 2* as an illuminated sphere of screens which is covered in rotating, overlapping Polaroid sheets responding to the light by presenting the viewer iridescent colors. The movement of each sheet is randomly generated, so the sphere the audience sees is constantly changing, emphasizing the perception of color as a lens-based process while the human eye would only see white when looking at a screen directly. Here, the moon is rendered a colorful kaleidoscope revealing wavelengths the human eye cannot detect.

8
One can access the various magazines at https://wholeearth.info/.

9
A comprehensive study of this Californian ideology can be found in Diedrich Diedrichsen and Anselm Franke, eds., *The Whole Earth: California and the Disappearance of the Outside* (Berlin: Sternberg Press / Haus der Kulturen der Welt, 2013).

10
Peckham, "Algorithm, Rendering, Object," 65.

capitalist society. This milestone was forever manifested in the seminal print magazine *Whole Earth Catalog*, initiated by Stewart Brand in 1968[8] with the picture of the Earth reprinted on the cover. The cover was in black and white but clearly evoked in readers' minds the televised pictures of the blue atmosphere and the vast expanse of the blue oceanic waters. The process of "worlding" and of imagining the interconnectedness of all living matter thus started with the moon and the blue globe, both seen from a remote position. It was the vision of a whole generation in California to link this macroscopic perspective to the microscopic lens of our individual lives—coloring them, so to speak, while being mindful of the blue globe.[9]

The technological, social, and ideological repercussions of that shift in perspective have not ended, leading to the global impact of Silicon Valley and its counterparts in China over the last decades. Emerging from his own artistic lineage within what was termed Post-Sense Sensibility in China around the early 2000s,[10] Wang's response has been complex, oblique, and enlightened, but at times obscure. A major shift in his conceptual approach and preoccupation with globes (another parallel to Yves Klein) and moons led him from the *Moon* series to the next large-scale sculptural work, his robotic *Dream*. Making the leap from visualizing a colored moon to literally visualizing the process of dreaming an automated painterly gesture was, to rephrase astronaut Neil Armstrong's famous quote, one small step for the artist, and one giant leap for art history.

I won't dwell on the equally important notion within *Dream* of giving material form to scientific data and the "inner" life of the artist himself, which clearly counters any romantic notion of self-expression that one might still harbor when looking at art. Theoretically, the transfer of a "dream" could be a matter of precision in representation, almost like a photographic reconstruction of imaginary worlds akin to what AI algorithms are currently engaged in. Wang's installation *Dream*, however, is not in the business of reconstruction. The wall text at the Shenzhen Art Museum identified the operation of the work as follows: "In a confined space made of transparent glass, a self-moving robotic hand roams freely, painting on the glass walls. Throughout the process, it continuously changes the color of the paintbrush it holds. The movement of the robot is controlled by the dream of the artist and the computer records the EEG waveforms and sleep data of the artist for several months in real time, after which it learns, trains, and generates a large amount of sleep EEG data." The dream is eventually dreamed by the machine. The artist's dream, by extension, is to refrain from consciously making art and let the robot be the coauthor, who, in a strange sort of codependency, relies on the artist to dream in the first place. It is a remarkable aspect of this installation that the dreaming happens elsewhere, in a remote location, possibly on the other side of the world.

But why is the dreaming process here generating a series of randomly generated painterly gestures with the full palette of paint tubes provided to the robotic machine? The realm of allusion is rich, and includes evocative gestures toward a history of traditional calligraphy as well as to Abstract Expressionism, in particular Jackson Pollock's dripping, performative painting process. While these references and obsessions of an art historian contribute to the rich resonance of the robotic installation, I argue that they are not helping the artist in his pursuit of "another dimension." It is a telling experience that over time the viewer is more and more fascinated by the robot itself, its speed and rhythm, its smooth movement or its precision in grasping the paintbrush or spray can. The machine emerges as the main protagonist, while the resulting traces of paint on the glass are obscuring rather than illuminating this staged performance. What precisely is driving these robotic moves? What dreams are activating the machine? Answering these questions in a technical manner with a record of the artist's brain activity while sleeping in the form of EEG recordings is missing the point. Is the artist not dreaming a constantly variable dream of the machine? It is the artist's stated mission or "dream" to eliminate consciousness from the process of making art, not unlike the Surrealists' "automatic writing" a hundred years ago, but now mediated through the symbiosis of technology and biology. On the other side, let us assume that it is the viewer's dream to watch a machine make more beautiful art than ever seen before. Paradoxically, the more the robot paints, the less we see it at work, as it is obscuring the transparency of its glass enclosure. Toward the end of the exhibition, we would simply see an opaque cube full of smears, with only the strangely disembodied sound of the active robot as a soundtrack to memories of an ongoing spectacle, a curtain of color having come down on this theatrical event.

COMPLICATING THE PICTURE

I have taken the time to focus on these earlier works because they signal an important stepping stone for Wang to now address what the exhibition in Shenzhen called "chaosmosis," or the symbiosis of natural and synthetic or artificial elements. To provide a sensorial process for the perception of color had already been the

11
The artist in an email to the author regarding the English translation of the title, July 24, 2024: "*Dubious* is the title of my past work, which is part of the *Untitled* series from 2012 onwards [and] was generated in 3D Max controlled by binary code converted from a text describing an experiment involving a child and a small monkey living together. And the title also was generated by computer. So, I think of *Dubious* as [a] noun or object."

12
While *Plant* is thematically linked to the works discussed here, it is ultimately a printed wallpaper devoid of any process of gestation, fermentation, or other biological and processual change, and thus not essential to my argument in this essay.

intention of *The Form of Formless, the Semblance of the Invisible* (2020), the title a direct reference to a quote by the Chinese philosopher Laozi, credited with the invention of the I Ching, the oracle of indeterminacy based on chance operations. In this immersive installation, the randomly sprayed colors on the walls changed when viewed from different angles by the viewers, who literally entered a complete surround-painting. As they moved through the space, they continued to have a field experience of an unstable kaleidoscope of concrete perceptions. Similar to a painter's random and yet personal mix of colors on a palette, the potentiality of an indeterminate field to become form was an emerging sensation more felt than understood, more dreamed than cognitively processed.

Biological Klein Blue embodies an indeterminate experience, less immersive but still sensorial, more a surface on the floor than a room, and yet also a three-dimensional space in which fluid matter hardens into a concrete form and events unfold in that process. In Shenzhen, the work was the centerpiece in a large gallery, surrounded by the metal sculpture with remnants of live matter and animals titled *The Dubious of Entanglement by Plants* (2012–24),[11] the two wall-mounted works *Define* (2022) and *Plant* (2024),[12] and *I Don't Know* (2024), a vertical container with a transparent screen front that both revealed and concealed a process of fermentation inside the fridge-like form with the wall text stating: "Images are generated by artificial intelligence, but it is the activity data of microorganisms in the container of the screen case that drives the AI generation. Simultaneously, inside the box, the viewer can observe these microorganisms as they grow." Not unlike *Dream*, the inside is defined as an organic generator of an external window displaying a rapid succession of seemingly unrelated images culled from the internet. The imaging of a random process looks very much like a contemporary take on Nam June Paik's electronic collage, but without the personal style of mixing. The images circulate in a symbolic world of their own. Despite the arresting change of the screen between transparency and rapid-fire activation, effectively taking the viewer's eye off the interior process, the apparatus of fermentation and visual generator remains obscure even when clearly visible for moments.

Nothing is obscured in *Biological Klein Blue*, accompanied as it is by this text: "This new Klein blue possesses biological properties, it is a work of synthetic biology. A mixed culture of genetically modified ingredients produces a brilliant blue color that is very rare in living organisms." The name Klein is not deemed worthy of any further explanation; instead, the description centers on the color but lacks any mention of the installation's

13 Email to the author on July 22, 2024, slightly edited for clarity.

processual change as the infused bacteria react over time to their environment. Foregrounding the color blue seems to mark the essence of the work as a process of colorization. This, however, is not what unfolded in the museum. Looking at the subsequent documentation of the work's temporality of gradual changes, it is striking to not only see the blue diminish over time to the point of complete absence, but also to realize that the process of exhibiting the work was tied to evaporation, which an email from the artist summarized as follows: "At the time of infusion it was in liquid form, then it began to solidify similar to jelly, and finally dried completely, somewhat like leather, but easy to break. When we were infusing the liquid, the frame was placed. After reaching its final solidity, the frame was demolished."[13] It is worth noting that this process was not visible to any visitor looking at the installation on any given day. At the opening, one saw an expanse of blue liquid on the floor, with some white bubbles floating around. The shallow surface was contained by a low frame. At the end, the frame was removed when a three-dimensional form devoid of any liquid had emerged, bearing cracks reminiscent of a dry riverbed.

Biological Klein Blue started where the *Moon* series left off, but then returned its matter to an earthen essence, a surface like an old piece of yellowed paper or a painting carelessly left exposed to harmful environmental conditions. The dream of *Dream*—the continuous unfolding of a beautiful movement—dried up when the slow interaction of bacteria and pigments, with its process of "painting" on its liquid canvas, reduced its aesthetic resonance with Yves Klein's IKB to a (metaphorically speaking) black-and-white matter as the blue evaporated and transformed. In a time of ecological disasters, we might think of the devastating effects of drought, but the change also signals something essential in a profound conceptual register. It had already been Klein's predicament that pure pigment needs support or binding matter, which in turn dilutes its vibrant hue. Whether we call it washed out, faded, or an object with patina, colored surfaces are not exempt from change over time. *Biological Klein Blue* is thus but a short-lived dream. The manifestation of a biological process in the clean and artificial environment of a museum has taken its toll. But is this a sad state of affairs? I don't think so. Just like the emergence of color in nature is seasonal, there will be another exhibition, another cycle of presence becoming absence.

Still, this development took me by surprise, and not only thwarted my expectation but complicated the notion of "picture." I had envisioned an effect where a colorful, vibrant, complex surface would have emerged over time, where bacteria would have bloomed in abundance and shown an ever-expanding growth, not unlike one of Wang's *Moon* paintings, which were the outcome of the mediated play between black and white and color. The wall text of Wang's other work with bacteria, *Define*, seemed to acknowledge this potentiality more directly: "Microorganisms that reproduce rapidly are selected, and the definition that humans decipher and describe (textual microbial characteristics) is coded in A, C, G, T. The coded genes are then genetically injected into the genes of the microorganisms, which are then multiplied and grown in the gallery space and on other artworks. At the same time, during the exhibition, these human-defined microbes are combined with microbes in the gallery or microbes brought in by visitors. The natural and the unnatural intertwine with each other in a perfect symbiosis that becomes the third nature." The "picture" on the wall or on the floor does not just execute a code or program; it resists interpretation, and thus complicates any intentionality attached to it.

ON THE CONDITIONS OF TRANSFORMATIVE CHANGE

To claim a new form of "third nature" in *Define* or grant access to "another dimension" in the *Moon* series are two ways of making the same claim: art transforms both matter and the viewer at the same time. The ultimate disappearance of blue was not intended. Its absence may even register with viewers as a loss. In fact, when asked about the generative growth of all the works in the exhibition, Wang responded by revealing that *Define*—displayed in the same gallery as *Biological Klein Blue*—did not behave as intended. In this particular case, the symbiotic process was designed to trigger at least change, if not growth, on the gallery wall—a nightmare for any museum, whose ultimate purpose is to protect artworks from damaging environmental conditions, whether drastic changes in climate or, as in this particular situation, meandering microbes and organisms. The pristine conditions of exhibiting art are predicated on control of the environment. This does not preclude the museum from allowing change to occur if it is part of the artistic intention and a condition of the work, but it must be controlled, and above all contained. But Wang's comment when sending additional visual documentation of the evolution of *Define* noted that, in Shenzhen, change did not happen. The bacteria did not do their "job." Conditions within the museum, we can deduct, were just not favorable. But it could have worked out differently. Wang pointed to documentation of the same process in other venues where growth and change were clearly visible and effective.

Whether the responsibility for making artistic decisions is delegated to algorithms or to bacteria, Wang sees himself as a practitioner who executes what nonhuman agents initiate and script. He merely sets the stage for a process that cannot fail artistically to unfold. If the viewer accepts the premise, any outcome is within the realm of what is possible and "intended." Preparing the conditions for change to happen is, on the other hand, not a guarantee of effecting change. Given the analogy with scientific processes of experimenting with the fusion of different elements in a controlled environment, possibly verifying results by repeating the same process, pristine lab conditions are not feasible in a museum setting. But Wang is the last agent in this scenario who would ask for complete control. It is precisely his approach and idea that he relinquishes some artistic control in the development of his works. What happens happens, and the artist can simply refer to the conceptual frame in which change is part of the imaginary of the work, part of the potentiality but not a necessity. In this way, even a material-based process is ultimately an effect of its conceptual premise: the artist makes decisions that prepare the ground or condition for something to happen—which is precisely the tautological definition of "happening" as proposed by Allan Kaprow more than sixty years ago.[14]

Wouldn't it be a dream come true if an artwork not only changed over time, but changed beautifully or dramatically or whatever adjective we might attach to our expectation as a viewer? Imagine we could watch bacteria at work replicating Claude Monet's *Water Lilies* or *Water Lily Pond*. I am reminded of Monet because of another personal experience: at the Chichu Art Museum in Naoshima, Japan, skylights open the Monet gallery to natural lighting conditions and thus to the whims of the changing weather. That's where I witnessed both darkness as well as brief bursts of sunlight falling on the largest of Monet's paintings. The temporality of this effect was like a spiritual epiphany. A dramatic change of lighting on a surface with an irregular sprinkling of colors produces potent effects—we experience "nature" even in a painting as an embodied experience and not just as a reading of the representation of a pond and its plants. The temporal appearance of a blue dot in the pond becomes the epiphany of "another dimension" within the painting.

The dream of *Biological Klein Blue* and *Define* is fugitive and yet present in its potentiality in every single moment of looking at them, or rather of sensing them. Wang's practice does not require

14
This is not the place to dig deeper into comparable artistic approaches, but I would be remiss if I did not at least mention Wang's proximity to the experimental and open-ended work done by the French artist Pierre Huyghe. For a most recent account of his complex oeuvre see the catalogue *Pierre Huyghe: Liminal*, ed. Anne Stenne and Jacqueline Feldmann (Venice: Marsilio Arte, 2024).

a particular aesthetic validation. I'm inclined to follow Nam June Paik, who stated programmatically at the beginning of his career that his experimental TV was like "nature, which is beautiful, not because it changes beautifully, but simply because it changes."[15] Whatever happens in a Wang Yuyang environment is a "beautiful" experience even when the color disappears, even when the robot is obscured, even when the pond dries up and the imagined lilies vanish in muddy cracks—in other words, when a transformation has happened. Transformative art transcends both idea and matter and opens up the senses to an imaginary realm of a colorful life, if only for a brief moment. That is what the viewers take home. They have sensed the artist's dream of color.

15
Nam June Paik, *AFTERLUDE to the Exposition of EXPERIMENTAL TELEVISION*, 1964, available at http://www.mediaartnet.org/source-text/31/.

EXHIBITION
WANG YUYANG: CHAOSMOSIS

Shenzhen Art Museum
March 24–May 5, 2024

CURATOR
Zhang Ga

ORGANIZED BY
China Artists Association Experimental Art Committee
Central Academy of Fine Arts
Shenzhen Art Museum

IN COLLABORATION WITH
School of Experimental and Sci-Tech Arts of CAFA
Art and Technology Innovation Center of BNU
Tsinghua Laboratory of Brain and Intelligence Seminar Series (THBI-SS)

ACADEMIC AFFILIATION BY
Long Museum

SUPPORTED BY
New Media Art Foundation
Beijing Yilanzhongxiao Co., Ltd.

GRAPHIC DESIGN
Yu Xiaodan, Liu Siran

PUBLICITY
Yan Lei

TECHNICAL CONSULTANTS
ZhangDan, Qu Xudong, Luo Yu

PHOTOGRAPHY
Zhang Hong, She Baihan, Hu Yi

PROGRAMING
Li Ke, Irene Gaumé, Xiao Tao, Wei Hao

TECHNICAL DIRECTORS
Chen Weimin, Cheng Zhanbing, Ding Shuo, Hu Yi, Huang Rongji, Adam Low, Min Taoling, Peng Zhijian, Wang Feng, Zhou Hu, Zhou Yong

TECHNICAL TEAM
Jia Songlin, Ling Shunyong, Luan Guangwei, Luo Rui, Rao Guangzhen, Wang Youbin, Xu Wenxuan, Yan Liangliang, Zhang Yueqiu

PRODUCTION
Factum Arte&Factum Foundation, Abiochem Biotechnology (Shanghai) Co., Ltd., Chengdu Sanyi Zhihui Technology Co., Ltd., JIAHONGJING Sculpture Art Design and Production, Guangzhou Billio Tech. Co., Ltd., Tianjin MiAmp Measurement &Control Co., Ltd.

PRODUCTION TECHNICIANS
Chen Changkun, Chen Changxing, Chen Chao, Chen Xiaobing, Chen Zhen, Lin Kaikai, Lin Liang, Ma Junjin, Peng Xianhui, Wang Chuang, Wang Longdong, Wu Bingsong

ACKNOWLEDGMENTS
Chai Zhikun, Adrian Cheng, Cheng Tan, He Jianfeng, Hu Dong, Xiaojun Lee, Lin Chenyue, Liu Yiqian, Lyn Pinjing, Tan Ping, Wang Bowei, Wang Wei, Wu Junxi, Xiao Xiangrong, Xing Li, Xu Qian, Yan Feng, Yan Weixin, Yang Lei, Yin Chunying, Zhang Zikang, Zhuang Fan

CATALOGUE
WANG YUYANG: CHAOSMOSIS

EDITED BY
Zhang Ga

TEXTS BY
Rudolf Frieling
Mark B. N. Hansen
Caroline A. Jones
Zhang Ga
Siegfried Zielinski

PUBLISHING EDITOR
Ilaria Bombelli (Mousse)

EDITORIAL COORDINATOR
Emma Passarella (Mousse)
Zhang Yiwei

PROOFREADING AND COPYEDITING
Emma Passarella (Mousse)
Lindsey Westbrook

GRAPHIC DESIGN
Anna Azzali (Mousse)

PUBLISHED AND DISTRIBUTED BY
Mousse Publishing – Contrappunto srl
via Pier Candido Decembrio 28,
20137, Milan–Italy
moussemagazine.it

PRINTED IN ITALY BY
Grafiche Zanini, Bologna

FIRST EDITION 2025

SUPPORTED BY
Art and Creative Science Education Foundation (ACSE Foundation)

€ 30 / $ 35
ISBN 978-88-6749-677-8

LEADING SUPPORT

DIOR

MEDIA SUPPORT

Robb Report 时尚甄选

ARTnews

SPECIAL THANKS TO

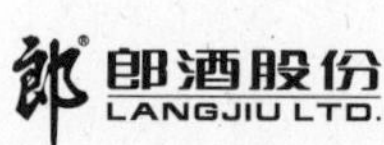

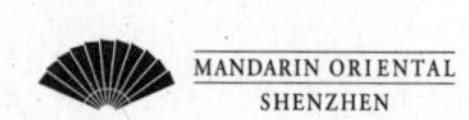

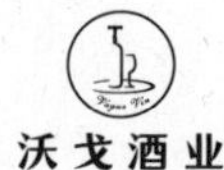